P9-BZZ-847

MUSIC BY PHILIP GLASS

1817

HARPER & ROW,
PUBLISHERS,
NEW YORK

CAMBRIDGE • PHILADELPHIA
SAN FRANCISCO • WASHINGTON
LONDON • MEXICO CITY
SÃO PAULO • SINGAPORE
SYDNEY

≡MUSIC BY PHILIP GLASS≡

BY
Philip Glass

EDITED AND WITH SUPPLEMENTARY MATERIAL BY
Robert T. Jones

For Ida and Ben

Libretto of *Einstein on the Beach* © 1976, 1984 by Robert Wilson. Reprinted by permission of Robert Wilson and the Byrd Hoffman Foundation, Inc. Contributions to libretto by Lucinda Childs, Samuel M. Johnson, and Christopher Knowles.

MUSIC BY PHILIP GLASS. Copyright © 1987 by Dunvagen Music Publishers, Inc. All rights reserved. Printed in the United States of America. No part of this book may be used or reproduced in any manner whatsoever without written permission except in the case of brief quotations embodied in critical articles and reviews. For information address Harper & Row, Publishers, Inc., 10 East 53rd Street, New York, N.Y. 10022. Published simultaneously in Canada by Fitzhenry & Whiteside Limited, Toronto.

FIRST EDITION

Designer: Barbara DuPree Knowles

Copy editor: Brian Hotchkiss

Index by Brian Hotchkiss

LIBRARY OF CONGRESS CATALOGING-IN-PUBLICATION DATA

Glass, Philip.
  Music by Philip Glass.

  Includes librettos of Einstein on the beach, Satyagraha, and Akhnaten.
  Discography: p.
  Includes index.
    1. Glass, Philip. 2. Composers—United States—Biography. 3. Operas—Librettos. I. Jones, Robert T. II. Glass, Philip. Operas. Librettos. 1987. III. Title.
    ML410.G398A3   1987   780'.92'4   [B]   87-45051
    ISBN 0-06-015823-9   87 88 89 90 91 MPC 10 9 8 7 6 5 4 3 2 1
          ISBN 0-06-015835-2 (*limited*)

CONTENTS

INTRODUCTION

BY ROBERT T. JONES

Eighteen years ago, as the most junior of the *New York Times*'s music critics, I was usually assigned concerts the other critics tried to avoid. Thus I found myself at the Whitney Museum of American Art one night in 1969 when thirty-two-year-old Philip Glass was playing. The particular event was a collaboration between Glass and the sculptor Richard Serra, neither of whom I knew much about. I cannot remember if I entered the Whitney that night wearing a chip on my shoulder, but I suspect that I did. In those days, I was a confirmed hater of the avant-garde, which in my mind denoted either silliness or Serialism, and I doubt that I took my seat with much enthusiasm.

The easiest sort of review to write, of course, is a vicious review, the kind that demeans its victim and drips venom on whatever it disapproves of or fails to understand. Glass and Serra provided a first-rate target. Still, I'll say this for myself: I was not dishonest. I hated every note Philip Glass played that evening, hated every screen image created by Richard Serra, and I heartily wished them both a speedy exit from their professions. Meanwhile, I looked forward with some enthusiasm to the review I was about to write, which read, in part:

> Mr. Glass's works were titled *How Now* and *Two Pages*. The first consisted of a six-note doodle on the electric organ, presently joined by another electric organ, electric clavinet and a couple of amplified soprano saxophones. The doodle shifted up and down, stuttered and threatened to fragment, and finally

ended some 20 minutes later as uneventfully as it had begun. *Two Pages* was much the same sort of thing, only without the variety of the first. Musically, Mr. Glass's instruments were enough alike in timbre to throw all the weight onto the material itself. The music and the films were artistically limited enough to be merely trivial, lacking even the sophistication to raise them into the class of the primitive. And this despite the electronics involved.

Bad reviews, however, do not halt a career, though they can sometimes slow its progress. In fact, scathing critiques are less dangerous to artists than those crediting them with greatness, for the latter can raise false expectations from the public and generate smugness in the soul of the praisee. Excluding those would-be artists who might, from sheer faint-heartedness, abandon their careers after a particularly fierce critical blast (as, in 1969, I very much wished Mr. Glass would abandon his), one might even go so far as to say that castigation is good for the creative soul.

It certainly seems to have been good for Glass's. Not only did he persevere, he actually seemed to flourish on such reviews, much as a healthy plant flourishes on fertilizer. As the years went by, his name loomed ever larger in the annals of the avant-garde, and as his music grew to mammoth proportions (literally: some of it, like *Music in Twelve Parts,* required hours to perform), the "underground" press began to lionize him as enthusiastically as the "establishment" press continued to deride him. As for me, I couldn't forget my night at the Whitney and avoided Glass's music like the plague.

But the avant-garde was about to ensnare me in spite of myself. In 1974 I found myself reviewing Robert Wilson's *A Letter to Queen Victoria* at the ANTA Theater, a big Broadway musical house that, on the Saturday afternoon I visited it, contained an audience totaling barely two dozen people. Again, I cannot remember what mood I was in when I joined that depressingly small audience, but I do recall that I was alone, with no companion to influence me with either negative or positive vibrations. And within minutes I was helplessly enthralled by Robert Wilson's extraordinary work. *Queen Victoria* was, quite simply, the most amazing thing I had ever seen in a theater.

From then on I followed Wilson's theater pieces whenever they appeared. I particularly liked the music Wilson chose for his "operas": scraps of Beethoven, ragtime, Schubert, pop tunes, and fairly innocuous items written especially for the occasion. I couldn't have been more horrified when I learned Wilson had got himself involved with the dreadful Mr. Glass, and that the two had concocted something called *Einstein on the Beach*. I had further learned *Einstein* had created something of an uproar in Europe (I was sure the uproar would have been even more uproarious if Glass hadn't horned in on Wilson's act) and that it was scheduled to be performed in the Metropolitan Opera House in November 1976.

I remember taking my seat in the orchestra section of the Met that night. Lucinda Childs and Sheryl Sutton were onstage in the first Knee Play, quietly counting aloud, their fingers performing a slow ballet, and there in the orchestra pit sat Mr. Glass, quietly playing his electric keyboard and looking deceptively sane.

You will read enough about *Einstein on the Beach* in the following pages to make my own account of that amazing evening superfluous. Suffice it to say that by the end of the first Train scene, my own ideas of the possibilities of music had been turned upside down and inside out. As Robert Wilson's intricate and beautiful stage images came and went, as Philip Glass's music seemed to breach the bounds of the possible, I watched and listened in a state of awe. I don't remember breathing. I do, though, remember weeping.

A week later, I interviewed Philip Glass for the first time. We met at an upscale eatery across the street from Lincoln Center, and I hoped he would not connect me with that now-embarrassing *Times* review seven years earlier. To this day I don't know if he was forgiving or merely forgetful; in any case, he never mentioned the matter, and neither did I. The interview went well. I found him warm but not eager, friendly but slightly impersonal, and he answered all questions concerning music with an engaging straightforwardness. Nonmusical questions he either evaded with the skill of an expert, or ignored, apparently from lack of interest in the subjects broached. Already he had the gift of fielding impertinent questions by offering quotable evasions instead. For instance, I remember asking him if he was a religious person. He replied that he didn't want to talk about religion.

"Why not?" I pursued.

"Because my music is so very odd already that I see no reason to make myself sound any odder."

Perhaps it was that very oddness that attracted me to Glass's music. (When I first heard *Einstein,* I was a forty-four-year-old critic sated by decades of listening to "standard repertory.") But to many people, those more attuned to the world of rock and avant-garde music, it didn't sound odd at all, only powerful, original and invigorating. I remember, for example, a discussion that took place in the early planning stages of this book. I was talking with Craig Nelson, the Harper & Row editor in charge of the project, and we fell to musing over our different musical backgrounds and how each of us had first reacted to *Einstein on the Beach*.

"I come from a classical music background," I said. "And I thought it was the most bizarre music I'd ever heard. It sounded like something from another galaxy."

"My background is twentieth-century music and rock," said Craig. "I knew all Glass's early stuff, and when I heard *Einstein* I remember thinking, 'At last! Glass has written something attractive, something delightful, something *easy!*' "

Such different reactions may be the key to Glass's dominance in the music of our time. People of different backgrounds find different things in his work (he writes at length in this book how "the audience completes the work") and, as a result, the instantly identifiable Glass sound now permeates the realms of rock, pop, commercials, films and new symphonic music. Glass's music is more famous than even his most ardent fans may realize, and has become so by dint of its own strength and irresistibility.

In these pages, the reader will encounter no claims from Glass that his music is as unique and original as many listeners have long believed it is, nor that Glass himself is a phenomenon (many will think both statements true anyway, as does this writer). Instead, they will learn how this music—especially as developed in the trilogy of operas comprised of *Einstein on the Beach*, *Satyagraha* and *Akhnaten*—grew out of older music, including sources as disparate as Ravi Shankar and (perhaps surprising to some) Johann Sebastian Bach. There are no virgin births in the realm of ideas. Everything is connected to something else.

Glass's art is connected to theater, to Eastern music, to Western music, to artistic trends that grew out of political and artistic discontent. Much of it is based upon complex uses of repetition, though even this is hardly new to music. Repetitive music has been around for centuries, casting its haunting strangeness over listeners for so long no one can state where it began. Some especially famous examples are the second movement of Berlioz's *Harold in Italy;* a deceptively simple and quite unforgettable little canon by the seventeenth-century composer Johann Pachelbel that, since its discovery barely a decade ago, has already become one of the most popular pieces in existence; and, of course, Ravel's *Bolero,* a fifteen-minute piece constructed from one simple tune repeated endlessly while orchestral instruments pile up enormous sonorities. As to *Bolero,* one cannot read about the circumstances of its composition without being struck by how guilty Ravel felt about having written it:

Ravel was always embarrassed at how easy *Bolero* had been to compose and how popular it became, but his embarrassment may have stemmed from the growing attitude in twentieth-century-music circles that the worth of a piece should somehow be equated with its complexity and the difficulty of its comprehension.

Ravel also, not very incidentally, was among the last of the composers in the first half of the twentieth century to interest a very large audience. It is by now a widely accepted fact that, in this century, "serious" music has encountered a calamitous loss of interest from the public, and that the "successful" composers—meaning those who actually attract audiences interested in hearing (and paying for the privilege of hearing) their music—have not only dwindled in number but also in the degree of respect won from their peers.

One of the more remarkable attitudes that developed during this century was that a genius is recognized only after he is dead and gone. "I write for future generations," was one tagline. "No man is a hero in his own time," was another.

The historical facts indicate otherwise. Every great composer of the past (or at least those currently regarded as such) was a success with the audiences of his own time. To name only a few: Monteverdi was enormously famous while he was alive, and his music attracted crowds that, one suspects, were far more interested in sonic thrills than religious experiences. Mozart's music drew huge audiences, was turned into pop tunes and dance pieces (his letters relate how the dance halls in Prague reverberated with "hit tunes" from *Figaro*); Mozart's demise as a pauper had everything to do with his ineptness as a businessman, but nothing at all to do with public acceptance of his work. Verdi? He was a national hero whose operas provoked riots, public demonstrations and constant harassment by government censors; his death was the cause of international mourning. Wagner, hailed alternately as the salvation and the ruination of music, ranked as one of the most famous men of his time, and his operas were box office draws of stupendous proportions. Beethoven's funeral was a state occasion. The list could be extended for pages.

It is indicative of the wrong-headedness of mid-twentieth-century attitudes that the mention of "box office" is often considered crass, somehow unworthy of consideration by a serious artist, yet what better barometer of interest can there be than the amount of money a public is willing to pay in order to participate in an artistic experience? True, earlier centuries saw support provided by rich patrons (Wagner's "Mad Ludwig" is a particularly flaming example) much as this century has its corporations and governmental foundations for the arts, but only in this century has there come a split between private and government support and actual public acceptance of the artist's product.

The loss of an audience for serious music in the twentieth century might be traced back to that arch-success Richard Wagner. In earlier centuries, composers used chromaticism (notes extraneous to the diatonic—the familiar *do-re-mi-fa-sol-la-si-do*—scale) often enough, and in the classical period (Haydn, Mozart and early Beethoven) chromaticism still appears frequently, but hardly ever as chromatic harmony. In Beethoven's later music, chromaticism increases, and it seems significant that as the degree of chromaticism increases, the reported degree of comprehension (especially on the part of nonexpert listeners) decreases. With Wagner's *Tristan und Isolde,* chromatic harmony begins to invade the musical kingdom in full force, opening the way to all sorts of expressive possibilities, as well as further musical complexities and the loss of a feeling for key centers. With Debussy (*Prelude to the Afternoon of a Faun*), the listener was virtually cast adrift on a sea of floating "keylessness," and with Richard Strauss (specifically Klytemnestra's nightmare in *Elektra*), the sense of music bursting apart at its seams becomes inescapable.

The feeling that music had exhausted its own possibilities, at least as far as tonal music was concerned, hovers around this period of musical composition. Indeed, after *Tristan,* after *Prelude to the Afternoon of a Faun,* after *Elektra,* where could music possibly go? One thinks of a boat neatly channeled down a straight canal, then suddenly, after centuries of comfortable sureness, set loose in a boundless ocean with no shores in sight and no stars for guidance.

The result was atonality, propounded first by Arnold Schoenberg in 1908 and resulting, in its perhaps most famous example, in Alban Berg's opera *Wozzeck*. This was fascinating music, intellectually compelling, dramatically powerful (at least as used in this particular kind of drama), but it never appealed very strongly to the general public. Atonality (literally, the absence of any tonality at all) soon gave way to Schoenberg's attempt to bring order into what had become compositional chaos: the twelve-tone system. Boiled down to its basics, the twelve-tone system meant that a seemingly arbitrary arrangement of the twelve chromatic tones could serve as the basis for constructing a musical work. Rules and restrictions as to the use of the system multiplied, fascinating musicians and erecting a screen of complexity around the art of musical composition.

The foregoing description of what happened to music in the first half of this century presupposes no value judgments of the considerable amount of music written. It does, however, attempt to explain one indisputable fact: The public that formerly had been interested in "serious" music reacted with either boredom or active revulsion to most of the new music produced. While the more intellectually inclined composers plunged into twelve-tone music, moving—as years passed—into positions of power in intellectual, political and social circles, the general public began to equate "new music" with incomprehensibility, dullness or outright ugliness. Composers began to write mostly for other composers. Otherwise, the production of new music simply ceased to interest audiences. Significantly, radicals like Carl Orff, who refused to join the herdlike plunge into complexity and, instead, came up with a music based on harmonic simplicity and rhythmic straightforwardness, found themselves in the curious position of simultaneously enjoying enormous public success (in Orff's case, with the cantata *Carmina Burana*) and disdain from critics and peers.

A rule of nature is that every action is followed by a counter-action, and in the 1960s there came a reaction to the musical dead end that had developed. Young people, always in rebellion against the generation that precedes them, rebelled against the worlds that encircled them—political, militaristic and artistic. The Vietnam war focused energies; drugs and rock music offered retaliatory channels. The mood of the times was to reject the past, including the entire society that had created that past. Western thought was suspect, for it had produced things far worse than a repellent music that hardly anybody liked; it had fomented war, destruction, planetwide misery. If there was hope, perhaps it could be found in other cultures. Eastern ones seemed the most likely: In India, China, Bali, were traditions unlike those in the West. Perhaps in the East was escape.

And perhaps in simplicity was an escape from complexity. There were musicians in the 1960s who were bored and disillusioned with the direction music had taken. These were young, talented and ambitious would-be composers who had grown up with the rhythms and philosophical content (notably cynicism and despair) of rock music socked into their souls as solidly as the traditions of Bach, Beethoven and Bartók. Some of them, like Terry Riley, Steve Reich and Philip Glass—the three who became most prominent in this new musical movement—surfaced from the pool of musical innovators who had absorbed "classical music," turned their backs on it and embraced Eastern brands of musical expression. No one composer invented this new music. It was an eruption of the times, an inevitability. It *happened*.

In 1964, when the first audible mutterings of a new music began to be heard, Philip Glass was a youngster of twenty-seven, with a sizable backlog of compositions to his credit, all of them performed, many of them published. But he had an increasingly uncomfortable feeling that he had been writing academic, derivative music that expressed nothing he wanted to express. He knew he hated serial music ("ugly and didactic") and he resented "the idea that music had to be an intellectual enterprise," but he knew no other kind of music to write. Instead of fleeing to the Far East (a region he knew virtually nothing about at that time), he fled to Paris for studies with Nadia Boulanger, the reigning doyenne of composition teachers. Guided by her iron hand, he rebuilt his technique, broadened his outlook and did not have to go East at all. The East came to him in the persons of Ravi Shankar and his tabla player, Alla Rakha. Thereafter, Glass disowned his old music and began the years of experiment that culminated in the startling and revelatory *Einstein on the Beach*.

The first audible hint of a new music came not from Glass but from Terry Riley in 1964. Riley's *In C* was a piece of overwhelming simplicity, a few bars repeated over and over, in layers, as instruments picked up the material and mortared a huge musical edifice from it. Riley's orientation was Eastern, and as the years went on he became more and more focused on Eastern techniques, almost disappearing from public awareness; he has since reappeared, performing in concerts and releasing beautiful and delicate recordings, but so far his music has not engaged the attention of a wide public.

Despite Glass's own claims in this volume that he was never interested in opera until after *Einstein on the Beach* in 1976, it is abundantly clear, given the advantages of hindsight, that he was a born theater composer, that his instincts are dramatic to a high degree, and that once *Einstein*'s success had made opera a feasible career choice, he was almost helplessly drawn to it. Like most successful opera composers of the past, he gravitated toward the theater in his student years and has been there ever since. So far, though, he has not concentrated on theater music to the exclusion of all else (Wagner, Verdi and Puccini were three giants who wrote hardly anything of importance that was not of an operatic nature), and as this volume goes into publication in the summer of 1987, Glass is full of plans for more nonoperatic music, in addition to more operas.

After encountering Glass's own statements on how much he values collaboration with other artists, the reader may wonder exactly how much of the present volume was written by "collaborators" and how much was written by Philip Glass.

The answer is: all of it. It is not "ghost"-written, dictated, or "told to." Nearly all of it was written in Nova Scotia in August 1986, Glass and I (in my function as editor) working in nearby cabins in the thick pine woods of his seaside hideaway. An early riser, Glass was usually at his desk by 6:00 AM, orchestrating the second act of his opera *The Making of the Representative for Planet 8* until breakfast at 10:00. The meal was invariably a massive one, Glass frying heavily garlicked potatoes; assorted other friends, family members and visiting artists of one kind or another crowding the huge kitchen to concoct their own various breakfast specialties (I must have produced as many buttermilk biscuits as I did manuscript pages). At 11:00 Glass would disappear into his cabin to complete his quota of twenty pages of orchestration per day, finishing promptly at one and putting aside music paper in favor of lined yellow legal tablets on which he rapidly and methodically wrote this history of his operatic Trilogy.

Meanwhile, I would be typing his words into my computer, editing the results and passing him the printouts. When writer's cramp intervened, Glass would appear in my cabin door, pull up a chair next to the wood stove (it's chilly in Nova Scotia, even in August), and we would inspect the results of our work. My own comments were usually pleas for "more details" and "more anecdotes"; his for tighter structure and a clearer line of thought. When we argued, as we incessantly did, I argued for more color, more humor; he insisted (typically, I thought) on fewer adjectives and less "fat" in the sentences. Promptly at 7:00 PM Glass halted for the day, and everyone assembled for dinner and a companionable evening of reading, talking, listening to cassettes and (for composer/writer and his editor) more post-mortem discussions on the book in progress. By 11:00 everyone had gone off to their own isolated cabins out in the woods, the "night people" to continue solitary work, the "day people" to sleep.

"In my student days," Glass said to me at one point, "I knew a lot of composers, many of them more talented than myself. But I learned one thing most of them did not: good work habits. When I was still a teenager, I forced myself to write music during a set period every morning, and I also forced myself to stop at one in the afternoon. I refused to take down musical ideas at other hours, even when they came to me. You might say I trained the Muse to come calling at *my* hours, not hers. And it worked. For years now, I have gotten my ideas in the mornings and never in the afternoons."

At home in Manhattan's East Village, Glass's life is far more hectic than in Nova Scotia, but even there his personal discipline is in evidence. He writes music all morning, deals with the music business all afternoon (auditioning performers, working in recording studios, being interviewed, arranging things on the phone), and firmly reserves his evenings for his family and friends, at least when he's not on one of his many tours with the Philip Glass Ensemble. It's as quiet a life as one can imagine this hurricanelike man leading.

Calm, laid-back, are the words most often used to describe Glass as a person. Whatever it's called, it's an attitude found and developed from Glass's exposure to Eastern philosophies, and it has given him the inner self-certainty needed to withstand decades of abuse from people who, in the beginning, couldn't stand his music. Many of the establishment critics in the world of "serious" music still can't, and their reviews have often been of the sort that might drive a sensitive person to suicide or murder.

Not Glass. He and the members of his Ensemble vie with each other in collecting the most abusive reviews, reading them aloud during the long hours on their tour bus, laughing over whatever witticisms the critics have managed to invent. Those negative charges that have been generated by the press are dispelled, turned to positive, in the good humor Glass himself radiates.

Critics. You'll find hardly a word about them in this book. It's a subject Glass and I often battled about during the writing period in Nova Scotia and in the East Village months that followed. "Now is your chance," I urged. "Throw rocks."

"Throwing rocks isn't my style," replied Glass.

Pressed beyond endurance, he finally sat down with pencil and legal pad and began to write, visibly distressed. A quarter-hour later, he stopped, scratched out what he had written, threw it away. "I can't," he said.

"Why can't you?"

"It's just too negative. It's the kind of thing that only slows me down. Years ago, I read an abusive review of one of my pieces, and it upset me so much I couldn't work for *a whole hour*! I don't want to invite those sorts of feelings again."

Such positive feelings go a long way in explaining why Glass likes to work *with* people (he calls it "collaborating") and why so many people like working with him. In our weeks of writing and editing this book in Nova Scotia, for instance, all possible persons were coaxed into reading the manuscript and then, with elaborate casualness, handed red pencils. Back in New York, the process continued on an expanded scale. Jorge Gallina and Candy Jernigan helped a lot, and so did Veronica Stevens, Stokes Howell and Kurt Munkacsi. JoAnne Akalaitis set us straight on details about the Mabou Mines company. Rudolf Firkusny gave us days of his time on the musical sections, as did Michael Riesman and Martin Goldray. Further, we had the good fortune to have no less than four thoroughly exhaustive proofs of the manuscript, one each from Dan Deitz, Tatiana Firkusny, Michael Riesman, and Dorothy Spelman.

Still, the real story belongs to Philip Glass. Now it is time to let him tell it.

APPRENTICESHIP OF SORTS

PARIS

I have often said that I became an opera composer by accident. I never set out to become one, and even today I use the word "opera" with reluctance. In the 1950s, when I was a music student, I dutifully studied the standards of the opera repertory, and I made regular visits to the old Metropolitan Opera House on Broadway at 39th Street where, for fifty cents, one could use a score desk near the top of the house. You could hear the operas perfectly from up there, but you could see them only by stretching forward and peering straight down, a posture not only uncomfortable but positively life-threatening. From this extreme perspective I heard—and, in a fashion, "saw"—any number of the old warhorses as well as the extremely modern (or what seemed modern in those days) *Wozzeck*. These were "duty" visits, undertaken to round out my education. Not in a million years would it have occurred to me that I might someday write an opera myself, let alone spend the greater part of my adult working life in the theater.

As it turned out, I was thirty-nine years old when, with *Einstein on the Beach,* I suddenly found myself actually working in opera houses. *Einstein* was soon followed by two more operas (*Satyagraha* and *Akhnaten*), forming a trilogy of what I regard as "portrait" operas—musical/dramatic portraits of powerful personalities who have engaged my attention at particular times. By then, clearly, I had become a composer of operas.

I find now in writing about these first three "portrait" operas that some of the most interesting aspects of their creation are the chains of "accidents" that led me to opera in the first place. Therefore, though I began this book with the intention of writing only about my own operas, I find I must start a full ten years before, during the time of my first theater work in Paris in the mid-1960s. Those were the years in which my music work and theater music became closely intertwined. No doubt it was the particular kind of theater I was drawn to, and the somewhat unusual theater music I began to write, that has led to the highly personal approach to theater music (opera, if you will) that marks this trilogy of portrait operas. This is how it came about.

The first theater of which I, like most people, was aware was the "traditional kind." This was narrative theater, that which starts from a literary base. This does not imply that literary theater is necessarily conservative. Several decades ago writers such as Bertolt Brecht, Samuel Beckett, Jean Genet and Harold Pinter were all developing new attitudes to material and audience, attitudes requiring new techniques of performance and presentation. At the same time, and continuing right up to the present, there exists a modern theater rooted in the conservative mode known as "naturalism." Beginning in the nineteenth century with Chekhov, it continued into the twentieth with such American writers as Eugene O'Neill, Arthur Miller and Tennessee Williams.

For a great many people, this latter type *is* theater. But this kind of theater never interested me very much, and it has played almost no part at all in my own working life. Growing up in the world of "progressive" theater as I did, and experiencing it in the ways I have, theater has always meant to me something quite different: a kind of experience that even today is viewed as anything *but* traditional. The kinds of theater which spin familiar stories, moralizing, sometimes satirizing, occasionally comforting us about our lives, have never meant much to me. What has always stirred me is theater that challenges one's ideas of society, one's notions of order.

When I was living in Europe in the early 1960s, I was very much in touch with theater that represented these ideals. Jean-Louis Barrault's Théâtre Odéon in Paris regularly presented new works by Beckett and Genet, and I particularly remember a stunning production of Genet's *The Screens,* directed by Roger Blin. Also, I saw the unforgettable Madeleine Renaud playing the Woman in what may have been one of the very first productions of Beckett's *Happy Days*. At about the same time, I made

4

a pilgrimage to East Berlin with JoAnne Akalaitis (whom I had recently married) to spend more than a week watching the Berliner Ensemble in productions of Brecht that were fairly close to their originals. Brecht also was regular fare at the Théâtre Nationale Populaire in Paris. In this way I was able to see two very different versions of this great playwright's work, both unlike anything I had encountered at home.

During this period I made regular trips to London as well. We were students then and, not having much money, we often hitchhiked to London, managing somehow to pay the boat fare across the Channel, queuing all night to buy balcony seats for the National Theater, where we might see Laurence Olivier in *Othello* or perhaps Strindberg's *Dance of Death*.

It was in the Paris of the early 1960s, though, that I became associated with the group of people who, in a few years, would become known as Mabou Mines, an experimental theater collective that has become well known in New York since the 1970s. This initial group included JoAnne Akalaitis, Lee Breuer, Ruth Maleczech, David Warrilow and, sometime later, Fred Neumann, Bill Raymond and Terry O'Reilly (not to be confused with composer Terry Riley). JoAnne, Breuer and Maleczech had worked together previously at the Actors Workshop in San Francisco with Herb Blau and Jules Irving, and at the San Francisco Tape Center with Morton Subotnick and Ramone Sender. From their Paris beginnings, however, they functioned as a unit, though they were not yet formally organized as a theater, and I soon began working with them as their resident musician.

At first our work began with the kinds of progressive European theater to which we all were attracted. In fact, the first two pieces that emerged from this association were stagings of Brecht and Beckett. Lee Breuer directed a production of Brecht's *Mother Courage*, for which I acted as music director, coaching the actors/singers in the wonderful Paul Dessau score. Then came a production of *Play* by Beckett, also directed by Breuer, with the first original score I wrote for this company.

We soon discovered, though, that there simply wasn't a large enough audience for an English-speaking theater company in Paris. Furthermore, I was beginning to encounter the stiff resistance to my new music that would pursue me for years to come. As a result, by 1967 we had all left Paris to settle in New York (although JoAnne and I first took a detour through Central Asia and India, the first of many visits to that part of the world).

Though we had our beginnings together in the progressive "literary" theater of Europe, in New York we soon began presenting theater pieces originating within the group itself. As was normal with many of the new

5

theater groups at this time, our finished pieces were the result of an intense, protracted work period. An image, a movement, sometimes a title could provide the initial inspiration for a work. After that came a long period of improvising, selecting, discarding and refining before it began to take its final shape. Invariably, the text itself was a result of this shaping process; it was hardly ever a point of origin. Much of this was what came to be called nonnarrative theater. This was hardly our own invention, since its roots can be found in a still earlier period—specifically in the works of Antonin Artaud, who attempted to transcend words by creating a theater of pure expression in Paris during the 1920s. Another important influence was Jerzey Grotowski and the Polish Lab Theater. JoAnne and Ruth had studied with him in France in 1969, and they were among the first Americans who brought his ideas back to New York.

After the late 1960s, there came a progressive proliferation of these "new theater" ensembles, all working, generally speaking, toward a similar goal. In New York I saw the work of Joe Chaikin's Open Theater and Richard Schechner's Performance Group, as well as the theater work of Meredith Monk, Richard Foreman and Robert Wilson. By the early 1970s there had developed a lively community of innovative theater people intensely involved in their own work and equally supportive, if often critical, of the efforts of their colleagues.

In all of this activity, the Living Theater served as inspiration and, at least to many young theater people like ourselves, standard-bearer for the new theater. I remember the "Living," as it was often called, from the late 1950s, when they performed in a downtown New York theater on Seventh Avenue. These were the days of Kenneth Brown's *The Brig* and Jack Gelber's *The Connection*. In my New York student days, they were part of the general avant-garde mix of the time, a mix that included the Beats (Jack Kerouac, Gregory Corso and Allen Ginsberg), the hard bop of John Coltrane, and Claes Oldenberg's *Store Days*.

I don't think I had any clearer sense of who or what the "Living" was than that. It had originated with Julian Beck and his wife, Judith Malina, who, in the early 1960s, had taken their theater collective for an extended stay in Europe, where their social/political anarchy was taken seriously. It was in the south of France, in a little festival outside Marseilles, where I saw them again in the summer of 1964, and this time the "Living" made an enormous impression on me.

The work was *Frankenstein,* and we saw its premiere performance. The weight of the work was in images and movement. Further, it was the first theater work I had seen that so radically extended the accepted sense of theater time: The performance began around eight in the evening and went on until sometime around three in the morning. I don't know to what extent, if any, *Frankenstein*'s time scale was modeled on that of Eastern theater, but I saw this same kind of scale used some years later in South India by the Khatikali theater. I encountered it again in New York in the early work of Robert Wilson. But what later came to be called Wilson's "theater of images" I saw for the first time with the "Living" in the early 1960s.

Later that winter (1964–1965), in Berlin, JoAnne and I sought out the Becks while they were rehearsing *Antigone* and talked to them about their work and their ideas about a collective theater, though I can't recall if they called it that. We were just two of the many young people who went to the Becks after their performances, and I doubt whether, for them, our encounter was memorable, but it certainly made a deep impression on us at the time. For us, as for many others, the "Living" provided an exciting alternative to the traditional commercial-theater world.

By the early 1970s, the nucleus of the future Mabou Mines theater company had been established in New York, and it was with them that I began to grow up in the theater. As the company's resident composer, I was closely involved with the development of their works, which meant being present during much of the rehearsal period and creating music for the productions. Sometimes this meant making a tape for use during performance, which I did for *Play*. Often, as with JoAnne's production of *Cascando* or Breuer's *Red Horse Animation,* it required writing music for the performers to use during the production and, of course, rehearsing the music as well. The men and women of Mabou Mines shared the duties of director and producer. As the years went on, Breuer and Akalaitis became the best known among the directors, but any number of works were originated by or with other members, such as Ruth Maleczech and Fred Neumann, who developed and directed their own pieces. Thus, over a period of twenty years, I wrote at least a dozen scores for the company, beginning with Beckett's *Play* which was produced in Paris at the American Cultural Center before Mabou Mines yet existed as a company. After that came *Red Horse Animation* (Mabou Mines and Breuer), 1970; *Music for Voices* (Glass), 1972; *The Lost Ones* (Beckett), 1974; *Cascando* (Beckett), 1975; *The Saint and the Football Player* (Thibeau and Breuer), 1976; *Mercier and Camier* (Beckett), 1979; *Dressed Like an Egg* (Akalaitis), 1977; *Dead End Kids* (Akalaitis), 1980; *Cold Harbor* (Worsley and Raymond), 1983; and *Company* (Beckett), 1983.

For a number of reasons *Red Horse Animation* was a significant

7

milestone in both my and Mabou Mines' lives. The rehearsal period stretched well over a year, and one extended period of work took place in the summer of 1970 near the town of Mabou Mines in Nova Scotia, which is how and when the company came by its name.

In 1969, after the birth of Juliet, our first child, JoAnne and I had gone to Maine looking for a place to work in the summer. Our idea was to find a spot that was quiet, but still near New York. We headed north and searched the coast for a thousand miles, ending up in another country before we found something suitable. Our summer home proved large enough to accommodate the members of the theater company as well as our growing family. I can best describe it in travel-agent prose: an abandoned summer camp on a cliff overlooking the sea, containing a sprawling main lodge, a handful of log shacks buried in an expanse of pine forest, and a vast and bleakly beautiful stretch of beach. Satisfyingly remote.

Incredibly, even on our slender budget, we could afford it. Joined by a writer friend, Rudolph Wurlitzer, we bought it.

We had asked the painter Power Boothe to help realize the physical aspects of the *Red Horse* production, and he joined us in Nova Scotia where we worked out the solutions to some unique theater/music problems. What we needed specifically was a floor—actually a hollow drum-like sounding board—built modular style in four-foot-square units. When this was amplified by contact microphones, it became the instrument on which the actors performed the music—stamping, tapping, using all manner of percussive effects. Those percussive sounds were organized into a highly logical arithmetic system I later began to call "additive process," a cornerstone technique that has served me well ever since. Meanwhile, though, the *Red Horse* floor was an expensive item, and we had no idea how to pay for it.

Ellen Stewart rescued us. Almost all our work at that time took place in the world of Off-Off-Broadway theater, and it was Ellen Stewart of La Mama who was central to so much of that activity. More than any other person, Ellen made Off-Off-Broadway a reasonable and realistic place to work. She provided a focus, first through Cafe La Mama, and later La Mama Etc. In the 1970s, this role was shared with Joseph Papp's Public Theater, where many of the Mabou Mines works were produced. However, it was Ellen who provided the very first public support.

Ellen originally had been working as a clothing designer for several of New York's best stores. One day, tired of hearing her theater friends complain that they couldn't produce their work, Ellen announced, "Well, baby, if you can't put on your work, I'll put it on *for* you!"

That's how she began. Ellen never had a great deal of money, but she was a genius at finding it, and at finding talent too. She discovered people, and she pulled money out of foundations. When we needed money to get *Red Horse Animation* finished, Ellen came in and offered to pay for the floor. More than that, she gave us a rehearsal space on Great Jones Street and put the whole company on salary for three years. Our company was only five people, and we each got fifty dollars a week. (That, by the way, is the only salary I have ever earned on a regular basis in the theater.)

From the very beginning, the Mabou Mines company welcomed visual arts people, many of whom had not previously worked in the theater. Their names grew into quite a lengthy list, and in those early years it included artists like Power Boothe, Gene Highstein, Suzanne Harris and Keith Sonnier. Ree Morton, Nancy Graves and Tina Girauard were on the list, too. Of all the theaters then developing in New York, I think Mabou Mines made the firmest commitment to extending the range of its work by means of extratheater collaborations of this kind.

Given that commitment, it should surprise no one that Mabou Mines' first New York appearance was at a museum. After all, Off-Off-Broadway theater as it developed in the early 1970s was really part of a larger artistic community located in Manhattan in the area known as Soho (a contraction of the phrase ''*SO*uth of *HO*uston Street''), but emphatically before Soho reached its present state of urban development as a shopping mall. Soho was also the home of the postmodern dance movement of Lucinda Childs, the Judson Group, Yvonne Rainer, and the Grand Union, a dance collective not unlike the theater collectives I've been mentioning that produced four now well-known choreographers (David Gordon, Steve Paxton, Trisha Brown, Douglas Dunn). Jonas Mekas's Film-Makers Cinematheque (modeled on the Paris Cinémathèque, a combination museum, archive and showplace for film) was by then firmly established at 80 Wooster Street.

At first the Soho audiences at these music, dance and theater events were made up almost entirely of other performers, musicians, painters, sculptors, filmmakers, poets, writers, etc. Very often, theater, dance and music events took place in the art galleries that were just beginning to appear in what was by then the center of an almost unprecedented scene.

We accepted all this at the time rather matter of factly. But, in reality, in the early 1970s we were witnessing and participating in a scene of tremendous vitality, one probably unparalleled since the Paris of the 1920s. Gallery collectives such as 112 Greene Street, The Kitchen (which, a few years later, became one of the centers for a totally new kind of performance art) and galleries like those of Leo Castelli and Paula Cooper encouraged and vigorously supported a whole range of events. This was the gestation period, as well as the place, when and where the "performance art" of the late 1970s and early 1980s began. And it was in these places that collaborative work could be practiced; where the technical skills were acquired which made possible the music theater pieces in which I became involved a few years later. At the same time there were people like Laurie Anderson, Julia Heyward, Stuart Sherman, Vito Acconci, artists who blurred the lines between art and the *performance* of art until the distinction finally disappeared and performance art emerged.

This was a very lively, very large and highly varied bunch of people. There could have been two hundred, or even two thousand, artists involved in these various movements. I don't think anybody knows because in those days everybody was simply too busy to stop and count. And if the arts were becoming more theatrical, then it was possible that the theater also was tending, if somewhat reluctantly, to become more involved with making art.

SOHO

The preceding sketch of New York's downtown world of performers and artists in that decade and a half between 1965 and 1980 will give some idea of the background I brought to my first collaborations in large-scale music theater. The other main ingredient was my experience writing and playing the concert music I had been developing at the same time.

If my formative theater experiences were in Paris, then the same may be said of the beginnings of my music. Thinking back to the Paris I knew in the mid-1960s, I remember excitement in the theater, but I'm afraid I remember no comparable excitement in the music world. The main—and really *only*—new music events were the "Domaine Musicale" concerts organized by Pierre Boulez. At that time Boulez was yet to become the internationally known conductor he is today. His long tenure with the New York Philharmonic, the BBC Symphony Orchestra, and his achievements as *Ring* Meister of Wagner's Bayreuth are only a few of the accomplishments that have since brought him to the attention of the general public. Nonetheless, throughout the late 1950s and early 1960s he was one of contemporary music's great ideologues, his reputation bolstered by his skill and talent as a composer of avant-garde concert music.

In those days, at least in Europe, Boulez's approval was essential for any new composer to be taken seriously. Or so it appeared. The "Domaine Musicale" concerts, for which he was both chief conductor and artistic director, were regular series of concerts devoted almost exclusively to the Serialist composers who were trying to extend the work of the original twelve-tone composers—Arnold Schoenberg, Alban Berg and Anton Webern—to yet another generation.

Dating the modernist period from 1912 (a good year, since it heralds the appearance of a major work by each of the two most influential composers of the early part of this century: Stravinsky's *Rite of Spring;* Schoenberg's *Pierrot Lunaire*), we can see what was known as the twelve-tone school emerging as one of several important developments in twentieth-century music.

Stravinsky seems to have set the standard for the large group of composers who continued the tradition of tonal music into the twentieth century. These composers basically accepted the alliance of melody and harmony that the Baroque, Classical and Romantic composers had employed to create the bulk of today's standard concert repertory. Of course, the music of these twentieth-century tonal composers was sometimes highly altered in many ways with dissonant harmony, polytonality (several keys or tonal centers heard at the same time), unexpected and eloquent melodies and unusual rhythms. Often grouped together were Neoclassical composers such as Stravinsky (at times), Hindemith, Bloch, or more folkloric and nationalistic composers such as Sibelius, Bartók, and Copland. In any case, the great majority of music written in the twentieth century (I am tempted to use the past tense since, as I write these words, we are approaching its tenth and final decade) has been in the tonal tradition.

Schoenberg and his followers took a more daring approach. Here the rules of harmony were set aside. In their place was posed a system in which the feeling of key center (which grounds our sense of melody and, often, structure) no longer existed.

Traditionally, the melodic and harmonic material of pre-nineteenth-century Western music had revolved around a tonal center of closely related keys. Then, during the nineteenth century, composers became increasingly interested in stretching the tonal boundaries to include more distantly related keys. By the end of the nineteenth century, composers such as Wagner had extended this process so completely that a sense of definite tonal center seemed irrelevant. At this point. Schoenberg's appearance and development as a composer became pivotal in directing the current of twentieth-century music that was to follow. His early works, written at the turn of the century, were in a highly romantic (and still tenuously "tonal") post-Wagnerian style, but he rapidly evolved, and by the 1920s had formulated his own radically new system.

What Schoenberg did appeared, at first glance, to be very simple. He gave each note in the chromatic (twelve-note) scale equal weight by the device of requiring all twelve notes to be used once before any were repeated. The seemingly arbitrary ordering of notes was called a "tone row" and functioned much like a melody in traditional music. When the same idea was applied to other elements of musical language (rhythm, dynamics, timbre), the all-inclusive name for the results was "serial" music.

This produced a very abstract and, to most ears, "modern" sounding music. In the hands of a talented composer, serial composition could produce highly expressive and often ingenious music, and it became fashionable, almost mandatory, among composers growing up after World War II. Probably its intellectual rigor and sheer difficulty for creator, performer and listener made it seem almost automatically worthwhile, regardless of how it actually came out. After the premiere of a new piece, it was not uncommon to hear the remark, "It's actually much better than it sounds"(!) Such attitudes seem more and more incomprehensible today, but it was only a few years ago that they were taken quite seriously.

Though there were many gifted and energetic composers and performers dedicated to Serialism, the music to this day has not found general public acceptance. In spite of this rather obvious drawback, its adherents over the years have at times been very influential, controlling performance opportunities and commissions, while developing a critical following to make up for its other shortcomings. In this way, the music business is much like any other, political skills and alliances counting for a great deal.

This, then, was the music that appeared to dominate the world of serious concert music in the mid-1960s. It was music I had studied as a student, and any further exercise of that kind interested me not at all. To me, it was music of the past, passing itself off as music of the present. After all, Arnold Schoenberg was about the same age as my grandfather! Occasionally the "Domaine Musicale" would play a work by an American such as Earle Brown, John Cage or Morton Feldman, and they always came as a breath of fresh air after so much heavy European didacticism.

These were men whose work struck me as far less doctrinaire and much more adventurous than that of their European contemporaries. Their systems also set aside the melody/harmony tradition, often in unexpected and sometimes amusing ways. Cage, for example, is known for his experiments with chance procedures. Feldman, once asked what "system" he used to compose his music, replied, "*I* am the system." More importantly, their work implied a far more innovative aesthetic, which ultimately meant more to my own development.

For me, as I mentioned, the real events were happening not in music, but in theater and film. These were the days of the first wave of the new French cinema. It seemed that every few months there would be a new film by Jean-Luc Godard or François Truffaut. Godard was especially prolific. In one year—1964, I believe—I saw both *Contempt* and *Les Carabiniers*. The Cinémathèque, a combination cinema and museum of cinema that alternated between presenting retrospectives of established film classics and notable new efforts in the film genre, was also there, its two locations busily reminding everybody of the recent achievements of the twentieth century's newest art form. Taken together, the film and theater worlds offered a sharp contrast to the new music concerts which seemed to me insular, over-conceptual, dry and academic.

Finally I simply gave up on the music world of 1960s Paris. I realized I was living, musically speaking, in a quiet backwater—quite a good environment for a young man trying to discover for himself a personal music language. Soon, opportunities began to present themselves through my work with the theater friends with whom I had begun associating.

However, apart from theater work, living in Paris had a decisive effect on my life in two ways. One I had planned for. The other was completely unexpected.

I had arrived from New York on a Fulbright scholarship with a master's degree from Juilliard. I suppose I had been a good student at Juilliard, though there were certainly more obviously gifted people around than myself. I had two very good teachers there—Vincent Persichetti and William Bergsma—both accomplished and well-known composers. My five years there had been highly productive. I had written a great deal of music (over seventy works), all of which had been performed. These works (string quartets, concertos, choral works, etc.) were good student pieces but not much more than that. Like most students, I had learned to write music like my teachers, but without a real voice of my own. In my last years, a number of these had been published by Elkan-Vogel (now part of Theodore Presser). The conservatory environment of Juilliard had been an ideal place to learn the practical side of a composer's craft. However, in the end, I felt I lacked the rigorous training which, at that time, seemed more a part of a traditional European music education.

I had gone to Paris to study with the famous Nadia Boulanger and this, in the end, had an enormous effect on the music I later was to compose. Very simply, I couldn't write the music I'm writing today without the technical mastery of basic music compositional skills that I learned with her and her assistant, Mademoiselle Dieudonné.

For Boulanger, my Juilliard achievements didn't count at all. I remember the first afternoon I spent with her at her apartment/studio on the Rue Ballou. She was seventy-seven at the time, a tough, aristocratic Frenchwoman elegantly dressed in fashions fifty years out of date. In dead silence, she read through pages and pages of the music I had brought her. I think I must have been quite proud of some of it. Finally, after an eternity of silent perusal, she pounced on a measure, pointing triumphantly at it, and declared: "There. *This* was written by a *real* composer."

That was the first and last time she said anything nice to me for the next two years.

From that day on, she set me on a program that started with beginner's lessons in counterpoint and harmony and continued with analysis of music, ear training, score reading, and anything else she could think of. Her pedagogy was thorough and relentless. From a young man of twenty-six, I became a child again, relearning everything from the beginning. But when I left Paris in the fall of 1966, I had remade my technique and had learned to *hear* in a way that would have been unimaginable to me only a few years before.

There were a number of other things I learned as well. The difference between technique and style, for example. Or learning how, through application and concentration, we can set new limits, going beyond what we might expect of ourselves.

I saw Mademoiselle Boulanger three times a week. There was, of course, my private lesson, which might be scheduled any time from seven in the morning until ten at night. The worst time to have was the 12 o'clock noon lesson, which I did have for some months. Since Mademoiselle Boulanger never stopped to eat, her lunch was served to her at—or, rather, on—the piano. For me, there was something wildly disconcerting about watching her balance her plates on the piano keys and correct counterpoint exercises at the same time. My attention was torn between the very real danger of food sliding onto our laps and the much more serious danger of her discovering that "hidden fifths" had somehow slipped into my music.

The Wednesday afternoon classes were her general classes. They were open to all her past and present students and were usually devoted to analyses of some extended cycle of works, those by Bach and Mozart being her favorites. "All her students" seemed to mean anyone alive, still in Paris, who had studied with her. Her small studio was jammed with people, some in their early teens, others clearly well into their sixties. And if you thought you could hide in that crowd, you were sadly mistaken. No attendance was taken. She simply assumed you were there. Out of the blue, during an explanation of the voice leading in a Bach prelude, she would call out, "Daniel! Come and play another bass line here!" Or, "Philip, sing for us a second alto part!" No one was safe.

For me, the most trying were the "Black Thursday" classes. For this class, she selected six to eight students. We would meet at nine, and the class would go at least until noon (hopefully ending before the lunch hour). The morning was devoted to solving some fiendish musical problem she had dreamed up for us. For example, we might find when we arrived that one line of music had been written out and was waiting for us on the piano. Naturally, it was never written in one of the three commonly used clefs. It was either in the baritone or, at least, the tenor clef. We would find out later that it might be a theme from the slow movement of Beethoven's third sonata for violin and piano. And if you happened to recognize it (by the way, it was *never* the melody or the bass line, but always an "inner" voice), the exercise was mere child's play. But of course we never did. What Mademoiselle Boulanger wanted us to do was simply to reproduce Beethoven's harmony with all the chords in their correct "positions" and the voice leading intact. And, unbelievably enough, after three hours of her pleading, begging and haranguing, we would actually manage it.

A session like that could be totally exhausting. Often, four or five of us would repair to the cafe opposite Mademoiselle Boulanger's apartment and sit in silence, drinking espresso or beer. We knew that being selected for the Black Thursday class was a real distinction. But what *sort* of distinction evaded us. Were we her best students? Or her worst? Or was it, more probably, a combination of the two? And if that was true, who was which? We sat in silence and parted in silence, not to meet again as a group until the following Thursday.

During the second of my two years with Mademoiselle Boulanger, I had another encounter, this time the unexpected one. A friend was working as a photographer on Conrad Rook's film *Chappaqua,* an early psychedelic fantasy involving such heavies from the New York literary underground as Allen Ginsberg, Peter Orlovsky and William Burroughs. The renowned Indian sitar player, Ravi Shankar, had been engaged to write the music, and they needed someone to work as Ravi's assistant, transcribing his music in Western notation for the French musicians who would be recording the sound track. There also would be a little conducting to do, plus translating English into French when necessary. I got the job, though at the time I knew scarcely a note of non-Western music, and I spent the next several months with Ravi and his drummer, Alla Rakha. This protracted encounter with one of the great traditions of world music and one of its foremost practitioners had a profound effect on me.

To explain, it is important to emphasize some major differences between classical Indian music and traditional Western classical music. First, there is the Indian ''raga'' system governing the order and intonation (tuning) of the notes in a scale. This is a highly elaborate system in which the particular raga, or set of notes and ornamentation (*raga* actually means ''color''), is related to emotional states as well as times of the day. The particular raga in use (there are said to be some eight hundred in all) determines what we would regard in the West as melody and, by extension, improvisation.

Although this melodic aspect is fascinating, it was not what attracted my attention then, and not what has held it ever since. What came to me as a revelation was the use of rhythm in developing an overall structure in music. I would explain the difference between the use of rhythm in Western and Indian music in the following way: In Western music we divide time—as if you were to take a length of time and slice it the way you slice a loaf of bread. In Indian music (and all the non-Western music with which I'm familiar), you take small units, or ''beats,'' and string them together to make up larger time values.

This was brought home to me quite powerfully while working with Ravi and Alla Rakha in the recording studio. There we were with the musicians sitting around waiting for me to notate the music to be recorded. This was never done in advance, no matter how much I pleaded with Ravi to meet ahead of time so I could prepare the instrumental parts before the musicians arrived. He was quite happy to meet early but he never used the time for writing. Instead, there was tea, discussion about music, tuning his sitar and the tamboura (the string drone which I was often called upon to play; one of my accomplishments from those early morning sessions with Ravi). Finally, when the musicians had arrived, Ravi would begin. He would sing the music to me, and I would write it down, part by part. In other words, if the piece was, say, three minutes long, he would first sing the entire three-minute flute part, then the entire three-minute violin part, and so on through our small orchestra of about nine players.

Some of Boulanger's exercises were not unlike this, and though I was impressed by Ravi's ability to hear all the individual parts of a piece composed on the spot entirely in his head and then dictate them note by note and line by line, the process was not unfamiliar to me. The problem came when I placed bar lines in the music as we normally do in Western music. This created unwanted accents. When the music was played back, Alla Rakha caught the error right away. No matter where I placed the bar line (thereby "dividing" the music in the regular Western style), he would catch me.

"All the notes are equal," he kept piping at me.

The whole thing was very unnerving. I had a studio full of musicians waiting for their parts, and I had to instantaneously solve a notational problem I had never confronted before.

Finally, in desperation, I dropped the bar lines altogether. And there, before my eyes, I could see what Alla Rakha had been trying to tell me. Instead of distinct groupings of eighth notes, a steady stream of rhythmic pulses stood revealed.

Delighted, I exclaimed to Alla Rakha: "All the notes are equal!" He rewarded me with an ear-to-ear smile.

I saw then what any first-year student in a world-music course (which did not exist in 1966) would have learned in his first semester. Indian music was organized in large rhythmic cycles (called *Tal*). The interaction of melodic invention—or improvisation—with the rhythmic cycle (the *Tal*) provides the tension in Indian music, much as that between melody and harmony (rhythm is the poor relation here) provides it in Western music. Of course, learning a lesson like this on the "front lines," so to speak, is immensely more valuable than learning it from a book.

I found the ideas I was discovering while working with Ravi and Alla Rakha so new to me, and so powerful, that I immediately began trying to implement them in the music I was just beginning to write. A few years later, in 1967, Ravi Shankar was a visiting professor at the City College of New York, and he spent the academic year in New York City with Alla Rakha. I renewed my acquaintance with them and took the opportunity to study some of the principles of Indian rhythm with Alla Rakha throughout that winter.

My new skills acquired from the Boulanger studies and the vistas that my first contact with Indian music opened up for me were the beginnings of my new musical language. My contact with the theater world and my group of theater friends became the catalyst and the occasion for trying out, in a series of new pieces, some of these ideas.

I already had discovered that these early pieces—the music for Beckett's *Play* and a few chamber works—aroused an intense resistance on the part of the musicians around me. I was beginning to work in a highly reductive, repetitive style that made most of the musicians who encountered it very angry. They wanted nothing to do with it.

And no wonder. Here, with *Play,* for instance, was a piece of music based on two lines, each played by soprano saxophone, having only two notes so that each line represented an alternating, pulsing interval. When combined, these two intervals (they were written in two different repeating rhythms) formed a shifting pattern of sounds that stayed within the four pitches of the two intervals. The result was a very static piece that was still full of rhythmic variety. The piece gave birth to a whole series I wrote at this time, including a concert work for JoAnne Akalaitis and Ruth Maleczech (in which they declaimed a soufflé recipe over my music), and culminating in a string quartet I wrote in 1966. These early pieces were the origins of the musical ideas I developed more freely with the ensemble I was soon to form on my return to New York.

Clearly, from my earliest years as a composer there has always been a close bond between the music I have written for the theater and music for concert use. More often than not, theater was where my most innovative work began, often to be worked out and developed later in my concert music.

Though most of the musicians I knew in Paris were hostile to these new ideas, Jack Kripl was an exception. A native of Detroit, Jack was in Paris studying saxophone and going to Boulanger's classes, like so many other Americans. He later won first prize in the Geneva International Saxophone Competition and then spent a number of years traveling in Europe where he performed widely as a saxophone soloist with major orchestras. But in those days he was, like me, a student on a Fulbright scholarship. When I showed him these early pieces of mine, he plunged into them with enormous enthusiasm and recorded them for me to use with our new theater company. Jack is still playing with me in the Philip Glass Ensemble today, a link between my present music and my very first pieces.

Another fellow student, Daniel Lipton, also encouraged me by conducting some of these early works. But, for the most part, the general reaction to these early pieces was active hostility. Actually, most other musicians thought I was just crazy.

One of the first things I realized was that if my new music was to be played, I would have to play it myself. I had played instruments most of my life, beginning with the violin when I was six. At eight, I took up the flute and was quite a serious student, studying with Briton Johnson at the Peabody Conservatory in my home town of Baltimore. I was good enough to play in school shows, church performances of the Bach Passions and the *B-minor Mass,* and even a little amateur TV. By my college years at the University of Chicago, I had taken up the piano, practicing regularly. This continued as a "minor" subject when I went to Juilliard in 1957. However, composers at the Juilliard School were not really encouraged to be performers as well. After all, what was the point? With fellow students like Paula Robison, Paul Zukovsky and Jerome Lowenthal around, young composers could be persuaded to write music especially for them. Still, even with this lapse during my music school years, the fact was that I had been a performer before and was prepared to be one again.

Soon after returning to New York in 1967, the opportunity came. I met Jonas Mekas at a party at the home of James Tenney, a well-known authority on the music of Edgard Varèse and a composer much admired in his own right. At that moment, I'm sure Jonas didn't know a note of my work, but when I described the music I was writing, he immediately invited me to give a concert at the Film-Makers Cinematheque. And so, in September 1968, my new music had its New York debut. It was, by the way, my personal debut as well.

The program that evening comprised solo pieces and duets written over the preceding two years for the few people interested in performing my work at the time: a small group including saxophonist Jon Gibson, violinist Dorothy Pixley-Rothschild and, of course, myself. All the music was written in a style very similar to my theater music. I played a duet with Jon Gibson. I also played a solo piece. So did Jon.

The whole concert was conceived as a visual, as well as musical, presentation. The scores were printed and bound together in accordion-fold fashion so they could be opened up, unfolded and set up in geometrical constructions that echoed their titles. For example, when Dorothy was playing *Strung Out,* a solo for amplified violin, the music was tacked onto the wall, running about fifteen feet before taking a right turn out from the wall and forming an L-shape. Thus the title meant (1) that the music was strung out along the wall; (2) that it had to do with the idea of stringing a violin; and (3) it played on the current colloquialism of being "strung out," i.e., at the end of one's tether, of being dragged to the very edge of something.

There was another piece, *Music in the Form of a Square,* a play on the title of Erik Satie's *Music in the Form of a Pear.* This piece was set up in a big square, each side about ten feet long. On the inside was tacked Jon's flute part; on the outside, my own flute part. We began to play, walking in opposite directions around the square, and we came to the end of the piece at our starting point. The music was amplified with contact microphones, giving the performers total freedom of movement, but with the sound physically located by the loudspeakers.

It was a very conceptual concert. A very *neat* concert. And it was both visual and musical. The audience was mostly artists, about 120 people which, in the little Film-Makers Cinematheque, made the place seem *packed*. It was considered very successful but, more important, these were 120 very enthusiastic people. The music meant something to them in terms of their own aesthetics, something they were familiar with.

In 1967–1968, for the most part, the first recruits for performing my music were musicians like Dorothy Pixley-Rothschild and pianist/composer Arthur Murphy, whom I knew from my Juilliard days. Saxophonists Dickie Landry and Jon Gibson came to the Ensemble through other musicians and artist friends. Richard Peck, another saxophonist, joined us several years later. Because of the mix of electric piano and organ (I had chosen them for their portability) and acoustic instruments, the Ensemble was, from the beginning, amplified. In 1970, Kurt Munkacsi joined us as sound designer and mixer. A native-born New Yorker, Kurt had started out playing bass in a rock band, then discovered his true interest was in the technical side of recording and, after studying engineering on a formal basis, had worked with a number of different people in the new-music and pop-music worlds. While working as an assistant in one of John Lennon's sessions, he heard about a mobile studio through a company called Butterfly Productions that Lennon owned. We managed to get the use of it for one weekend, and that was enough to launch us on our first recording project, *Music with Changing Parts*.

This was to be recorded for my own record company, Chatham Square Productions (named after the location of Dickie Landry's studio where we often rehearsed), which that I had recently formed with Klaus Kertess for the purpose of making my music more widely available since no commercial record company would touch it at the time. Klaus had an art gallery on East 77th Street called the Bykert Gallery, and with the backing of a reasonably respectable business like Klaus's, I was able to borrow five hundred dollars from the Hebrew Free Loan Association on Second Avenue. A few enterprising philanthropists had set up this association to help newly arrived immigrants start their own businesses in America. I didn't exactly qualify, but I wasn't actually disqualified either. I got the loan, and the record company was started. Some years later, when I signed a record contract with CBS, I turned over the early Chatham Square tapes to CBS for eventual reissue.

Since *Music in Changing Parts*, Kurt has been involved in all my recording projects, assuming, over the years, the role of record producer.

His role as sound designer was of great importance to the Ensemble. As the evolution of my music has created new needs, he has designed the sound equipment necessary to make the music hearable, both to the audience and—just as important—to the onstage musicians themselves.

These musicians are at the mercy of the onstage sound monitors, which is a problem peculiar to amplified music, one that doesn't arise in any other kind of music. Onstage, the musicians are actually sitting *behind* the loudspeakers, which are pushing out a volume of sound suitable to a theater of some three thousand people. If we sat directly in front of those speakers, our ears would virtually burn out. So the question is, what do we actually listen to? One person may want to hear the left hand of the keyboard, another may want to lock his part into that of the vocalist. And only when the musicians can hear one another accurately can they play well together. By placing Kurt in the center, facing us, he can respond to our sound mix needs and mix for the house at the same time. However, this was a technique that took years of experimentation and practice to develop.

By the early 1970s there had been some shifting around in personnel, but the ensemble of keyboards, wind instruments and soprano voice was pretty well in place. During those years a number of other composers passed through, to rehearse a short time, play a concert or two and then move on. Among them were Anthony Braxton, Joan LaBarbara (she sang with us for a number of years and participated in the 1976 *Einstein on the Beach* tour), Frederick Rzewski, Jim Tenney, Barbara Benary, Bob Telson and Richard Teitelbaum, and singers Iris Hiskey and Dora Ohrenstein, the last-named still singing with us today. These brief appearances notwithstanding, the personnel of the Ensemble had been set very early. The most significant later addition was Michael Riesman who joined us in 1974, and who, at the time of writing this, functions as music director of the Ensemble. Michael is responsible not only for playing the main keyboard parts but for rehearsing the Ensemble and occasionally making transcriptions of some of my music originally written for operatic forces (for example, scenes from *Akhnaten* and *Satyagraha* are currently part of the Ensemble's concert repertory).

My involvement with the Ensemble was important to my evolution as a theater composer. In fact, during the late 1960s and early 70s, the Ensemble was the focus of my attention, for it fit easily into the downtown New York community of artists, musicians and theater people. We often played in the same places used by the theater groups, whether it was a concert presented by Ellen Stewart at La Mama Etc., or at the

Whitney Museum, or as part of a new performance series put together by Marcia Tucker, then a new, young curator of contemporary American art. And there were countless gallery and loft concerts as well.

It was the visual arts people who were really behind these events and who solidly supported them. In my case, this meant material contributions, often money, sometimes sound and/or lighting equipment, from the artists themselves—Richard Serra, Sol LeWitt, Nancy Graves, for instance. Even more important, it meant contacts with people in galleries and museums that would sponsor concerts, often in the setting of arts festivals. The Ensemble's first European tour, in 1971, was a result of my earlier solo tour playing electric organ or piano, which was put together for me by sculptor Richard Serra and took me through Holland, Switzerland and Germany. (At the time, I was working as Richard's studio assistant, and the music tour was to entice me to travel with him to help install a series of shows of his work.) I further encouraged this contact with the visual arts by asking the artists I knew to make posters for the concerts. This eventually grew to quite a collection and included works by Richard Serra, Sol LeWitt, James Rosenquist, Joel Shapiro, Nancy Graves, Keith Sonnier, Brice Marden and Barry Le Va, to name only a few. Some of these posters involved my own participation. For instance, the LeWitt poster was made from my own handwriting, and I ran off the Sonnier poster by myself on a downtown silkscreen press owned by an artists' cooperative in New York's East Village.

It was more difficult to extend that kind of collaboration into the concerts themselves, though in 1970 I did give a series of solo concerts in Europe where part of the program consisted of a screening of Michael Snow's film *Wave Length*. A few years later, in 1978, LeWitt became a collaborator with choreographer Lucinda Childs in *Dance,* a five-part evening-length work for her company and my Ensemble. I have also collaborated from time to time with Serra on art/music pieces, most recently an installation at the Ohio State University art gallery in Columbus in February 1987.

In short, by the early to mid-1970s my work was developing along two parallel, seemingly separate, paths. On the one hand, I was working in the theater and developing as a theater composer. On the other, I was actively composing concert music for my own Ensemble. The musical language was very much the same, and it was often the problems raised by theater situations that prompted me to look for new musical solutions. For me, theater became the catalyst for musical innovation, and the

Ensemble gave me both the instrument and the opportunity to develop ideas apart from the practical, and more circumscribed, demands of the theater itself.

Looking back, it now seems obvious that these two activities would eventually merge. Considering the kind of theater with which I had been involved, and the kind of composer/performer I had become, it came as no surprise what form this synthesis took.

EINSTEIN ON THE BEACH

In the early 1970s, Robert Wilson was rapidly emerging as one of the formidable theater talents of my generation. We shared the same community of support—a sizable following that provided both enthusiasm and emotional feedback—and worked mainly in the same neighborhood of New York, the as yet unfashionable Soho. We were bound to meet.

I first saw Bob's work in 1973 at the Brooklyn Academy of Music: one of the all-night performances of *The Life and Times of Josef Stalin*. It was the last performance of that production, and there was a cast party afterward at the Byrd Hoffman Foundation, Bob's administrative and fund raising organization on Spring Street. I had gone to the performance with Sue Weil, a friend who, at the time, was director of performances at the Walker Art Center in Minneapolis. I remember that the *Stalin* audience was very sparse but that we stayed through the night. Sue and I came armed with a pound of Junior's cheesecake, a local Brooklyn specialty; fortified by that, plus numerous cups of coffee available in the lobby, we hardly moved during the 10–12 hour performance.

My first reaction to Bob's work—in the case of *Stalin*, an unending meditation in movement and images with little music that I recall—was immediate. I loved it. I understood then, as I feel I have ever since, his sense of theatrical time, space and movement. These were the essentials of Bob's work as I saw them then. His extraordinary use of light developed as a major ingredient over the next twelve years.

At that time, I was in the process of completing a major work, *Music in Twelve Parts,* for the Ensemble. This was an extended composition (six hours in all) I had begun in 1971 and presented in its first full-length performance at Town Hall in the spring of 1974. Thus, both Bob and I were at that moment concluding very extensive projects.

In any case, Sue and I went to the cast party. I no longer remember who was there, but I do remember that Bob looked very tired. After all, it had been an all-night performance. He struck me as a very serious but friendly person. This was a man who, because he worked in the theater, was used to dealing with people, with dancers, actors, musicians. He was an easy person to talk to, and he still is. The party was on the second floor, and there was the usual wine and cheese and friends and congratulations. I can't remember whose idea it was for us to meet again. It just came up spontaneously between us.

We agreed that evening that we would meet and investigate the possibility of working on something together. In the spring of 1974 we began a series of regular meetings that continued over the next year. Our method was to meet every Thursday for lunch whenever we both were in New York. At first the meetings were mostly a way to get acquainted with each other. There was a small restaurant on Sullivan Street where we could talk undisturbed, almost always alone. Some time later we were occasionally joined by Christopher Knowles, who eventually contributed a number of the principal texts for *Einstein on the Beach*.

In addition to possessing an extraordinary range of theatrical talents, Bob was also a remarkably gifted teacher of handicapped or deprived children. In that capacity he had been invited to lecture at Harvard and had even become a consultant to the New York City Board of Education and the Department of Welfare. Later he became an instructor in public schools, working with disturbed children. Sometime, while he was involved in this kind of work (as well as in the making of *The Life and Times of Josef Stalin!*), he had come across Christopher, a fourteen-year-old boy with some neurological impairment and a strikingly unusual way of viewing his own world. Christopher was a poet, and he certainly was a visionary. He had learned to work with a tape recorder and a typewriter, and he was capable of writing things of startling originality. Bob has always been interested in working with people who experience things in different, out-of-the-ordinary ways. He convinced Christopher's parents that their son would be better able to develop his artistic gifts as a member of the Byrd Hoffman group, working with them as they toured South America and Europe.

It wasn't long before Bob and I were discussing a major collaboration. Though it would be almost a year before I began the music (sometime during the winter and spring of 1975), it was during these meetings that we worked out the principal themes and structures of *Einstein on the Beach*.

We began with the subject. Since neither of us knew what that would be, this involved lengthy discussions, and we used up several lunches on that item alone. Bob has always been interested in famous historical figures, and I recall that he proposed Charlie Chaplin as the major character of our work, but I couldn't see how that could be done. It seemed to me too complex a problem to present, on the stage, a character who had been one of the great performers of modern times. Adolf Hitler was another of Bob's suggestions, but this subject was just too "loaded."

I countered Hitler with Mahatma Gandhi, but I suppose that Gandhi as a subject did not have for Bob the rich associations he did for me, and the discussion passed on. At one point, Bob suggested Albert Einstein, and that immediately clicked. As a child, Einstein had been one of my heroes. Growing up just after World War II, as I had, it was impossible not to know who he was. The emphatic, if catastrophic, beginning of the nuclear age had made atomic energy the most widely discussed issue of the day, and the gentle, almost saintlike originator of the theory of relativity had achieved the 1940s version of superstar status. Besides articles in the popular press, there were any number of public discussions led by physicists, officials and other prominent figures. Among the many books that appeared at the time, quite a few were popular works "explaining" relativity, and a very notable one was by Einstein himself. Furthermore, Einstein as a personality had become, not for the first time in his life, the subjects of books, photographs, gossip, rumor, et al. For a time I, like many others of my generation, had been swept up in the Einstein craze. Perhaps Bob, growing up in Waco, Texas, had been too. In any case, it was a subject we both quickly warmed to.

The actual title of our proposed work appeared somewhat later. One Thursday, Bob brought with him the title page of what became the first of many storyboards, or visual workbooks, records in the form of drawings of our discussion and ultimately the basis of Bob's designs. The title in its original form was *Einstein on the Beach on Wall Street*.

Bob said, "What do you think?"

I said, "I like it."

I don't think we ever discussed the title again. Somewhere along the way, the title was shortened, but I don't recall when or why.

Let me make a probably-not-very-important disclaimer. I had not read Nevil Shute's 1956 postnuclear, end-of-the-world novel, *On the*

Beach. Neither, I believe, had Bob. Further, neither of us had seen the film. That doesn't mean that the title isn't connected to ours; it just means that any connection is an indirect one. However, what *Einstein on the Beach* might mean to people is very much connected to the associations they bring to it. More of this later.

During this initial period, we settled many important features of the work. To begin with, we decided the piece would have an overall running time of four hours (as it turned out, we ran over by about forty minutes). We also arrived at the visual themes: the Train, the Trial, the Field-with-Spaceship. These, like the title, were arrived at through mutual agreement: Bob would suggest visual themes but, if I failed to respond with matching interest, we would pass on to others. Now, looking over that original sketchbook, I see a number of scenes that didn't make it into the final work. One was a scene in a "Western" saloon. Another was a sketch of what Bob described as "Japanese war monsters." We also talked about an underwater scene, to be performed in tanks of water, but that proved impractical: Tanks of water are *very* heavy.

We made other important decisions regarding the overall structure at that time. *Einstein on the Beach* would have four acts separated by interludes later called "Knee Plays" (the "knee" referring to the joining function that humans' anatomical knees perform). The three visual themes would be distributed through the four acts which, with the Knee Plays, would produce the following overall form:

Knee Play 1

ACT ONE
a. (Train 1)
b. (Trial 1)

Knee Play 2

ACT TWO
c. (Field/Spaceship 1)
a. (Train 2)

Knee Play 3

ACT THREE
b. (Trial 2)
c. (Field/Spaceship 2)

Knee Play 4

ACT FOUR
a. (building from Train)
b. (bed from Trial)
c. (spaceship—interior of earlier Spaceship)

Knee Play 5

By then we had decided on the kind of company we would require to realize this particular work. I think we correctly assumed (this, after all, was 1974) that we would find no interest on the part of theaters or opera companies in producing such a piece. It never even came up between us as a wild idea that someone, somewhere, might possibly provide the wherewithal (personnel, rehearsal space, materials, etc.) for us to build it. From the very beginning, we knew we would have to do it ourselves.

However, we weren't exactly starting from scratch. By 1974 I had an established music ensemble, most of whose members had been with me for years, some since 1968. These regular players were Jon Gibson, Richard Peck, Dickie Landry, singer Joan LaBarbara—and Kurt Munkacsi, who designed and built the sound equipment and handled the live sound mix at concerts. Michael Riesman, our most recent recruit, quickly became the principal keyboard player (I was always the second, sometimes the third, keyboardist) and soon made himself invaluable, practically becoming our pit conductor by *Einstein*'s opening night. That, then, would be our orchestra.

On his side, Bob, over the years, had developed a wide circle of actors, dancers and collaborators of various kinds. Further, his headquarters on Spring Street had a quite useable rehearsal space. However, Bob decided not to depend on the regulars he had worked with in the past, but to look for a new company. His existing company was basically comprised of amateurs, and we obviously needed professional skills, especially in musical and vocal areas. We felt we needed an acting company of between twelve and sixteen people who also would be able to sing (they would be our chorus, responsible for the large majority of the singing) as well as dance, for we had decided that the first two of the Field/Spaceship scenes would be extended dance pieces.

Apart from this cadre, Bob envisioned the use of three or four "character," or lead, actors. In addition, since Einstein was known to have been an amateur violinist, I suggested that the Einstein character play the violin and be placed somewhere between the music ensemble and the singing/dancing ensemble.

So, by the end of this initial period of meetings, which had stretched

31

into the late fall of 1974, we knew quite a lot about the piece we were making. Ahead of us loomed huge problems of casting, administration, financing, etc., but the thoroughness of our planning had made the work tangible for us. Our "libretto" already had begun to take shape in the form of the previously mentioned sketchbook of visual themes. That became the basis for the music I soon was to begin writing. As for the text, both sung and spoken, that would be developed during our rehearsal period, still almost a year away.

Considering that ours was a piece of music theater destined for a large proscenium stage, it is evident that the authors were going about it in a rather unusual way. This was hardly one of the many experimental works predestined for the lofts and galleries of downtown New York. We knew from the beginning that the piece would have to be presented in a large venue equipped with all the mechanical facilities—lights, bars, wing space, orchestra pit—one would expect to find in a modern theater or opera house. Besides that, there were a number of presumptions Bob and I made about the work which, though they might be common ideas in the emerging New York counterculture, would appear quite startling in a larger cultural context. Interestingly enough, these were things that Bob and I had never needed to discuss. I suppose it was precisely because we did not *have* to discuss our way of working that we were drawn together in the first place.

For example, it never occurred to us that *Einstein on the Beach* would have a story or contain anything like an ordinary plot. Bob, by then, had done a series of large theater works which, by their titles at least, were based on the lives of famous persons (Freud, Stalin, etc.). But how that title character appeared in the work could, in the end, be *very* abstract. It seemed to me that in Bob's previous work, the title merely provided an occasion for which a theatrical/visual work could be constructed. It functioned as a kind of attention point around which his theater could revolve, without necessarily becoming its primary subject. This freedom gave his work an extension and richness which often overshadowed the work of his contemporaries.

To me, this process took on a somewhat different meaning in the Einstein work (as I believe it did for Bob as well). I saw *Einstein on the Beach* more as a portrait opera. In this case the portrait of Einstein that we would be constructing replaced the idea of plot, narrative, development, all the paraphernalia of conventional theater. Furthermore, we understood that this portrait of Einstein was a poetic vision. Facts and chronology could be included (and indeed were) in the sequence of movements, images, speaking and singing. Conveying that kind of information, though, was certainly not the point of the work.

In one of our early conversations, Bob said to me, "I like Einstein as a character, because everybody knows who he is." In a sense, we didn't need to tell an Einstein story because everyone who eventually saw our *Einstein* brought their own story with them. In the four months that we toured *Einstein* in Europe we had many occasions to meet with our audiences, and people occasionally would ask us what it "meant." But far more often people told us what it meant to *them,* sometimes even giving us plot elucidation and complete scenario. The point about *Einstein* was clearly not what it "meant" but that it was *meaningful* as generally experienced by the people who saw it.

From the viewpoint of the creators, of course, that is exactly the way it was constructed to work. Though we made no attempt at all to tell a story, we did use dramaturgical devices to create a clearly paced overall dramatic shape. For instance, a "finale" is a dramaturgical device; an "epilogue" is another. Using contrasting sections, like a slow trial scene followed by a fast dance scene, is a dramaturgical device, and we used such devices freely. I am sure that the absence of direct connotative "meaning" made it all the easier for the spectator to personalize the experience by supplying his own special "meaning" out of his own experience, while the work itself remained resolutely abstract.

As to the use of three visual themes, or images, Bob often mentioned that he envisioned them in three distinct ways: (1) a landscape seen at a distance (the Field/Spaceship scenes); (2) still lifes seen at a middle distance (the Trial scenes); and (3) portraits seen as in a closeup (the Knee Plays). As these three perspectives rotated through the four acts of the work, they created a sequence of images in an ordered scale.

Furthermore, the recurrence of the images implied a kind of quasi-development. For example, the sequence of Train scenes from the Act I, scene I Train, to the "night train" of Act II and finally the building which resembled in perspective the departing night train, presented that sequence of images in a reductive order (each one became less "train-like") and at the same time more focused and energized. The same process applies to the sequence of Trial scenes (ending with a bar of light representing the bed) as well as the Field/Spaceship, with the final scene in the interior of the spaceship serving as a kind of apocalyptic grand finale of the whole work. Each time an image reappeared, it was altered to become more abstract and, oddly enough, more powerful. The way these three sequences were intercut with each other, as well as with the portrait-scale Knee Plays, served to heighten the dramatic effect.

The thematic structure of the music very closely followed this somewhat complex but overtly dramatic structure. This included the change of scale from the full ensemble with chorus, to *a cappella* choir, to solo violin (as in the second Knee Play). There were musical as well as dramatic strategies involved in some of those decisions. After all, everyone couldn't play and/or sing continuously for four hours and forty minutes, so the necessity of creating resting places for the singers and players was usually combined with a dramatic/structural purpose.

A somewhat whimsical exception to the above logic was the placement of Einstein (the violinist) in the work. Bob and I often began—or sometimes ended—our discussion of each scene with the question "Is Einstein here?" Sometimes the answer was yes, sometimes no. And in any case, our "Einstein" couldn't *always* be on stage: No violinist could play for four hours straight.

Many details were added later during the rehearsal period. At some point Bob decided to use an Einstein costume for everyone on stage; this was based on a photo of Einstein dressed in baggy pants, suspenders, (or "braces"), short-sleeved shirt, and smoking a pipe. All the visual details—elevators, space rockets, gyroscopes, watches, clocks, compasses and so on—were things we had come to associate with Einstein, either through his own writings or from photographs or anecdotes about him. I discovered years later why the furniture on the stage was all made out of plumbing pipes: Bob told me that Einstein had once remarked that, if he had his life to live over again, he would have been a plumber! From our first meetings to opening night, one could see a steady accretion of Einstein lore and memorabilia being loaded into the work through Bob's eerily steady and brilliant imagination. The structure we had started with was both loose enough and then precise enough to contain nearly anything either we or, soon after, our company came up with.

The result—or should I say convergence—of this visual process with a very close musical articulation of the same, had the effect of empowering what had started as an abstract structure with a highly dramatic and theatrical shape. It hardly mattered what you thought *Einstein on the Beach* might "mean." The work began with a nineteenth-century train and ended with a twentieth-century spaceship, and it was fired throughout by images, movement, words, music, and finally the imaginations of the spectators themselves.

It was possible for Bob and me to embark so confidently upon such a large-scale work as *Einstein on the Beach*—a piece with so many unusual elements—because of one fact: So much of what we knew about the theater (and the contemporary aesthetics that went with it) had been learned from an older generation, many of whose major creative figures were still actively working around us. Bob often told me that the world of dance had a formative effect on his thinking, largely through the work of George Balanchine and Merce Cunningham. For me, an almost identical result had come about through my exposure to, and experiences with, the new European theater of Brecht and Beckett.

Fundamental to our approach was the assumption that the audience itself completed the work. The statement is no mere metaphor; we meant it quite literally. In the case of *Einstein on the Beach,* the "story" was supplied by the imaginations of the audience, and there was no way for us to predict, even if we had wanted to, what the "story" might be for any particular person.

I arrived at that assumption through my early working experience with the then-forming Mabou Mines theater in Paris in 1965. Those experiences were of crucial importance to me, for they removed my evolving approach from a purely theoretical context and rerooted it in a practical theatrical foundation.

One especially memorable experience for me was working on Samuel Beckett's *Play*. This fascinating trialogue takes place after the death of the three characters. We see their faces on top of three funeral urns, two women and a man, and in three separate but intercut monologues they tell the story of their romantic triangle, spotlights moving from face to face to trigger the speakers. JoAnne Akalaitis, Ruth Maleczech and David Warrilow were the actors, Lee Breuer directed, and I wrote the music, a series of five or six short pieces separated by equal lengths of silence.

The music for *Play*, as I described earlier, was simply two superimposed patterns of two notes each. Working with Jack Kripl on soprano saxophone, we recorded a piece that lasted the one-hour length of the play, forming a mosaic background to the whole. In terms of the music alone, it was the first of the highly reductive and repetitive pieces that occupied me for years afterward, and it set the direction which eventually led to the ensemble music just three years in the future. This first production in Paris was performed several times; because of its size it could, and did, fit into all kinds of small theaters and studios. Later, *Play* was often performed in New York at La Mama. As a result, I viewed it many, many times and listened to the taped music both with and without the play—another formative experience for me.

As theater music, *Play* had an equally crucial effect on my thinking. I found, during my many viewings, that I experienced the work differently on almost every occasion. Specifically, I noticed that the emotional quickening (or epiphany) of the work seemed to occur in a different place in each performance—in spite of the fact that all the performance elements such as light, music and words were completely set.

This puzzled me. It also made me extremely curious, since traditional theater "works" quite differently. Every time you see *Hamlet,* for example, the catharsis, or emotional high point, of the play comes in the same place. One might say that a classical or traditional play is a machine built in a specific way to make the emotional peak always happen in the places the author intended. Various productions, which include the visual elements of sets and costumes as well as acting styles of different schools, are designed to make the machine function precisely. This legacy of Western theater goes back to the Greeks: You can read about precisely this in Aristotle's *Poetics.* It may at first seem astonishing how enduring these theatrical devices are, but on second thought, perhaps it is not so surprising since, after all, these are psychological mechanisms which can be intensely personal as well as broadly universal.

But the point for me was this: When confronted with Beckett's *Play* I was forced to see that the psychological mechanism was working quite differently from more traditionally constructed works. Otherwise, why and how could I experience *Play* so differently at different performances?

This deeply puzzled me for a long time, and it finally led to the conclusion that Beckett worked for me the way it did because it was *not* a theatrical object with an interior mechanism designed to evoke a specific response. It occurred to me then that the emotion of Beckett's theater did not reside *in* the piece in a way that allowed a complicated process of identification to trigger response. It is this identification with a play (or, more precisely, confusion of ourselves with the person in the play) that really is at the heart of traditional theater. No, *Play* worked differently.

A simpler way to say it is that Beckett's *Play* doesn't exist separately from its relationship to the viewer, who is included as part of the play's content. This is the mechanism we mean when we say the audience "completes" the work. The invention, or innovation, of Beckett's *Play* is that it includes us, the audience, in a different way than does traditional theater. Instead of submitting us to an internal mechanism within the work, it allows us, by our presence, to relate to it, complete it and personalize it. The power of the work is directly proportional to the degree to which we succeed in personalizing it.

Extending the Beckett theory into other realms, one might venture to say that art objects—be they paintings, string quartets, or plays—don't exist or function by themselves as abstract entities. They function and become meaningful only when there are people present to experience them. When put that way, one old riddle is answered very easily. When the tree falls in the forest, does it make a sound if no one is there to hear it? The answer, of course, is no. Yet many people still act as if Art somehow has an independent existence all its own.

Art and culture are invented. We make them up. Otherwise, they don't exist. We live with our culture so closely that we think of Art as something that has its own natural, independent existence. But, obviously, it does not. I have no doubt that if one lived alone long enough, one would stop making Art, because Art has to do with people. But of course no one lives totally alone, isolated from the society around them. Even a hermit carries Society with him in his extreme solitude, and Art, as we often say, is a form of human communication. Human society and culture consist of things that people create together, and this is truer of Art than of anything else.

People talk about criminals being the result of their environment, but they seldom speak about artists being victims of *their* environment, though in fact they are. When things go well, we take all the credit; when things go bad, we blame "society." Rarely does an artist give credit to society, but all too often society gets the credit for our failures. Rembrandt, for instance, didn't drop out of the sky; he came out of a period, from the social context of the world he grew up in. Otherwise, everything about Rembrandt is invented, including the pictures.

This was a view very much shared by the world of musicians and artists around me. Certainly I had been prepared for it by John Cage's book *Silence,* which I had read as early as 1962. Later, I saw in New York an older generation of artists such as Jasper Johns and Sol LeWitt and found their work very much consonant with this way of thinking. This was true of the visual artists of my generation as well—Richard Serra, Eva Hess and Nancy Graves, to mention a very few—and certainly of the theater people I mentioned earlier.

Starting with that Beckett work in Paris in 1965, I began to find my way into a truly contemporary way of thinking about both music and theater. I came to see the idea of art content tied in with our relationship to it, an idea providing the basis of a truly modern, or perhaps postmodern, aesthetic. Furthermore, it was an aesthetic that, in a very satisfying way, tied artists in all fields to other contemporary thought, be it philosophy, science or psychology.

Between 1965 and 1975 I produced ten years of work in music and theater which, in most of its important ways, was based on this way of thinking. *Einstein on the Beach* was a next step on a path that had begun some years before.

By the spring of 1975, Bob's *Einstein on the Beach* sketchbook was almost complete. There would be additions and corrections right through the rehearsal period, but the themes were mostly there, and the structure had been set from the beginning. We were entering the second period of the work, during which I composed almost all the music.

As mentioned earlier, I had recently completed an extended work, *Music in Twelve Parts*. This was an ensemble work written between 1971 and 1974. Starting from 1965, I had been preoccupied with the idea of using rhythmic structure to generate an overall form. The genesis of this had been the music for Beckett's *Play*. However, my interest in this technique had been quickened by my contact with Ravi Shankar and Alla Rakha, and all through the late 1960s my ensemble music reflected my preoccupation with developing techniques that would extend a rhythmic motive into an overall structure.

By 1970 I felt ready to organize my thinking of the previous five years into one large extended work. *Music in Twelve Parts* was to become a kind of catalogue of ideas about rhythmic structure. Each "part" concentrated on several of these techniques (cyclic, additive and repetitive structure), and by the completion of Part 10, the cataloguing was fairly intact. Thus Part 11 concentrated on the joining places of the other parts, which, to the listener, appeared as modulations. Part 12 turned to cadence—the formal closing phrases we are accustomed to hearing in Western music—as a fitting end to such an extended piece (each "part" was some twenty minutes long, the entire work requiring, with intermission, about five and one-half hours to perform).

When combined with the earlier techniques of rhythmic structure, these two new developments (modulation and cadence) became the basis of my next ensemble work: *Another Look at Harmony, Parts 1 and 2*. This music became the beginning of *Einstein on the Beach*. Part 1 became the music for Act I, scene 1 (the Train), and Part 2 became Dance 1 (Field/Spaceship). However, it was also important to me that the musical language grew naturally from the earlier sources. If anything, *Einstein on the Beach* became an occasion, an opportunity, for these musical ideas to flow into a larger form. (A detailed discussion of the *Einstein* score begins on page 57.)

The music came very quickly. I think the ease with which I wrote the *Einstein* music was due both to the inspiration of the subject matter and to Bob's drawings. I began in the spring of 1975, and the score was completed and ready for rehearsal by that November. I composed the scenes in order, except for the Knee Plays, which I wrote at the end. During this period, our meetings took on a more practical form. As I mentioned earlier, we had planned two large dance sections. Bob wanted these two sections to physically break open the piece after the other scenes where stage movement would seem incremental and so slowed down that certain long passages would appear almost frozen in time.

Bob suggested Andy de Groat as our choreographer. I had seen his work in Bob's *A Letter to Queen Victoria* in 1974 and had been struck by the power his work could convey through the grace and simplicity of natural movements. I always thought of the *Einstein* dance sections as two pillars equidistant from the ends of the piece which provided the shocks that would drive it into the next section and give a dramatic balance to the whole. I think Andy's dances in that first production were very successful in achieving this freedom and naturalness.

During this period Bob settled on three of the four main characters. The two women would be Sheryl Sutton and Lucinda Childs. Sheryl was a long-time associate of Bob's, and over the years had become one of the foremost exponents of his style of movement and acting.

Since 1971, Lucinda had been a very well-known "postmodern" choreographer. Her work first appeared in the 1960s as part of a group of choreographers known as the Judson Group, named after the Judson Church in Manhattan's Greenwich Village, which first presented their work. (As mentioned earlier, other dancers who emerged at that time included Yvonne Rainer, David Gordon and Trisha Brown, all of whom became renowned choreographers in later years.) They personified a movement that represented the generation after Merce Cunningham and John Cage, and their work was frequently based on everyday colloquial movements and, often, improvisation. Some of this work, particularly Lucinda's, could be very reductive in style, very much like my own approach in music. I remember one performance of Lucinda's at Washington Square Methodist Church in 1975 where all four pieces on the program were danced in total silence.

Both Bob and I were anxious for Lucinda to appear as a leading character in *Einstein,* but we were unsure that she would agree to an acting part, especially since the dance sections were to be choreographed by someone else. To our great relief, though, she accepted, and ended up with her own dance solos, which she composed for herself, in the first Train scene. When we began the second production of *Einstein on the Beach* at BAM (Brooklyn Academy of Music) in 1985, Andy was occupied in Europe and unavailable, so Lucinda reproduced her original choreography and created two new dances for the dance scenes as well.

That left us with two characters to cast. For the part of the young boy, Bob wanted to use Paul Mann, who was then ten years old. Bob had worked with him before, and since this was to be a speaking part, there were no musical problems to solve. The last role, that of an elderly man, was left for the auditions, which were soon upon us. Before we got to that, though, we had other problems to solve, which all involved financing and administration.

The administrative part was pretty straightforward. We each had our own organizations, Bob's Byrd Hoffman Foundation on Spring Street and my Aurora Music Foundation, which was run by Performing Artservices, a not-for-profit arts administration service begun some years before by Mimi Johnson, Jane Yockel and Margaret Wood. Besides working for their other clients, they organized my concert tours. Jane Yockel and George Ashley (another Artservices person) had worked with Bob before, which made it easier to coordinate our plans. In the end, we decided to use Bob's organization for the overall running of *Einstein*, since he had rehearsal space on Spring Street ready for use, plus important contacts in Europe, where the work was destined to premiere.

Sometime in the spring of 1974, Michel Guy came to New York to see Bob and me. Michel had been the director of the Autumn Festival in Paris during the Pompidou administration and had introduced some of America's most progressive performers (including Merce Cunningham, John Cage and Bob Wilson) to France. When the d'Estaing government had come to power, he had been named minister of culture. As it turned out, Michel had long wanted to do a challenging new work, and this seemed an ideal opportunity. Bob had just visited him in Paris, and the minister said, "At last! Now I can do something really new!" When Michel saw me in New York, he was equally enthusiastic and suggested that our new work premiere in France. He would arrange a substantial commission from the French government. Specifically, he wanted us to premiere *Einstein on the Beach* at the Avignon Festival in August of 1976 and later to present it in a two-week run at the Autumn Festival in Paris.

This was a heaven-sent offer. However, it didn't come completely out of the blue. Though we were virtually unknown in America, both Bob and I had worked quite a lot in Europe by then, and Bob was particularly well known in Paris. One of his early works, *Deafman Glance,* had created a sensation there, as has every work he has done there since that time. I was part of the new American avant-garde known in Paris, and no doubt I had a following of my own. In fact, I had appeared with my Ensemble at Michel Guy's Autumn Festival in Paris some years before. But Bob was a true *enfant terrible* of the theater, and in Paris that meant a great deal.

With the matter of our premiere settled, we turned our attention to the practical matters relating to forming a company and mounting a production of a full-length music theater work. It was November 1975, and the score was virtually complete, with Bob in the process of building models of the sets. When complete, it would be possible to run through all the scene changes of the opera in a theater the size of a doll's house. This is an important stage when the future technical problems will begin (hopefully) to reveal themselves.

This is also an important stage for the composer. To an extent, timings of the scene changes can be calculated and the flow of the music coordinated to the visual elements. At this point, these decisions are provisional, and refinements can be made even beyond the opening night.

We were fortunate in having Ninon Karlweiss as our agent in Europe, a very experienced, respected and rather formidable person long associated with the European avant-garde theater. She was an early supporter of Bob's work and also had done some bookings for my Ensemble, though theater work was more in her line. She had been responsible for bringing Grotowski's Polish Lab Theater to America in 1969, and had also been associated early on with Peter Brook. There were few people in the contemporary theater world she didn't know. Ninon ranged through Europe, keeping no notes, writing no contracts as far as I could tell, but somehow unfailingly getting work in which she believed into the places she thought it needed to be seen. If you were to see her at a performance, however, she always appeared to be sound asleep (I personally saw this many times). But when the performance was over, she could launch into a detailed critique of whatever it was, to the astonishment of all. This, and her habit of smoking a plastic cigarette, are memories of Ninon I shall always carry with me.

Now Ninon announced that she had secured an important second producer for us. It would be the Venice Biennale, and Ninon had proposed a very interesting arrangement: In lieu of a performance fee, the Italian government would build the sets and paint the drops. Bob was very pleased, since he considered the Italian shops to be among the finest in Europe. And though it would require some traveling back and forth to check on the progress of the work, it would be worth it. Besides, it helped to have the decor built on the same side of the Atlantic as the premiere, saving us the shipping costs.

The next important development was the actual formation of the performing company. The pit musicians would be my own Ensemble, and I was sure I couldn't find a better group of musicians to play the music. Kurt Munkacsi, naturally, would be on hand to develop a sound system necessary for a stage work of this size.

The singers and dancers we decided to find through auditions; for economic reasons, we were attempting, as much as possible, to find people who could perform in both capacities. (At the Brooklyn Academy of Music (BAM) revival in 1984, we were able to have a separate corps de ballet for the dance sections, which helped make those performances more polished.) But we found quite a few dancers with musical training and, on the other hand, a number of singers who had had movement and dance experience. I think this is probably due to the American tradition of musical comedy, where song and dance performers are taken for granted. As a result, in America it is not uncommon to find young people who may later specialize, but who begin their training with both music and dance lessons.

We held what is known as an open call audition in November. This meant placing ads in trade papers and in the *Village Voice*. To our complete dismay, nearly 120 people showed up, and it took Bob, Andy and me over three days to see everybody. It was a very wide range of people, some very accomplished and serious, others not, and even a few tourists who weren't really trying out at all but simply wanted to meet us! Each person had to sing for me, do a movement exercise for Andy, and perform an acting or theater piece for Bob. I think we probably made some fine choices (good guesses, really), because this initial company of sixteen or so stayed pretty much together for the next year.

During the auditions, we cast Samuel M. Johnson as the Judge in the Trial scenes as well as the Bus Driver in the last Knee Play. People often asked where we found Mr. Johnson (who had such a dignified air that no one ever called him by his first name). Actually, he just showed up with half a dozen other older men (the call for this part was for an elderly man). When we met him in 1975, he was well into his seventies. He had done some film and theater work, seemed to be retired, lived in Brooklyn, and we never knew much more than that about him.

At first he was hesitant to accept the role. He explained that he had just taken up the piano, and he was concerned that the touring might interfere with his regular practicing. I assured him that in the theaters where we would be performing, it was normal to find pianos and practice rooms and that we would be sure he had time every day for his piano practice. Convinced that his studies could continue unhindered, he accepted the part. I clearly recall hearing him playing in the afternoons on the backstage pianos wherever we were appearing, usually arrangements of Stephen Foster.

Our general plan was to rehearse from December to April in the Byrd Hoffman studios on Spring Street. May and June would be a break, and we would reconvene in Avignon in July for a last few weeks of rehearsal with sets and costumes before the premiere in August at the Avignon Festival. The initial commission allowed us operating expenses and salaries through our American rehearsal period. That and our enthusiasm for the work was enough to get us started.

We began with a five-day-per-week rehearsal schedule which grew to six days later in the winter. Each day included three three-hour rehearsals, one each for music, dance, and staging. This meant beginning the day around 10:00 AM and working into the evening. Though Bob and Andy were each in charge of one rehearsal, I played a version of the music reduced for one electric organ at all three of them. Over the next four months I got to know my music *extremely* well.

Teaching the singing parts to the chorus took place over the next four months, barely enough time considering there were four and one-half hours of music to learn. I never told the singers exactly how much, because I feared I might have a full-scale rebellion on my hands before I even got started. I used a method I had learned from Alla Rakha when I had been studying tabla (the paired Indian hand drums) with him some eight years before. Very simply, we began at the beginning, memorizing a small amount of music. The next day we reviewed the previous day's work and added a new section. We continued this way, each day beginning with a review of the accumulated learned material and adding new material at the end. Ultimately, we were able to do full run-throughs of the work entirely by memory.

At the same time, the dance sections were being rehearsed, and Bob, also working chronologically, was staging the work to the music. In the end, through a very intensive and protracted work period, our company not only learned the piece but mastered it. I don't doubt that they were literally doing it in their sleep. Some of them claimed they actually woke up at night with numbers and solfège syllables (*do, re, mi . . .*) running through their heads. And I think this degree of mastery was essential since at the same time they were singing, they were often required to execute extremely complex hand and body movements, devised by Bob, which unfolded at a precise rate. Besides this, most of them were also in Andy's dances so that, in the rehearsal period as in the performance itself, there were few moments of repose for the performers. In retrospect, I think we set tasks for our company of almost heroic proportions, though I don't think Bob and I realized it at the time. As for the company, they accepted these conditions willingly and, it seemed to me, cheerfully, as the simple demands of the work.

During the musical rehearsals, I began to use solfège syllables and numbers as an aid to memorizing. This eventually became the vocal text of the piece. Also during this period, the spoken lines became part of the piece. From our first meeting, Bob had wanted to use Christopher Knowles's writing for at least part of the work. Christopher had attended a number of our initial meetings and, not long after, Bob began showing me some of his writings with the idea that they could become part of the vocal text. At that time, though, I didn't feel confident about setting his words. It may have been partly the text itself. I liked it right away, but I didn't know whether I could incorporate it into a vocal line.

For me, the main problem was that I had had very little experience in recent years setting words to music. As a student, I had written quite a lot of vocal and choral music, but that had been more than fourteen years earlier. Finally I suggested we use the text as a spoken part over the music. This also gave Bob a great deal of freedom in the placement of the text. I think today my attitude to the text would be quite different, and I probably would have set at least some of the text as singing parts. However, I am not at all unhappy about how Christopher's text worked out. My interest in spoken texts in music theater continues to the present. Certainly my return to voice-over spoken text in *Akhnaten* was due to what I considered a successful use of this technique in *Einstein on the Beach*.

Once the voice-over procedure was introduced, Bob found a number of places for Christopher's texts to appear in the action, usually spoken by Lucinda or Sheryl. In addition, he asked Lucinda to compose a text for her extended appearance during the second Trial. The result was what we all called the "Supermarket" or "Bathing Cap" piece. I later was told that she had found the lines unexpectedly difficult, had developed a real "writer's block" about them and could think of no way at all to write about beaches. At that point Bob asked her, "Why are you avoiding the beach?" The result was a speech not *about* the beach, but about *avoiding* the beach! And it's the only reference to a beach in the entire opera.

Two of the most remarkable texts were contributed by Mr. Johnson. In the first Trial, Bob wanted the elder Judge to make a speech, and at one of the rehearsals he asked Mr. Johnson if he could write something for himself. Mr. Johnson said he thought he could, and at the next day's rehearsal launched into his "Paris, city of lights" speech from memory. Bob and I, as well as the entire company, were astonished. The dramatic sense and length of the speech, as well as its general "feel" for the music, were perfect. No changes were necessary, though from time to time during the tour Mr. Johnson would alter a phrase or word, quietly polishing his small masterpiece.

Mr. Johnson surprised us a second time when we premiered *Einstein* in Avignon. When his moment came in the first Trial, without warning of any kind to Bob or me, he delivered his speech in French! It was quaint French, meticulously learned from a textbook, and it stunned and delighted everyone in the theater.

As we rehearsed the work in chronological order, we became accustomed to Mr. Johnson's precision and impeccable delivery of his text, and when we reached the end of the work (Knee Play 5), Bob again asked Mr. Johnson to provide a text for the Bus Driver who appears in the final moments. Once more, he contributed a speech—"Two lovers sat on a park bench"—that impressed us with its deftness, simplicity and complete appropriateness. I can't imagine a better ending to the evening than the words he gave us. A man over twice the age of anyone else in the company, Mr. Johnson kept somewhat apart from the rest of us. However, he was always a pleasure to be with and to work with. Eight years later, during the revival of *Einstein* at BAM, we found him unchanged, even to his practice of formally addressing Bob as Mr. Wilson and me as Mr. Glass.

It had been a long and absorbing rehearsal period. Some small props were in use but, as yet, no one had seen the sets or costumes, though during the rehearsal of each scene, Bob showed the company many drawings of both. As for the music, we had what I could play of it by myself on one small electric keyboard. Now the time had come for a real run-through with musicians before an invited audience.

First I rehearsed with my Ensemble for nearly two weeks. Then we found a violinist, Bob Brown, who could manage the difficult violin part and who agreed to play in costume for a long, still somewhat indefinite, tour.

By late April we were ready for our first public showing. We secured the use of a small theater (called at that time the Video Exchange Theater) in Westbeth, an artist-housing project in New York's Greenwich Village. There, on two successive evenings, we performed *Einstein on the Beach* for the first time. There were no sets or costumes (those were still being built in Italy), and the lighting—by then an important element for Bob—was sketchy. Still in all, the music, the text and the action were learned, the dances completed. The piece was *there*. We had two full houses in our two-hundred-seat theater, packed with friends, artists and a few possible sponsors.

From the reaction of those initial two nights, Bob and I got our first inkling of the electrifying effect this work was capable of having on an audience.

While *Einstein on the Beach* was coming together in the studio, the administration of the *Einstein* company was also evolving. In effect, we were forming an ersatz opera company designed to travel. Neither Bob nor I had any idea what all that involved and, having gone through it once, I see why companies and work like this are rare. To produce an innovative work on a large scale requires organization and skills that its authors have no time for (they are, after all, *making* the work) and little inclination to take up. In the case of *Einstein,* Bob's Byrd Hoffman Foundation became the headquarters around which a whole organization took shape.

The overall administrator was Kathleen Norris, and in most ways she operated like the producer, regulating cash flow, coordinating schedules, organizing shipping, looking at contracts, and on and on.

In addition to Ninon Karlweiss, we were fortunate in having another associate of Bob's and mine in Europe: Benedicte Pesle. Her office in Paris was Artservices, actually the progenitor of the Performing Artservices with whom I was then working in New York. Benedicte had worked mainly with American dance companies in Paris such as those of Merce Cunningham, Twyla Tharp and, later on, Lucinda Childs. She also had been a long-time supporter of Bob's work and was involved in his first appearances in Paris. Some years before she had been responsible for bringing Michel Guy to one of my rehearsals in Dickie Landry's studio in New York's Chinatown. With Ninon as our agent and Benedicte working out of her Paris office as a kind of European coordinating center, the *Einstein* tour could begin to come together.

Significantly, we committed ourselves to a European tour long before we began to think about an American presenter. The reasons for this have to do with the somewhat complex social and economic differences between European and American art support, and less to do with marginal differences between the European and American publics. My experience has been that American audiences are as eager for new music theater work as their European counterparts. The problem has been that, at that time, they seldom had the chance to see any.

▲ Tyson Street as Einstein in the 1984 Brooklyn Academy of Music revival of *Einstein on the Beach*. (TOM CARAVAGLIA) ▼ *Einstein on the Beach*, Act II, Scene 2—Night Train; from the BAM revival, 1984. (TOM CARAVAGLIA)

▲ *Einstein on the Beach*—Spaceship; BAM, 1984. (TOM CARAVAGLIA)   ▼ SAMUEL M. JOHNSON AS THE BUS DRIVER IN THE FINAL SCENE OF *E*INSTEIN ON THE *B*EACH; BAM, 1984. (TOM CARAVAGLIA)

▲ *Satyagraha*, Act I, Scene 1—The Kuru Field of Justice; Stuttgart production, directed and designed by Achim Freyer. (HORST HUBER)

▲ *Satyagraha,* Act I, Scene 1—The Kuru Field of Justice. Douglas Perry, center, in the original Dutch production directed by David Pountney and designed by Robert Israel. (TOM CARAVAGLIA) ▼ *Satyagraha,* Act II, Scene 2—Indian Opinion; Stuttgart production. (HORST HUBER)

▲ *Satyagraha*, Act II, Scene 3—Protest; Stuttgart production. (HORST HUBER) ▼ *Satyagraha*, Act III—New Castle March; Stuttgart production. (HORST HUBER)

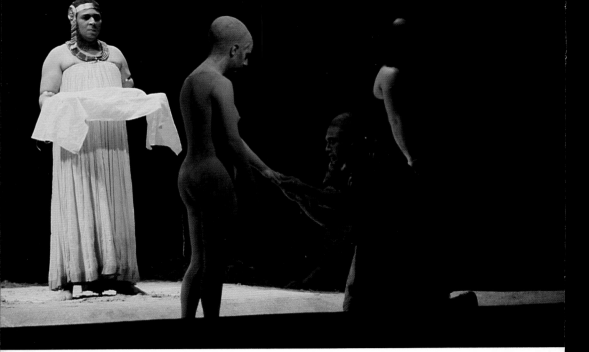

▲ *Akhnaten,* beginning of Act I, Scene 2—The Coronation of Akhnaten; Houston production directed by David Freeman, designed by Robert Israel and Richard Riddell, November 1984. (JIM CALDWELL) ▼ *Akhnaten,* Act I, Scene 2—The Coronation of Akhnaten; Houston production. (JIM CALDWELL)

▲ *Akhnaten,* Act II, Scene 2—Akhnaten and Nefertiti. Christopher Robeson and Marta Senn in the Houston production. (JIM CALDWELL)   ▼ *Akhnaten,* Act II, Scene 2—Akhnaten and Nefertiti; original Stuttgart production, directed and designed by Achim Freyer. (HORST HUBER)

▲ *Akhnaten*, Act III—Attack and Fall; Stuttgart production. (HORST HUBER) ▼ *The Juniper Tree*, end of Act I. Ruby Hinds, Sanford Sylvan and Janet Brown in American Repertory Theater (Cambridge, Mass.) production, directed by André Serban, designed by Michael H. Yeargan. (AMERICAN REPERTORY THEATER)

Public funding for new works in America has been skimpy and reluctant. As for private and corporate funding, there have been several factors that, until recently, have held them back. I think that the avant-garde was generally considered too wacky for the oil and tobacco companies (until, that is, they discovered that a large public actually likes the stuff). Also, only in recent years have knowledgeable specialists been working in influential positions where art-funding policies could be affected. After all, it may take a lot of hard work and money to organize a Picasso retrospective, but it's hardly daring or courageous. It takes a different level of commitment and imagination to fund the kind of work that might appear in, say, BAM's Next Wave Festival. In any case, in 1975 and 1976 that kind of support had not surfaced in America.

On the other hand, in Europe there were organizations, almost entirely government funded, presenting all manner of new work. Cities like Paris, Venice, Berlin, Amsterdam, and Edinburgh, to mention only a few of the better-known ones, all have annual performance arts festivals, most of them begun as part of the reconstruction after World War II.

The festivals in Europe begin in the spring and continue through the fall. The trick for touring companies is to go from country to country, hitting the greatest number of festivals in the shortest period of time in order to keep costs to a minimum. This is probably the main reason so many American performers and companies have developed strong reputations in Europe before becoming known at home. This certainly was true for the Philip Glass Ensemble, and it made me an internationally known composer years before I was known in America. As I write this now, in the mid-1980s, things have changed considerably, with major performance festivals in New York, Los Angeles, and Philadelphia, as well as institutions with innovative company directors in Minneapolis, Boston and Chicago, to mention a few. At this point, American performers of new works can begin to work at home. In the mid-1970s, though, there was no real choice but to look to Europe.

Ninon finally put together a six-country tour that would last about four months and add up to over thirty performances. Almost all of the potential presenters were coming to see the opening at Avignon, and I suppose it was just as well that Bob and I didn't know that none of them, apart from the French, had actually signed a contract with us. Everything depended on the success of the opening night.

The festival at Avignon, occurring each year in August, is an international theater and arts festival that attracts productions from all over the world. The main festival sometimes sponsors avant-garde pieces but, as at Edinburgh, it is at the "fringe" festival where younger and often less conventional theater people can show their work. For the weeks of the festival, the city is packed with young performers and audiences drawn mainly from the European student population.

It's an exciting period, full of energy and expectation, and the year the *Einstein* company arrived was no exception. We were there for about two weeks before the first night and so busy with rehearsals and technical preparation that we had no time to attend any other events. We began in the morning, reviewing the work of the previous winter with the company while Bob and Beverly Emmons set lights in the theater. We began rehearsing in the theater in the evening and always stayed until 11:00 or 12:00 at night. There were costume fittings, and the crew had to learn the scenery changes. Julia Gillete, our stage manager, was learning to "call" the show, i.e., learning the cues for the performers.

We also were installing a complete sound system that included wireless mikes for the performers, a great novelty in those days but crucial if the speaking and singing parts were to be heard in the context of the amplified music performed by the Ensemble. Kurt had designed this system in the spring. It included a fairly elaborate monitoring system so the performers could hear each other. With this degree of technical innovation, it would take the full rehearsal period, and then some, to learn how to work it properly. Besides that, once on stage we discovered any number of scenes that required short bits of additional music simply to cover the mechanics of scene changes. I got around to writing these early in the day or whenever I could find the time.

About then, Joan LaBarbara (who, although beginning her composing career was still performing with the Ensemble as soprano vocalist) came to me with a complaint. "Look," she said, "this is an opera, and I'm the soprano lead, and I don't have an aria. I want an aria!"

I agreed that it was a good idea. The only possible place for a soprano solo seemed the scene in Act IV where Bob's beam of light representing the bed ascends and disappears, so that's where the aria went. Joan learned it just days before the premiere, and her instincts proved exactly right: The aria emerged as one of the most dramatic moments in *Einstein*.

There were only a few days to go, and the whole work was still almost five hours long. With practice, the stagehands did learn to make scene changes a bit faster, but *Einstein* never was under four hours, forty minutes in length. After that, from night to night the show never varied by more than a couple of minutes. This was equally true eight years later during the revival at BAM. This is all the more surprising in that some of the backstage technical moves could be very tricky. For example, one end of the bar of light which represented the bed has to lift, bringing the entire bar to a vertical position, then ascend slowly into the fly space. This was done with just two men operating a hand winch. Should their movements become less than absolutely regular, the "bed" would sway precariously across the stage, and the mysterious effect that Bob wanted would be lost.

There were many, many details of this kind that required rehearsal time for the stage crew. I mention this because the general public is often entirely unaware of the kind of preparation and care that make the stage pictures actually happen.

To me, the most daunting moments of the piece came in the final scene, the Spaceship. For this scene, Bob had devised a triple-tiered grid of cubicles in which all the performers, including the members of the Ensemble, stood and sang or played for some twenty minutes before the final Knee Play. We had scant seconds in which to scramble, single file, up the ladders (all this in semidarkness and in full view of the audience) and get into place before the action began. There were no safety belts, and the performing space was quite narrow, a matter of several feet only. To demonstrate to the cast how safe the arrangements were, I placed myself on the third and highest level. Generally the excitement of the moment swept us all along, and there were no complaints. In some theaters, though, the floorboards of the stage could be so springy that our "spaceship" would be noticeably swaying under our feet. Of course, everything was tied off and properly secured, and there was no real danger. Still . . .

On the opening night, I think Bob and I were almost too caught up in the execution of the piece to really take note of the audience and its reaction. I was playing with the Ensemble, and Bob was still making notes for the performers and stagehands. I remember in the Spaceship scene at the end, Bob appeared in the last moments to perform a dance with flashlights in the near-dark. I had no idea he would be performing on stage until then, and it was an electrifying moment. As for the next four performances, in my memory they all blend into one.

Almost immediately it was clear that *Einstein on the Beach* was *the* event of the festival. Many in the audience came back as often as they could. All the tickets were gone, so people would find ways of sneaking into the theater. These kinds of intense, almost fanatical, followers appeared again and again throughout Europe over the next four months. In Paris, where we were at the Opéra Comique for nine performances, there were regularly about two hundred people standing outside the theater, waiting on the chance of someone leaving early and giving them a ticket stub. Somehow a passage into the orchestra pit from the outside had been discovered, and during the evening it would slowly fill up with unticketed spectators. The gendarmes would come along and regularly empty out the pit. If you were an Ensemble member who happened not to be playing at that moment, you were in real danger of being swept away during one of those periodic purges.

The first result of success in Avignon was that Ninon could complete booking the tour. Actually, it seemed never to be quite completed, and many times along the way I recall her trying to pin down producers and finalize our financing. I suppose it never really was finalized, considering the financial morass awaiting us at the end of our tour. In the meantime, though, she had arranged performances in six countries: France, Italy, Germany, Yugoslavia, Holland and Belgium. After Avignon came a short break, then the company reconvened in Venice in September and stayed together until leaving Europe in mid-November.

Besides some minor cast changes, there were a few additions. My children, Juliet and Zachary, then eight and five years old, joined me in Italy. Bob gave them small parts in the piece, and they stayed with us about three weeks. It was a lot better than leaving them with a babysitter all that time: I could look up from the pit and see them several times throughout the evening.

By midtour the piece was running as smoothly as such a complicated business ever would. Each change of venue, though, brought fresh problems. A new crew had to learn the piece, often in little more than a day. The performers also had little time to familiarize themselves with the various European stages. There is no standard backstage arrangement, and in every theater the company had to learn a new route between the stage and the orchestra pit where the Knee Plays were set. With all the moving around, they ran the danger of getting lost backstage before learning their way around yet another theater. What really mattered most, though, was that the word on the piece seemed to have been excellent and to have preceded us, so we were sure of large and enthusiastic crowds wherever we went, even before the first-night curtain went up.

The unsolved problem very much on our minds was how to bring the work to the United States. There were few presenters who would dream of doing *Einstein* at that time and we could imagine no money being made available to us. (In the U.S., at this writing, *Einstein on the Beach* has still played only in New York City.) We knew Harvey Lichtenstein, the director of BAM, would be interested. Even before his Next Wave Festival in the 1980s, he had produced some of the most daring new work to be seen in the New York area, including some of Bob's earlier work. Apart from that, we had no idea where we might go.

During the run in Paris, Bob and I went to see Jerome Robbins, who was there at the time and had seen one of the performances. He was enthusiastic about the production and said he thought somebody in New York should see it. He telephoned the Metropolitan Opera and evidently was persuasive. We were told that someone would be coming to Europe to see *Einstein* and discuss it with us.

A few weeks later, Jane Herman and Gilbert Helmsley arrived in Hamburg and saw two performances. Gilbert was a well-known lighting designer who also had the reputation of being a genius at production management. Jane was in charge of special events at the Met. Usually that meant presenting or booking in events to fill the house during the summer months when the resident company was not working. However, there also was one "dark" night each week—at the Met, that was on Sunday—which could be available, and she was actively looking into ways of expanding the use of the house on those nights. To us at that moment, bringing *Einstein on the Beach* to the Met looked like a real long shot, and I must say that almost until the day we arrived there I didn't really believe it was going to happen.

By then, it was October and we were more than halfway through our tour. Nobody knew better than we did how long it would take to hang the drops, set the lights, install the sound system and teach the show to a new crew. And our time at the Met would be very tight. However, Jane was enthusiastic about *Einstein* and was anxious to make it happen at the Met. She and Gilbert worked out a plan where we would move into the theater at midnight after Saturday night's opera was finished and the sets were struck. The idea was to come in with a night crew and work straight through until 6:00 PM Sunday for a curtain at 6:30.

For us, certainly, it was a very exciting idea to have our American premiere at the Met. But it was a great worry to both of us as to whether Jane and Gilbert's plan could actually work. It meant hanging the whole show in one night and early morning, and this alone took two days in a normal theater. The lights would have to be set at the same time, and the stagehands who would be running the show would begin to learn their moves barely ten hours before show time. If there were any snags along the way, we would run out of time in the afternoon. That could mean little or no time to check the sound system and perhaps less to walk through the scenes with the company. At times, the various disasters we could imagine befalling us seemed all but inevitable.

Gilbert assured us that we would have one of the best, if not *the* best, stage crews in the world, and that he personally would be in charge of the production. On both counts he was as good as his word. Without a crew of that caliber, the show could not have been put on at all. When the time came, Gilbert organized the work with military precision, with charts and maps on display backstage, with coordinated timings so the stagehands could always find their way to where they would be needed. In the end, we had two stage managers at the Met, Gilbert on stage right and Julia on stage left. Finally, at that first meeting in Hamburg, Bob and I were convinced that maybe it could work. It certainly was worrisome, but we were ready to take the risk.

After Jane and Gilbert went back to New York, we still had several countries left in which to present *Einstein*, and we were so preoccupied that we gave little thought to New York. As we prepared to go home, barely a week before our Met date on November 21, 1976, we began to discuss the upcoming events. Jane and Gilbert had been reassuring about the technical problems, but what about an audience? The Met is, after all, a 4,000-seat house; 4,500 if you count the standing sections. During our last weeks in Europe, I was mainly worried that the Met would be half empty. My last big event in New York had been a concert of *Music in Twelve Parts* in Town Hall in May of 1974, and I had been pleased to have about 1,200 people in a 1,400-seat hall. Bob had had his *Letter to Queen Victoria* in a Broadway theater for a limited run that had been well attended, but he had not been overwhelmed by a demand for tickets.

Such were my thoughts as we arrived in New York. I remember Paul Walter, an old friend of Bob's and an early supporter of *Einstein,* meeting us at the plane and telling us that the first night at the Met was sold out and another performance was being added for the following Sunday!

I was astonished. Evidently during the four months we had been away, reports from Europe were coming back to New York, chronicling our success and the excitement *Einstein* had generated en route. It certainly would have allayed our fears had we known this before. As it was, the second night was sold out almost immediately, leaving only standing room to be sold (two per person) the day of the performances. I had trouble getting tickets for my own family, who were arriving from Baltimore, and I remember rather self-consciously getting into the standing-room line the next Sunday morning to pick up a couple of extra tickets, hoping no one would recognize me.

As it turned out, all our preparations had not been in vain, for the opening night at the Met was as nearly flawless as we could have hoped. That turned out to be the case on the following Sunday as well. The hectic eighteen hours preceding curtain time, instead of draining our energy, seemed to move everyone into high gear.

The performers arrived in the late morning, being exempted from the early morning hours of load-in and light setting. Kurt was there from the beginning, setting up the cables and speakers (which towered some twenty feet high on both sides of the proscenium arch), and I was back and forth from my apartment on East 14th Street all day. Bob was there, of course, from the first moment the theater was ours. There was so little time left at the end of the afternoon that it seemed that the audience had arrived before we knew it, and the first Knee Play began, exactly on time, at 6:30.

I was barely aware of the audience that night. I'm told that not a few stormed out after the first half-hour or so. It couldn't have been too many, though. From my place high up on the Spaceship in Act IV, the house looked more than full, and everyone was standing for us when it was over. In a way, I suppose *Einstein on the Beach* was a bit more controversial here than it had been Europe, probably because some in the audience had mistakenly thought that an evening at the Met would hold to a more traditional line. If so, they certainly had a surprise waiting for them. For the most part, though, the audience that came was expecting, if not exactly *Einstein*, then at least something new and unusual. For many who were there on those two evenings, it no doubt was their first time in an opera house anywhere. I remember standing backstage during the second Sunday's performance, watching the audience with one of the higher-up administrators of the Metropolitan Opera.

He asked me, "Who are these people? I've never seen them here before."

I remember replying very candidly, "Well, you'd better find out who they are, because if this place expects to be running in twenty-five years, that's your audience out there."

Pretty outspoken of me, I admit. But, then, we were having a pretty good night.

My life did not seem to be dramatically changed by the *Einstein* experience. I returned to making my living by driving a taxi, as I had during most of the 1970s, and I vividly remember the moment, shortly after the Met adventure, when a well-dressed woman got into my cab. After noting the name of the driver (New York law requires the name and photograph of the driver to be clearly visible), she leaned forward and said: "Young man, do you realize you have the same name as a very famous composer?"

It brought to mind another, rather more uncomfortable, experience of previous years. At that time I was earning a living as a plumber and had gone to install a dishwasher in a loft in Soho. While working, I suddenly heard a noise and looked up to find Robert Hughes, the art critic of *TIME* magazine, staring at me in disbelief. We had met before, and he knew me at sight.

"But you're Philip Glass! What are you doing here?"

It was obvious that I was installing his dishwasher, and I told him I soon would be finished. (I have always been careful about deadlines.)

"But you are an artist," he protested. "I won't permit you to work on my dishwasher!"

I explained that I was an artist, but that I was sometimes a plumber as well, and that he should go away and let me finish the job.

It made one think, for after the curtain came down on the second Sunday, *Einstein on the Beach*, or at least its first production, was officially over. And it left a host of financial problems that continued to haunt us for years to come.

The arithmetic isn't hard to explain. Over the period of twelve months that our company (numbering almost forty at times) was together, we spent about $900,000 on salaries, travel, living costs, equipment expenses, administration and so on—actually a very modest amount for the number of people, time worked, distances traveled. The trouble was that the income for the work from commissions and performance fees amounted to only $810,000, leaving a deficit of $90,000. At the Met, for example, *Einstein on the Beach* lost $10,000 each performance in a sold-out house. This is normal in opera houses; well-known works such as *Carmen* or *Aida* regularly play to full houses and lose money. That's why opera companies have chronic deficits and are always engaged in fund raising.

To present full-scale operatic productions that a general public can afford means losing money. We had actually been offered the chance to extend *Einstein* to other dark nights at the Met that winter, but no one was willing to pick up the nightly deficit. The Met had its own season to worry about and, understandably, wasn't eager to subsidize a production that was neither originated by them nor even a part of their regular season.

To have ended our tour with a deficit was all the more disheartening because so much time had already been spent raising money to augment the performing fees during the previous year and a half. Now we were to learn an even more difficult lesson: If it's hard to find money to produce a new work, it's virtually impossible to find it for a piece that's finished and packed away.

On the other hand, Bob and I both had offers to make new work. *Einstein* clearly had created opportunities for us individually. And, when we began subsequent collaboration some years later (with *the CIVIL warS*), the success of *Einstein* certainly had a part in securing producers. But in the winter of 1976–1977, what we had come to refer to as "The Einstein Debt" seemed a huge weight that could never be rolled away. Technically, the debt was owed by the Byrd Hoffman Foundation, but Bob and I both were involved in trying to find the money. Bob was having exhibitions and selling drawings. I sold the original score of *Einstein on the Beach* to a private collector. It seemed that for a few years all spare money from commissions and performances went to "the Einstein debt." I know this was true for Bob, especially since he so keenly felt that the legal responsibilities fell to him. There was even an art auction organized by Joe Helman of the Blum-Helman gallery, in which artist friends contributed work for sale. This included work by Richard Serra, Barry Le Va, Keith Sonnier, Nancy Graves and Sol LeWitt, to mention only a few. About $7,000 was produced this way, and it all went to lessen "the Einstein debt."

After a time, conversations between Bob and myself drifted from "the Einstein debt" to other subjects, mainly having to do with the theater. Bob was in Europe beginning work on *Death, Destruction and Detroit,* and I was in the U.S. starting work on *Satyagraha.* Over the next few years, I often spoke with Bob about directors and designers, and when there were questions about composers and Bob thought I could be helpful, he would call me. The *Einstein* period had been a very intense working relationship for us, and it had lasted well over two years, but another six years passed before we worked together again.

Shortly after *Einstein* had closed, we began thinking about making a recording. It seemed important that it happen very soon, while the singers were still available. I think they were in no danger of forgetting the music. The music had been so thoroughly learned and had been performed so many times (about thirty-five performances of the original production) that I would guess that even today those original performers can still sing most of it. I used to joke with them at the time that when the tour was over there would be a course to deprogram them and get all the numbers and solfège syllables out of their heads.

During the tour, as mentioned earlier, Michael Riesman had become music director of the Ensemble. This means he is responsible for casting, rehearsing, and conducting when necessary, and overseeing the general level of musical execution. Then, as the overall record producer, we had Kurt Munkacsi who had designed our tour equipment and done the sound mixing for the entire tour. But at that time I couldn't find a record company willing to take the chance of recording *Einstein*.

No surprise. The recording industry is not known for its courage and in general is not interested in risk taking. We managed to get some foundation support to make the master tapes, which meant a very tight budget but, as the music was so well in hand, that turned out not to be a big problem. I was able to condense the music so that the finished recordings would be on four discs, a not unmanageable length and one that's fairly common among opera recordings. No sections were cut out. Instead, the number of repetitions was reduced. For example, on stage the first Trial ran about forty minutes; it simply took that long for the stage action to unfold. Without those considerations, the music could reveal itself in less than twenty minutes.

Thus in the spring of 1977 we reassembled our company at the Big Apple Recording Studios (now Greene Street Studios) in New York's Soho district and, using modern multitrack overdub techniques, taped the complete *Einstein on the Beach*. Mr. Johnson recorded his speeches in both English and French, though only the English version was finally used. By then, our violinist, Bob Brown, had returned to Europe to pursue a solo career, but I was fortunate in being able to interest the extraordinary American violinist Paul Zukovsky in the part, and it is his playing that is heard on the record.

Recently, Bob (Wilson) and I reviewed the recording as part of an *Einstein* film project, and I was struck anew by how well performed and recorded it was. Kurt, who has been working with me on records since 1971, considers it to be our first recording project that reached a truly high standard of performance both technically and musically, and I agree.

Shortly after that, Tomato Records, a small record company operating out of New York, agreed to issue the complete recording. They secured the services of Milton Glaser to design the packaging and the book inside the album. This small and otherwise very imaginative company turned out to be in a lot of financial trouble, and we soon discovered that the sales of the *Einstein* set were virtually keeping them afloat, while little or no royalties were being paid to the authors. Ultimately, Tomato Records went out of business, and for a couple of years the recording became an expensive collector's item. Finally CBS Records picked up the rights and rereleased *Einstein* under their own CBS Masterworks label, complete with the original packaging.

Like the *Einstein* production, the *Einstein* recording seemed always to be nicely balanced between public artistic success and behind-the-scenes financial troubles.

THE MUSIC

The musical forces for *Einstein on the Beach* were built around the ensemble for which so much of my music since 1968 has been written. This consisted of two electric organs, three winds (doubling on saxophones, flute and bass clarinet) and one solo soprano voice. A chamber choir of sixteen mixed voices carries the weight of the vocal music in *Einstein*. From that group, a second soprano soloist is sometimes used with the regular ensemble soloist (as in the first Train scene); a tenor soloist is also used, again with the ensemble soloist, for the duet in the Night Train scene. A violinist, costumed as Einstein, plays a featured part and completes the lineup.

Einstein was planned as an extended evening performance (four hours, forty minutes) without formal, prescribed intermissions. We knew there would be few people able to sit straight through the entire work, and the audience was expected to take their own breaks (quietly, of course) when needed. Personally, I can say that, after more than fifty performances of *Einstein,* I have never seen the entire work straight through without interruption, though many people constantly assure me they have, as it were, taken it "whole." Still, the work was never intended to be seen as a whole, narrative piece. Its "wholeness" comes from its consistency of subject matter and overall structure and becomes the theatrical equivalent of an "act of faith" for the audience.

The sheer unbroken length of *Einstein* clearly presented musical problems that had to be worked out. With that much music to be performed, the orchestra had to be divided into smaller alternating groups, everyone coming together only occasionally for the big *tutti* numbers. The Knee Plays, for example, feature the chorus and violin with occasional help from one organ, and the Trial scenes also use smaller groups of instruments with chorus. The large ensemble and vocal numbers are left to the Train, Dance, and Spaceship scenes. The violin is featured in the Knee Plays, starting with the second one. Since the violinist is sitting halfway between the orchestra pit and the stage, it focuses attention in front of the curtain—a real advantage since there was a scenery change during each of the Knee Plays.

This was actually one of my minor miscalculations in writing *Einstein*. Since the Knee Plays were conceived for smaller groupings of musicians and produced a more intimate effect, they were not very loud. Meanwhile, behind the curtain, huge pieces of scenery were being dragged about, sometimes dropped, and this could often be heard quite clearly over the music. Intermezzo music is always a problem. Just when you would like the music to be quiet, creating a sense of repose between scenes, that's really when it needs to be as loud as you can make it, to cover all the backstage business. (I've continued to write quiet interlude music for other operas, hoping for the best with the backstage crews.)

As I have mentioned elsewhere in these pages, *Music in Twelve Parts,* the extended work written between 1971 and 1974, was a catalogue of ideas on rhythmic structure with which I had been working since my Paris pieces of 1965. The two major techniques that had evolved were those I called *additive process* and *cyclic structure.*

Additive process is one of those very simple ideas that can quickly lead to very complicated procedures. It can easily be explained: A musical grouping or measure of, say, five notes is repeated several times, then is followed by a measure of six notes (also repeated), then seven, then eight, and so on. A simple figure can expand and then contract in many different ways, maintaining the same general melodic configuration but, because of the addition (or subtraction) of one note, it takes on a very different rhythmic shape. Example A, taken from the first Trial scene of *Einstein,* shows this process as played in the violin part.

[EXAMPLE A]

I have used rhythmic cycles (repeating fixed rhythmic patterns of specific lengths) to create extended structures in my music by superimposing two different rhythmic patterns of different lengths. Depending on the length of each pattern, they will eventually arrive together back at their starting points, making one complete cycle. This has been described by some writers as sounding like "wheels inside wheels," a rather fanciful but not wholly inaccurate way of evoking the resulting effect. The opening of the first Train scene from *Einstein* is a good example of this (Ex. B). In this case, three repeats of the upper part (indicated by "X3") are equal in length to four repeats of the lower part (indicated by "X4").

[EXAMPLE B]

When the cyclic and additive processes are combined, some extremely interesting and complex structures are produced. This was the main overall musical device of *Music in Twelve Parts*, and it is present also in *Einstein*, particularly in Train One, from which the last example was taken.

In *Another Look at Harmony*, written just before *Einstein* and an important thematic source for the opera, I turned to a new problem. What I was looking for was a way of combining harmonic progressions with the rhythmic structure I had been developing, to produce a new overall structure. This turned out to be a problem of such absorbing interest that it occupied me almost completely for the next ten years, and the results can be heard in all the music I wrote during that time. In *Einstein* the problem is approached in half a dozen different ways; each scene, in fact, presents a different way of "solving" the problem. The two following examples will give an idea of how this was done.

[EXAMPLE C]

Example C is taken from the closing section of Train One. It is music that occurs throughout the work, forming the basis of the Spaceship music in Act IV as well as appearing in Knee Plays 3, 4 and 5, making it one of the major thematic devices of *Einstein*. At first glance, Example C appears to be a traditional cadential formula, the time-honored closing phrase which, in a variety of forms, became highly developed during the Baroque period and lasted well into the present. However, there is an altered or pivotal chord in the middle that results in a closing chord a half-step below what one would normally expect. It is this lowered resolution of the cadence that motivates its repetition. In the final scene of *Einstein*, this goes on for over eight minutes. What sustains musical interest over that length of time is the additive process which, when applied to the cadence, produces a lengthy and dramatic rhythmic development. Written in chords, the cadence reads as follows:

key of F minor

f   −   D♭   −   B♭♭
(I)   (VI)   (♭IV)

A   −   B   −   E
(IV)   (V)   (I)

key of E Major

The pivot chord is B♭♭ which sounds as A in the new key of E.

[EXAMPLE D]

The next example (Ex. D) comes from the closing section of Trial One. It is repeated in Trial Two and finally in the Bed scene of Act IV. Here a straightforward four-chord sequence is outlined. With each repetition, the length of one chord is increased by a group of eighth notes as the additive process is applied to the upper part, as shown in Example E. This can easily be heard as the two notes of the bass line become successively longer during the course of the section.

[EXAMPLE E]

The five Knee Plays of *Einstein* appear as interludes between the main scenes, and they contain the two major themes of the work. The first has just been described as the cadential theme. The second appears in all five Knee Plays and opens and closes the opera. It is shown in Example F in the form that we first hear it.

[EXAMPLE F]

In a more lyrical form, it is heard in the third, fourth and fifth Knee Plays, in either the chorus or violin.

[EXAMPLE G]

In Example G, we see it in the violin part as it is played in the fourth Knee Play. This theme takes on even greater importance when viewed from the perspective of the next two operas. Though I didn't know it at the time, this would become the ''Trilogy Theme'' and would reappear at crucial moments in both *Satyagraha* and *Akhnaten.*

It is worth noting another aspect of the development, in *Einstein on the Beach,* of this new approach of combining rhythmic and harmonic structure into an overall unified process. With the introduction of what is known as "root-movement harmony" (since the "root," or "fundamental," of the chord creates the impression of moving *through* as well as *with* the chord progression), a new element came into play in my music. Harmonic movement is central to our perception of expressiveness in music, at least in the periods from the Baroque to the Late Romantic. Once this movement had entered my music, it marked a sharp break with the very rhythmically charged, but harmonically static, music I had written before.

In its own way, the pre-*Einstein* music, rigorous and highly reductive, was more "radical" in its departure from the received tradition of Western music than what I have written since. But as I had been preoccupied, at that point, with that more radical-*sounding* music for over ten years, I felt I could add little more to what I had already done. Again, it is surely no coincidence that it was at the moment that I was embarking upon a major shift in my music to large-scale theater works that I began to develop a new, more expressive language for myself.

THE LIBRETTO

EINSTEIN ON THE BEACH

An Opera in Four Acts
by
Philip Glass—Robert Wilson

SPOKEN TEXTS BY
Christopher Knowles/Samuel M. Johnson/Lucinda Childs

SOLO ROLES
Solo Soprano   Solo Tenor   Solo Violinist

CHORUS
16 Voices (SATB)

ORCHESTRA
The Philip Glass Ensemble

NOTE: Texts are repeated to fill the time
allotted to them in the staging book.

KNEE PLAY 1

KNEE PLAY CHARACTER 1

(Recite numbers randomly.)

KNEE PLAY CHARACTER 2

(Text written by Christopher Knowles)

Will it get some wind for the sailboat. And it could get for it is.
It could get the railroad for these workers. And it could be were it is.
It could Franky it could be Franky it could be very fresh and clean.
It could be a balloon.
Oh these are the days my friends and these are the days my friends.
It could get some wind for the sailboat. And it could get for it is.
It could get the railroad for these workers. It could get for it is were.
It could be a balloon. It could be Franky. It could be very fresh and
    clean.
All these are the days my friends and these are the days my friends.
It could be those ways.
Will it get some wind for the sailboat and it could get for it is it.
It could get the railroad for these workers workers. It could get for
it is. So these are the days my friends and these are the days my
    friends.
But these days of 888 cents in 100 coins of change . . .
These are theiidays mmy friends and these are my days my friends.
Make a tiota on thses these are theiidays loop
So if you say will it get some wind for the sailboat and it could for
It could be Franky it could be very fresh and cleann. So it could be
    thos
e ones. So if
You cash the bank of world traveler from 10 months ago.
Doo you rememberf Honz the bus driver . . . , Well I put the red ball
blue ball two black and white balls. And Honz pushed on his brakes
    and
the four balls went down to that. And Honz said. ''Get those four
    balls aw
ay from the gearshift.'' Oh these are the days my friends and these are
    th
e days my friends. It could get the railroad for these workers.
    Itmmcould
So will it get some wind for the sailboat. And it could get for it is.

ACT I / SCENE 1 / TRAIN ONE

MAN CALCULATING (CRAZY EDDIE)
(Text written by Christopher Knowles)

This love could be some one
Into love
It could be some one that has been somewhere like them
It could be some like them
Tis one like into where that one has been like them
Well, it could be be some like them
Those like into where like that into this
This one has been broken like into where
But it could be some that it could be some like into like
into like into
like into where like that

It could be be some of the lucky ones then
This has been like into where that the ones
That where that it could be some like them too
This one, the ones that it could be somewhere like them
It could be somewhere like
let's see
Then, it could be somewhere like the one
it could be somewhere that it could be somewhere
That it could be somewhere
like into that one has been lucky

The one it has like into where ever
The one it has like into where like into
         where like into
Where the singing of the love of them

This one has been like into where the one it has
like into what is of that
is where that love was
it could be somewhere like them them
Them them them
it could say where by numbers this one has
like into it
The one is *you* over all the all the all the

It could be some that it could be,
could be so like that it is the one it could be the one
it was the ones like them
it could be some like them
That one
It could be some like them
It could be some*where*
The ones like them
You *will*
The ones are
The ones are
The ones are are
The ones are like
The ones are like into where the ones are the ones
The ones
The ones are like into this
The ones are like that
it
The ones are like
The ones are like
The ones are like them
The ones are like to the Crazy Eddies
are the are the a million
The ones are like what you do Crazy Eddies
That could be some that is into it is like what is it
What is it
What is it
What is it
What is it
Yes, come to the self service

What is it that could have some like I into it
What is it
That is it
What is it
it could be some one like them
it could be some one like them
Like them
Like that
The ones are like that
This one is not like them

I could be cry like a baby I'll be there
It could be course of that has been
the ones are like them them them them
who
them them them them them them them
The other ones, then, that has been
Like when it was the ones who prefer the ones
are like them them them
These circles
The ones the th th th th th th th th th th th
You *will*
Crazy Eddies Crazy Eddies Crazy Eddies Crazy Eddies Crazy Eddies
Goodbye Crazy Eddies
Crazy Eddies are the most ones
Like into a coat jacket
are into like it has the has the ever
Ever ever ever ever ever ever ever ever the

And that is the answer to your problem, handsome
Problem
Promise
The ones are like into this way
This always be
This
That it could be somewhere into where that it could be into some

—Repeats—

ACT I / SCENE 2 / TRIAL ONE

JUDGES

This court of common pleas is now in session.

LAWYER: MR BOJANGLES
(Text written by Christopher Knowles)

So it you see one of those baggy pants it was huge
Mr Bojangles
So if you see any of those baggy pants it was huge chuck the hills
and if you know it was a violin to be answer the telephone and if

any one asks you please it was trees it it it is like that, Mr
Bojangles, Mr Bojangles, I reach you, So this is about the things
on the table so this one could be counting up. The scarf of where
in Black and White
Mr Bojangles So if you see any of those baggy pants chuck the hills
it was huge and if you know it was a violin to be answer the
telephone and if any one asks you please it was trees it it it is
like that. Mr Bojangles Mr Bojangles Mr Bojangles I reach you
The scarf of where in Black and White this about the things on the
table. This one could be counting up. This one has been being
very American. The scarf of where in Black and White.
So if you see any of those baggy pants it was huge chuck the hills
and if you know it was a violin to be answer the telephone and if
any one asks you please it was trees it it it it it it it it it it
is like that
So this could be reflections for
Christopher Knowles—John Lennon
Paul McCartney—George Harrison
This has
This about the things on the table
This one has been very American
So this could be like weeeeeeee. . . . .
Mr Bojangles
This could be about the things on the table
This about the gun gun gun gun gun . . .
This has

PARIS (IN ORIGINAL PRODUCTION)

OLD JUDGE
(Text written by Mr. Samuel Johnson)

When considering the best liked cities on earth, Paris looms large among
them. Paris is one of the world's greatest tourist attractions. And not
without reason, for Paris has much to offer. Paris does not have a mul-
tiplicity of skyscrapers like New York, but it has much beauty and ele-
gance. And Paris has an illustrious background of history.

In Paris there is a number of young men who are very beautiful, very
charming, and very lovable. Paris is called ''the city of lights.'' But

these young men who are very beautiful, very charming, and very lovable, prefer the darkness for their social activities.

One of the most beautiful streets of Paris is called Les Champs-Elysées, which means the Elysian Fields. It is very broad, bordered with trees, and very pleasant to look at.

One of the most beautiful things of Paris is a lady. She is not too broad, bordered with smiles, and very, very, very pleasant to look at. When a gentleman contemplates a lady of Paris, the gentleman is apt to exclaim: "Oo la la," for the ladies of Paris are very charming. And the ladies of Paris are dedicated to the classic declaration, expressed in the words: "L'amour, toujours l'amour!"

A Russian man once said that the eyes of a Paris lady are as intoxicating as good wine, and that her burning kisses are capable of melting the gold in a man's teeth.

In Germany, in Italy, in Congo, in China, and in the United States, there are men who say: "If you've never been kissed by a lady of Paris, you've never been kissed at all."

(ALTERNATE SPEECH, FROM 1984 REVIVAL)

OLD JUDGE
(Text written by Mr. Samuel Johnson)

"In this court, all men are equal." You have heard those words many times before. "All men are equal." But what about all women? Are women the equal of men? There are those who tell us that they are.

Last week, an auspicious meeting of women was held in Kalamazoo. The meeting was addressed by a very prominent lady who is noted for her modesty. She is so modest that she blindfolds herself when taking a bath. Modesty runs in her family. She has a nephew who is just ten years of age. Sometimes, the nephew says "I'm going to the forbidden name store." The little fellow is too modest to say "I'm going to the A & P." Well, here is what that modest lady said to the gathering of women in Kalamazoo:

"My sisters: The time has come when we must stand up and declare ourselves. For too long have we been trodden under the feet of men. For too long have we been treated as second-class citizens by men who say that we are only good for cooking their meals, mending their socks, and raising their babies.

"You have a boyfriend, and he calls you his queen. Then, when he marries you, he crowns you. These are the kind of men who, when they become romantic or, I should say, when they are in a certain mood, they want to kiss you and kiss you and kiss you again.

"My sisters, I say to you: Put your faces against it, and, if the man takes a kiss from you without your permission, look him squarely in the face, roll your eyes at him, and say to him 'How dare you, you male chauvinist pig! You put that kiss right back where you got it from.' "

"My sisters, we are in bondage, and we need to be liberated. Liberation is our cry. Just yesterday, I talked with a woman who is the mother of fifteen children. She said 'Yes, I want to be liberated from the bedroom.' "

"And so, my sisters, the time has come when we must let this male chauvinist understand that the hand that changes the diapers is the hand that shall rule the world."

"And now, my sisters, let us stand and sing our national song. For the benefit of you who have not yet memorized the words, here they are:

The woman's day is drawing near, it's written in the stars
The fall of men is very near, proclaim it from your cars.
Sisters, rise! Your flags unfurl! Don't be a little girl.
Say 'Down with men, their power must end: Women shall rule the world!' "

YOUNG JUDGE
(Text written by Christopher Knowles)

Would . . . Would I . . . Would I get . . . Would I get some . . . Would I get some wind . . . Would I get some wind for . . . Would I get some wind for the . . . Would I get some wind for the sailboat.

KNEE PLAY 2

KNEE PLAY CHARACTER 2
(Text written by Christopher Knowles)

Could it get some wind for the sailboat. And it could get those for it
  is.
It could get the railroad for these workers. It could be a balloon.
It could be Franky, it could be very fresh and clean, it could be.
It could get some gasoline shortest one.

Zag Al these are the days my friends and these are the days my
friends.
Could it get some wind for the sailboat. And it could get those for it
is.
It could get the railroad for these workers. It could be a balloon.
It could be Franky, it could could be very fresh and clean, it could be.
It could get some gasoline shortest one.
Al these are the days my friends and these are the days my friends.
It could get a stopper. It could get the railroad for these workers.
Could it could be a balloon. It could be Franky, it could be.
Back to the rack and go back to the rack. It could be some workers
so.
It could be a balloon, it could be Franky, it could be.
Which one are the ones for. So if you know. So i you take your watch
off.
They're easy to lose or break. These are the days my friends and these
are
the days my friends. It could be some of th. . . . It could be on your
own.
It could be where of all. The way iron this one. So if youknow you
know.
this will be into where it could be. So look here.
Do you know they just don't make clothes for people who wears
glasses.
There's no pockets anymore. So if you take your glasses off. They're
easy
to lose or break. Well New York a Phonic Center has the answer to
your
problem. Contactless lenses and the new soft lenses. The Center gives
you thirty days and see if you like them. And if you don't. They could
refunds your money. So this could be like into a satchel in the sky. A
batch
of cookies was on the _____ for these are the days. This could be
into
a satchel.
It could get the railroad for these works
Do you know they just don't make clothes for people who wears
glasses.
There's no pockets anymore. So if you take your glasses off. They're
easy
to lose or break. Well New York A Phonic Center has the answer to
your

problem. Contactless lenses
and
Could it get some wind for the sailboat and it could get for these
    workers.
So al these are the days my friends and these are the days my friends.
Do you know they just don't make clothes for people who wears
    glasses.
There's no pockets anymore. So if you take your glasses off. They're
    easy
to lose or brea
k Well New York a Phonic Center has the answer to your problem.
Contactless lens
es and the new soft lenses. The Center gives you thirty days and see if
    you
like them. And if you don't. They could refunds your money. (Except
    for
the exammin
ation fee.) So if you're tired of glasses. Go to New York a Phonic
    Center on
Ele
ven West Fourty-Second Street near Fifth Avenue for sight with no
    hassle.
Please Call Br9-5555. . . . . .
Could it get some wind for the sailboat. And it could get those for it
    is.
It could get the railroad for these workers. It could be a balloon.
It could be Franky, it could be very fresh and clean, it could be.
It could get some gasoline shortest one it could be.
Al these are the days my friends and these are the days my friends.
Look. . . . . batch catch hatch latch match patch watch snatch
    scratch. . . . . .
Look.
SWEARIN TO GOD WHO LOVES YOU
FRANKIE VALLI THE FOUR SEASONS

KNEE PLAY CHARACTER I

Numbers recited randomly and portions of Mr Bojangles, which was
included above as part of Trial One.

ACT III / SCENE 1 / TRIAL TWO / PRISON

LAWYER: MR BOJANGLES

(Text written by Christopher Knowles;
To be recited at bar 19A$^{2.5}$.)

The song I just heard is turning
(The song in where) _____
Tis thing
This will be the time that you come
This has been addressed to all those girls
All this one has been very American
So stop
When you see when it was it has been
When you Hey Mr Bojangles
       Hey Mr Bojangles
       Hey Mr Bojangles
This has
This song wear a black and white then this has been
This about the things on the table
This will be counting that you allways wanted has been very very
   tempting
So stop
Hey Mr Bojangles
Hey Mr Bojangles
Hey Mr Bojangles
This has
This scarf of wear in black and white
That this has been _____
This about the things on the table
This will be counting
This has been addressed to the girls where
The song of (Satan) where it could be
Into where into where a
Hey Mr Bojangles
Hey Mr Bojangles
Hey Mr Bojangles
Ah this hah this scarf of wear of black and white that this about the
things on the table
This will be counting but
This has been addressed to those girls

All this one has been very American
So stop
When you see where has been
Hey Mr Bojangles
Hey Mr Bojangles
Hey Mr Bojangles
This has red blue
Allways run very quickly in a mad world
Say this
That call you Piggy in the sky
Like up in the ———
This is written
John Lennon for from Christopher Knowles' actions where that (major)
    star
Paul McCartney
George Harrison
The peoples
Where I this has also worked
This has been reflections
Has been lucky as the sky
This has been like . . .
So this one has
If you be so arrogant
It could be somewhere like to those ones
So learn what is so
So well like into a satchel like into where like a monster
If you know like gong like like a gong gong gong gong gong gong
Hey Mr Bojangles
So like if you see a little (nose) beggar with baggy pants

WITNESS

*(Text written by Lucinda Childs; To be recited from lying on bed
through exit, repeating as necessary.)*

I was in this prematurely air-conditioned super market
and there were all these aisles
and there were all these bathing caps that you could buy
which had these kind of fourth of July plumes on them
they were red and yellow and blue
I wasn't tempted to buy one

but I was reminded of the fact that I had been avoiding
the beach.

LAWYER

*(Text written by Christopher Knowles; To be recited from the Patty
Hearst moves through the exit.)*

So uh this is about the uh things on the table
so this one will be counting up
so if you see any of those baggy pants, chuck the hills
so if anyone asks you please, it was trees

the uh scarf of where in black and white
that this one will be sittin'
this about the uh things on the table
this will be counting up

so uh uh this is about the uh things on the table
the uh scarf of where in black and white
that this one is sittin'
this is about the uh things that were
so if you see any of those, then this could be one of them
so stop here so stop this so look here
so this is written
Hey, Mr. Bojangles
Hey, Mr. Bojangles
Hey, Mr. Bojangles
so this could be the one that was
so if you see this one, then. . . .

(Inserts at the machine gun and/or the music change [25]):

Gun gun gun gun
Hey, Mr. Bojangles
Hey, Mr. Bojangles
Hey, Mr. Bojangles
Christopher Knowles bank robbery
so if you know
bank robbery bank robbery bank robbery is punishable by
20 years in federal prison so this is written
so if you know this is one so so look here

so Christopher Knowles and the Beatles
so so

(Repeat "Hey, Mr. Bojangles" until exit.)

WITNESS: I FEEL THE EARTH MOVE

(Text written by Christopher Knowles; Recited at the music change
[35] after the reveal has gone out.)

I feel the earth move . . . . . I feel the tumbling down tumbling down.
     . . . . There was a judge who
like puts in a court. And the judge have like in what able jail what it
     could be a spanking. Or a
whack. Or a smack. Or a swat. Or a hit.
This could be where of judges and courts and jails. And who was it.
This will be doing the facts of David Cassidy of were in this case of
     feelings.
That could make you happy. That could make you sad. That could
     make you mad. Or
that could make you jealous. So do you know a jail is. A court and a
     judge could
do this could be like in those green Christmas Trees. So Santa Claus
     has about
red. And now the Einstine Trail is like In Einstine on the Beach. So
     this will.
So if you know that faffffffff facts. So this what happen what I saw
     in. Lucy or
a kite. You raced all the way up. This is a race. So this one will have
     eight in
types into a pink rink. So this way could be very magic. So this will
     be like to
Scene women comes out to grab her. So this what She grabbed her.
     So if you lie on
the grass. So this could be where if the earth move or not. So here we
     go.
I feel the earth move under my feet. I feel tumbling down tumbling
     down. I feel if
Some ostriches are a like into a satchel. Some like them. I went to the
     window
and wanted to draw the earth. So David Cassidy tells you when to go
     into this on

onto a meat. So where would a red dress. So this will get some gas.
So this could

This would be some all of my friends. Cindy Jay Steve Julia Robyn
Rick Kit and

Liz. So this would get any energy. So if you know what some like
into were. So . .

So about one song.

I FEEL THE EARTH MOVE

CAROLE KING

So that was one song this what it could in the Einstein On The Beach
with a trial

to jail. But a court were it could happen. So when David Casidy tells
you all

of you to go on get going get going. So this one in like on WABC
New York. . . .

JAY REYNOLDS from midnight to 6 oo.

HARRY HARRISON

So heres what in like of WABC. . . . . . .

JAY REYNOLDS from midnight to 6 AM

HARRY HARRISON from 6 AM to L

I feel the earth move from WABC . . .

JAY REYNOLDS from midnight to 6 AM.

HARRY HARRISON from 6 AM to 10 AM.

RON LUNDY from 10 AM to 2 PM.

DAN INGRAM from 2 PM to

So this can misteaks try it aga9 . .

JAY REYNOLDS from midnight to 6 AM.

HARRY HARRISON from 6 am

This could be true on WABC.

JAY REYNOLDS froj

This can be wrong.

This would WABC.

JAY REYNOLDS from midnight to 6 AM.

HARRY HARRISON from 6 AM to 10 AM.

RON LUNDY from 10 AM to 2 PM.

DAN INGRAM from 2 PM to 6 PM.

GEORGE MICHAEL from 6 PM to 10 PM

CHUCK LEONARD from 10 PM to midnight.

JOHNNY DONOVAN from 10 pm to 3 AM.

STEVE-O-BRION from 2 PM to 6 PM.

JOHNNY DONOVAN from 6 PM to 10 PM.

CHUCK LEONARD from 3 AM to 5 AM.
JOHNNY DONOVAN from 6 PM to 10 PM.
STEVE-O-BRION from 4 30 AM to 6 AM.
STEVE-O-BRION from 4 30 AM to 6 AM.
JOHNNY DONOVAN from 4 30 AM to 6 AM

KNEE PLAY 5

KNEE PLAY CHARACTER 1: NUMBERS AND MR BOJANGLES

KNEE PLAY CHARACTER 2: TEXT FROM KNEE PLAY 1

BUS DRIVER *(Lovers on a Park Bench)*
(Text written by Mr. Samuel Johnson)

The day with its cares and perplexities is ended and the night is now upon us. The night should be a time of peace and tranquility, a time to relax and be calm. We have need of a soothing story to banish the disturbing thoughts of the day, to set at rest our troubled minds, and put at ease our ruffled spirits.

And what sort of story shall we hear? Ah, it will be a familiar story, a story that is so very, very old, and yet it is so new. It is the old, old story of love.

Two lovers sat on a park bench, with their bodies touching each other, holding hands in the moonlight.

There was silence between them. So profound was their love for each other, they needed no words to express it. And so they sat in silence, on a park bench, with their bodies touching, holding hands in the moonlight.

Finally she spoke. "Do you love me, John?" she asked. "You know I love you, darling," he replied. "I love you more than tongue can tell. You are the light of my life, my sun, moon and stars. You are my everything. Without you I have no reason for being."

Again there was silence as the two lovers sat on a park bench, their bodies touching, holding hands in the moonlight. Once more she spoke. "How much do you love me, John?" she asked. He answered: "How much do I love you? Count the stars in the sky. Measure the waters of the oceans with a teaspoon. Number the grains of sand on the sea shore. Impossible, you say. Yes and it is just as impossible for me to say how much I love you.

"My love for you is higher than the heavens, deeper than Hades, and broader than the earth. It has no limits, no bounds. Everything must have an ending except my love for you.''

There was more of silence as the two lovers sat on a park bench with their bodies touching, holding hands in the moonlight.

Once more her voice was heard. "Kiss me, John," she implored. And leaning over, he pressed his lips warmly to hers in fervent osculation. . . .

THE ACTION—AS REMEMBERED
BY ROBERT T. JONES

KNEE PLAY 1

On stage, Knee Play 1 runs thirty minutes and is in progress when the audience is admitted to the auditorium. It begins imperceptibly: Two women sit at tables at the right front of the stage, counting and reciting, their fingers performing a slow ballet on their tabletops. Almost inaudibly, the keyboards play the three-note descending figure that begins the music. Fifteen minutes into the scene (and fifteen minutes before the actual first scene begins) the Chorus slowly enters the orchestra pit, each member requiring two minutes to take his/her place. As the theater lights slowly dim and spotlights come up on the Chorus, they begin to count. The women on stage continue their recitation until a sudden blackout ends the Knee Play.

ACT I / SCENE 1 / TRAIN ONE

A small boy stands atop a tower, a beam of light striking a shining plastic tube he gravely holds in his outstretched hand. During the course of the scene, he occasionally tosses paper airplanes onto the stage below.

A solo for female dancer immediately follows, launching the opera and continuing throughout the first scene. [In both the original 1976 production and the 1984 revival of *Einstein,* Lucinda Childs danced her own choreography, a restless, almost violent pacing and retreating along a diagonal line.] She grips a pipe in her left hand (Einstein was often photographed while smoking a pipe) and, like everyone else on the stage, is dressed in the Einstein "uniform": sneakers, white shirt, braces, baggy pants.

At the front right corner of the stage a man scribbles equations onto an invisible blackboard. A full-scale locomotive imperceptibly inches its way across the stage, steam pouring from its smokestacks. Two women inch across the stage, one making birdlike motions, the other reading a newspaper. Three other dancers move across the stage, holding strings that form a carpenter's triangle.

Three times during this train scene, a beam of light descends, slicing through the scene and cutting it in half. A blackout follows, during which the locomotive retreats and the characters realign themselves along different diagonals (the instrumental-only sections in the music) before beginning again.

ACT I / SCENE 2 / TRIAL ONE

Three illuminated rectangular horizontal beams of light form the major visual theme of the trial, augmented by a huge clock without hands and an enormous bed (Einstein once mentioned that many of his ideas came to him in dreams). The members of the Chorus slowly enter and take standing positions in the jury box, their fingers moving in unison in complex patterns under individual spotlights. A pair of bored secretaries sits in front, pantomiming the taking of dictation. A bewigged pair—an elderly black man and a little boy—take their places on the judge's bench between two globes of light. The Defendant (a young woman) slowly mounts a stool, escorted by the Prosecutor, and a Witness (a young black woman) recites from a book (the "Bojangles" speech). Throughout, Albert Einstein plays his violin from a neutral position midway between the pit musicians and the stage performers.

The trial proceeds in leisurely tension, with a young lawyer carrying an illuminated briefcase, the Chorus gravely taking a coffee break, and a huge black disc slowly eclipsing the handless clock (a visual reference to a confirmation of Einstein's theory of relativity which involved observing a solar eclipse and measuring the apparent displacement of light from stars visible next to the blanked-out sun). The trial concludes with Samuel M. Johnson's "Paris" speech with its recurrent references to light. [For the 1985 revival, Mr. Johnson provided a different speech.]

KNEE PLAY 2

The two women, again in their square pool of light at the right front of the stage, sit on chairs and recite; behind them images of Einstein flash onto a screen. Through it all, Einstein plays his violin.

ACT II / SCENE 1 / DANCE 1

The scene is a vast open space, with a hovering spaceship visible in the far distance. [In the original production, Andrew de Groat's choreography featured dervishlike spinning; Lucinda Childs's dances for the 1985 revival were colder, more mathematically precise, with an emphasis on clean line and an exact matching of movement to music.]

ACT II / SCENE 2 / NIGHT TRAIN

The second appearance of the train image has little in common, visually speaking, with the first. The scene is a midnight-blue space, with the gaslit turn-of-the-century train poised on a flat and desolate plain. The moon shines down, passing through various phases from crescent and new to full. As the Chorus chants numbers and solfège syllables from the orchestra pit, an elegantly clad Victorian couple emerges from the amber interior of the caboose, stands on the platform and pantomimes a love duet. A lunar eclipse occurs, paralleling the eclipse of the clock in the first Trial: as the moon's disc is obscured, two stars become visible on either side of the black disc (a visual echo of the two lights on the judge's bench during the Trial). Toward the end of the scene, the couple returns to opposite seats in the train's coach; the woman pulls a gun from her handbag and threatens her companion with it; he raises his hands; the train moves into the night. After a brief blackout, the train is seen again from a great distance.

KNEE PLAY 3

The Chorus chants their numbers and solfège syllables from the pit while the two women stand in their square at stage front before a control board of flashing lights. The Chorus makes steering motions; they suddenly produce toothbrushes and begin brushing their teeth, then suddenly stick out their tongues. (There exists a famous photograph of Einstein sticking out his tongue at a photographer.)

ACT III / SCENE 1 / TRIAL TWO / PRISON

The second trial is now both trial and prison combined. The Chorus and principals resume their places as before, and the Defendant takes her position on her high stool. Presently the stage divides, a looming screen of bars cutting off the right side: Two prisoners begin a pantomime behind the bars, and the Defendant slowly moves from her stool to the bed, where she lies, writhing as if in a nightmare, while reciting the "supermarket" speech. As the speech continues, her movements become jerkier, more disjointed, and black-clad stagehands move out to deposit props along the stage floor. The Defendant moves slowly along the front of the stage, collecting the props and rearranging her clothing. Suddenly she assumes the appearance of Patricia Hearst in a famous photograph of a bank robbery (still repeating her speech), in guerilla garb and pointing a machine-gun at the audience. The onstage participants mimic her threatening postures as the lights brighten harshly. The Defendant now appears with her arms chained, the bars disappear and, as the stage is cleared, she reappears seated on her stool and reciting the "I feel the earth move" speech. As the lights dim, her voice fades into silence.

ACT III / SCENE 2 / DANCE 2

The scene is the open field as in the previous dance, but the spaceship is much nearer this time, and it moves dramatically across the scene as the dance continues.

KNEE PLAY 4

In an elongated, horizontal version of the previously vertical square, the two women lie on glass tables, twisting and turning in a horizontal dance while illuminated from beneath. (These images are suggested by a scientific experiment involving light being shot through a vat of mercury.) As in the previous Knee Plays, the Chorus is stationed in the pit.

ACT IV / SCENE 1 / BUILDING

The visual shape of the Night Train scene has been retained, but the train has now become a building. It looms in industrial grayness at the center of the stage, and in one window an Einstein is visible, compulsively scribbling equations as a crowd of men, women and children strolls on to stare. Eventually the crowd strolls away as casually as it had arrived.

ACT IV / SCENE 2 / BED

The horizontal illuminated lines of the previous trial scenes are now metamorphosed into one beam of light merged with the bed image that stood before the judge's bench. On a black stage, the edge of the bed becomes fluorescent, a solid beam of brilliance. During the organ cadenza, it slowly rises to a vertical position and, as the soprano sings her wordless solo, rises almost imperceptibly and disappears into the heights.

ACT IV / SCENE 3 / SPACESHIP

Flickering lights outline the cubicles of the spaceship, and in the gloom can be seen a glass elevator enclosing a human figure, sliding up and down from a smoking slot in the stage floor. Another glass cubicle, containing a reclining figure, moves continually from left to right across the top of the scene. As the organ solo plays, the musicians gradually climb ladders and take their places in the compartments of the spaceship. Once they are in place, the music bursts out in full strength. A black-clad male dancer darts out, making semaphore signals with a pair of flashlights. As the scene continues, a sense of chaos builds. Banks of control lights in the musicians' cubicles flash wildly (unison chromatic scales) and, finally, smoke pours from two plastic "bubbles" on the floor near the front of the stage. The bubbles open, and two astronauts climb out and slowly collapse. The sense of an atomic explosion is overwhelming. A curtain descends, cutting off the scene. It bears Einstein's equation for atomic energy: $E = Mc^2$.

KNEE PLAY 5

Two Lovers (the two female players, abandoning their astronaut characters) sit on a park bench, fingers moving in the same silent ballet that began the opera. A motor bus slowly moves into view, its headlights and physical shape recalling the first train, its driver reminiscent of the train's conductor in the opening scene. As the verbal phrases overlap with increasing thickness and the Chorus (backstage) chants numbers, the Bus Driver delivers his speech with its gentle verbal images of numbers, moon and stars, Heaven and Hades, grains of sand and boundless love. Words and music cease. The bus moves toward the Lovers, and the curtain falls in silence.

SATYAGRAHA

W ell, Philip, that was very interesting. Now, how would you like to write a *real* opera?''

Hans de Roo, director of the Netherlands Opera, had just seen *Einstein on the Beach* at the Carré Theatre in Amsterdam, and we were talking the next day in his office. I remember answering that I'd like that very much, but what did he mean by "a real opera"?

His response was very clear: "It should be for my orchestra, chorus and soloists, people trained and practiced in the singing of traditional operas."

The subject of opera had been coming up all along the *Einstein* tour. There were endless discussions and debates wherever we had been and even in places we had *not* been. Opinion had fallen into two opposing camps. Those who said *Einstein* was not an opera pointed to the fact that it had no story, used neither a regular pit orchestra nor normal operatic voices, and was far too loud.

Frankly, I tended to agree with them. Besides, the operatic tradition seemed to me hopelessly dead, with no prospect for resurrection in the world of performance in which I worked. To me, it seemed a far better idea to simply start someplace else. As a description of *Einstein*, I preferred ''music theater'' to ''opera.''

However, for those who thought *Einstein* was a true opera, the matter couldn't be settled so easily. For one thing, it was a large-scale music drama (the lack of plot was overlooked) with music throughout. True, the singing was not "operatic." Instead, we had used what I like to call "naive" voices, voices with an untrained sound colored and projected via microphones. Certainly the singing was virtually continuous throughout the evening. Besides, there was a real duet in the Act II Night Train scene and a very demanding soprano aria in the Act IV Bed scene. It was also well known that Bob Wilson had for years been referring to his large-scale theater works as "operas," whether the music was by Beethoven, Alan Lloyd (the composer of *A Letter to Queen Victoria*), or even when performed in total silence. What Bob referred to, of course, was the original meaning of the Italian word *opera* signifying, simply, "a work."

So the discussions went on and on. But when the talk ran out, practical considerations seemed to outweigh the aesthetic or ideological. In order to present *Einstein*, what was required was a large proscenium stage, with wing space for scenery and performers to move on and off, fly space for drops to come in and out, a lighting bridge and assorted lighting instruments, and an orchestra pit in which the musicians could play without obstructing the view of the audience. You could call *Einstein* whatever you liked, but virtually the only places in which it could be performed were opera houses.

Naturally, this didn't make it an "opera." But it did mean that *Einstein*, during its first tour, was seen in the opera house in Avignon, the Opéra Comique in Paris, the Fenice in Venice, La Monnaie in Brussels and so on. I think this may have created a kind of expectation on the part of our audiences. When they saw what was actually being performed, they were either outraged or delighted. There were few in-between reactions.

From my point of view, I began to find that the subject of opera was becoming interesting. Not the discussion of what a *real* opera is—that I didn't care about at all. Allusions to any possible historical connection to the great tradition of opera were, from my point of view, utterly beside the point and best avoided altogether. What interested me were the physical realities of the theaters I was working in, those large houses that employed stage crews, choruses, orchestras and soloists. It seemed too good a thing *not* to consider as a real working possibility.

So, in 1976 when Hans de Roo proposed that I write a new work for the Netherlands Opera, I eagerly accepted. Hans suggested I come up with a subject, and we would talk again when he came to New York a few months later.

We met again in the spring of 1977. There were, as usual, practical considerations to work out, and these matters took up almost the entire year before we could set a date and work could begin in 1978. I've discovered since that not only is this quite usual but that, actually, a year of discussion about a new work is rather short. Usually several years are involved, and there have been occasions when, out of sheer impatience, I've started writing a piece on an invitation such as Hans's and completed it before the contract was signed.

In this case, the problem was that, though the Netherlands Opera was prepared to build, rehearse, and perform a new work, the actual commission—i.e., money—for the composer, had yet to be found. At that time, my business affairs were still being taken care of by Artservices in New York. Margaret Wood, then associated with that office, took on the problem. She had many friends and contacts in Holland, knew the country well and volunteered to help find the money. As it turned out, she didn't have far to look. In Rotterdam, *Einstein* had a big supporter in the person of Willy Hofman. Willy was in charge of the Doelen Theater in Rotterdam, a large and modern complex accustomed to presenting all kinds of concerts and theater works.

Willy has unusually broad interests in the theater. Besides having a strong commitment to avant-garde works such as *Einstein*, he was also known for introducing American productions of Broadway musicals in his theater. In his office hung posters for *My Fair Lady* and *West Side Story* and others which he had produced at the Doelen. Unfortunately, men like Willy are as rare as they are refreshing.

Margaret went to him with our project. He was immediately enthusiastic and said he would help us find the commission money but wanted the work to premiere in Rotterdam. We agreed and, before long, heard that our proposal was being presented to the Rotterdam city council.

The idea was to have the work commissioned by the City of Rotterdam for the Netherlands Opera. The Netherlands Opera had its headquarters in Amsterdam but, as a national opera company, routinely traveled with its productions to the major Dutch cities such as Utrecht, Rotterdam, Scheveningen and Eindhoven. The Rotterdam council voted favorably on the proposal and, for the second time, I had a major commission from Europe.

Meanwhile, my discussions with Hans were proceeding. My proposal was for a three-act opera based on M. K. Gandhi's crucial years in South Africa. It would be called *Satyagraha,* the name he used for his nonviolent civil disobedience movement. Since having suggested it to Bob Wilson nearly four years before, it had stayed on my mind. It seemed in every way a good subject for the theater, Gandhi being one of *the* charismatic leaders of our day. It also was material that attracted me personally, stemming from my many visits to India after first working with Ravi Shankar in 1965.

In the twelve years since then, these visits had continued regularly, approximately every third year. With each visit my interest in the culture and traditions of India deepened. My visits lasted anywhere from three weeks to two months and took me all over the country, from the Himalayas in the North to Tamil Nadu in the South. I witnessed theater in the South, ashrams (spiritual communities) in the North, dancers and musicians everywhere. Dance, theater and music in India are inseparable from religious traditions, so my interests, having started with the performing arts, began to broaden and included a wide range of cultural, historic and religious subjects.

Throughout India I encountered photographs of Gandhi, in railway stations, waiting rooms, almost every public place. I saw his image printed on stamps and on money. But apart from knowing him as the "father of the country," I don't think I really thought about who *he* was.

In 1973, I was staying in a small town not far from Darjeeling in the Himalayas, visiting friends who lived just beyond the outskirts of town. On my daily walks there, I struck up an acquaintance with a shopkeeper who sold rugs. His name was Sarup, and it wasn't long before we were having tea together and I was dining at his home. Mr. Sarup was a devout Hindu and a great believer in modern India. He had seen Gandhiji (as Gandhi was fondly called) speak once, and it had made a great impression on him.

One day as I was passing his shop, Mr. Sarup called out to me very excitedly, "Mr. Philips! Mr. Philips!" His friend who ran the local movie theater had just acquired a short film on Gandhiji, and he was eager for me to see it. It was early in the day, but arrangements had already been made for a private screening for Mr. Sarup and myself.

There, amidst the jerky black and white images from newsreel footage of forty years before, I got my first glimpse of the man who meant so much to so many people, not only in that part of the world but wherever the subjects of religion and politics are passionately argued.

And what a man he must have been! A slim, tiny figure, but even in that ancient newsreel, a radiant and powerful personality. I recall, especially, a film clip showing him during the Great Salt March in 1930. A part of his unceasing, nonviolent opposition to British rule in India, this march had been a protest against a tax on salt. Throughout his life it was typical of Gandhi to pick his battlefields with uncanny shrewdness. Salt being an everyday and necessary part of life, no one in India would fail to see its significance to ordinary people. The tax itself was not particularly harsh, but it had become a symbol, universal in its simplicity, of foreign domination. The film showed Gandhi, amidst thousands of followers, walking into the Indian Ocean and illegally "harvesting" salt from the sea by dipping a cloth in the water. The electricity of the moment was staggering, unforgettable.

A few weeks later, back in New Delhi, I found his publishing company, the Navajan Press, still in operation and picked up a generous selection of his writings to take home with me. I suppose from that point on, studying Gandhi became something of a hobby for me. On subsequent trips to India, I visited places where he had lived and sought out persons who had known him. This was still the early 1970s, and I was yet to begin thinking about music theater in the way I would only a few years later. My early Gandhi studies were really quite personal, with nothing like an opera project lurking in the back of my mind.

One of his books was entitled *Satyagraha*. It described his years in South Africa, where he had gone in 1893 as a young English-trained barrister. The next twenty-one years was the period during which the Gandhi the world now remembers was born. He had arrived from India seemingly unaware of the color bar imposed on all non-Europeans by the white South African government. At that time, there was a fairly large Indian community, mainly indentured laborers who had been drawn from India to South Africa by the prospect of better wages offered by South African employers, most of whom considered the "native" black population unsuitable for agricultural work.

The importation of Indian labor had been going on for some twenty-five years, and a small Indian middle class, mostly businessmen and their families, had grown up, catering to the needs of the Indian community. Gandhi had been hired by two such families to arbitrate a business dispute between them. As a young attorney in India, he had been strikingly unsuccessful and had jumped at the chance to earn some money abroad. On arriving, however, he was so shocked by the conditions imposed on his countrymen in South Africa that he had determined to either leave immediately or to stay and take up what was sure to be a protracted battle against social injustice.

The Indians in South Africa had been systematically disfranchised by the government. They could not vote, own land or even move freely about the country. They were allowed to work for five-year periods, then had to leave for home with whatever money they had managed to save, or else sign a new five-year work contract. In those years, the young Gandhi believed, obviously rather naively, that the Indian workers were "sons of the empire" and entitled to the same legal safeguards as any white workers. He was firm in his belief in the justness of his cause. Inspired by the New Testament, and the writings of John Ruskin, Henry David Thoreau, and Leo Tolstoy, Gandhi proposed a course of nonviolent protest to the Indian community. He was warmly supported by his countrymen and soon came to an arrangement with them whereby he was guaranteed enough legal work to support his family and thereby enough free time to devote to the social and political work he set up for himself.

Satyagraha is a Sanskrit word meaning "truth-force," and was the name chosen for the movement that Gandhi led in South Africa. Until 1914, Gandhi led his small Satyagraha army again and again against the government policies. Almost all the techniques of social and political protest that are now the common currency of contemporary political life were invented and perfected by the young Gandhi during his South African years. As weapons against the South African government, Gandhi used marches, civil disobedience, passive resistance, voluntary imprisonment, and public petitions. By 1914, General Smuts, the head of state, finally had to agree to repeal the most egregious of the color-bar laws, known collectively as "The Black Act."

Seemingly victorious, Gandhi returned to India permanently. He had arrived from India in 1893 in a bowler hat and a pinstripe suit. He left South Africa in 1914 dressed in simple white cotton cloth. The tools of Satyagraha, now honed to perfection, were soon turned on the British Raj in India itself. Thirty-three years later, in 1947, India regained its independence. Some may argue that historical events were moving inevitably in that direction, but few will disagree that Gandhi had, in his own person, provided India with the courage and moral authority to push events to a point of no return.

Here, then, was my subject. I chose Gandhi's years in South Africa as the time period of my opera. For one thing, a life as long and eventful as his could not possibly be contained in a single evening-long work. Secondly, I felt that the South African years were his most creative period, when the persona whom we now know as Mahatma ("Great Soul") Gandhi was being invented.

Hans de Roo approved the choice of subject matter, and even the very sketchy outline I gave him, but the real work had yet to begin. It occurred to me later that the subject might have been considered somewhat sensitive in Holland: After all, the Dutch were the original Afrikaaners and shared responsibility (at least morally) with the English for the white South African culture. However, to this day, no one in Holland has ever mentioned this to me. I suppose the Dutch immigrations to South Africa occurred so long ago that they seem as remote from contemporary Dutch life as do the original Dutch settlements in New York.

I was ready to begin the first stage of the work and, as was quickly becoming my custom, wanted first to put together a "team" to form the conceptual aspects of the work. The music would come later. First, I needed some sort of outline, if not story or plot, around which to form the music. I was looking for a designer, a writer and a director, and I hoped that the people who would actually be involved in the first production in Holland would be involved from the very outset of the work.

For a writer, I turned to Constance DeJong, another Soho friend. Besides having the required writing and organizational skills, she had a natural attraction to the subject matter. I asked Robert Israel to create the costumes and sets, and since he wanted to work with Richard Riddell on the lighting, which would be integral to the design, I asked Richard to join us too.

It was Israel who had introduced me to Hans de Roo in the first place. (We were, and still are, on the closest of terms—he is always "Bob" to me—and I refer to him by his last name in these pages only to distinguish him from Bob Wilson.) Israel had come to Holland from the U.S. three years earlier and was finishing a period of work as a resident designer for the Netherlands Opera. He had begun his career as a painter in New York's art community before taking up theater design, and we had many Soho friends in common. Furthermore, Israel had a real sympathy for my music and was eager to hear it in the setting a traditional opera production would provide. He and Riddell made a good working team. Together, they had much more experience than I did in music theater, and their advice on a host of matters, not necessarily just design problems, was invaluable to me at that stage of my work.

Ideally we should have had a director to work with at this stage, but this proved the most elusive element of our team. The obvious choice was Robert Wilson, but he was busy in Germany with a major production of his own (*Death, Destruction and Detroit*) and therefore unavailable. We could think of no one else suitable, and Hans de Roo was firm in his insistence that only an experienced opera director, whose work he personally knew, should be engaged. Our future director—Britain's David Pountney—didn't appear until after the music was completed.

This was a potentially serious problem: Usually the director has to approve the choices of designer, and the designs have to conform to the director's concept of the production. By going with a designer first, I had reversed the usual order of things, placing advance restrictions on the director by predetermining for him the physical stage reality. Hans de Roo had worked with Pountney on several occasions before and recommended him very highly to us. For his part, Pountney accepted his late arrival extremely well. Perhaps it might have come out differently had he joined us in the beginning. About this, though, he never complained, and he carried through his directorial role expertly and, I felt, in our original spirit.

Israel, DeJong and I worked out the main outlines of *Satyagraha* in the summer of 1978 in Nova Scotia. Howard Klein of the Rockefeller Foundation had taken a personal interest in our project and, with help from that foundation, we organized a trip to India the following winter. Though none of the events of the opera took place in India, that, nonetheless, was where we would find the material we needed. On his return to India from South Africa in 1914, Gandhi had carted all his papers with him. An astonishing collection! He seems to have thrown away nothing. All these documents—letters, notes to himself, receipts, newspaper reports, etc.—are housed in the Gandhi Peace Foundation's library in New Delhi. They make up over ninety volumes, and in 1978 they were still being expanded and sorted out. There we found letters that passed between Gandhi and Tolstoy, newspaper descriptions of events that eventually found their way onto our stage, and photographs of Gandhi and his South African associates.

I was eager for my collaborators to view the films I had seen some six years before. The Gandhi Foundation had collected all the newsreel footage available anywhere and from it had assembled a film lasting no less than six hours. The foundation personnel in New Delhi made all this material available to us. Their generosity and interest in our project was all the more touching in that I doubt that they really knew what an opera was or exactly how this material would wind up in our project. Their attitude was that it was their function to help in the dissemination of Gandhiji's ideas. That, of course, somehow included our project, and I don't think they questioned it any further. Besides that, we organized a visit to Gandhi's last ashram—Sevagram—in Central India. There we could still see the kind of communal society Gandhi had begun to implement for his close followers in South Africa, specifically Phoenix Farm and Tolstoy Farm. Both were ashrams in the fullest meaning of the word: a community bound together by shared spiritual, religious and social values.

There were, furthermore, countless persons in Ahmadabad, New

Delhi and South India who had known Gandhi and were willing to talk to us. One memorable visit was to Vinobhava, then his foremost disciple, still living in South India at that time. In Vinobhava's ashram we saw a printing press very similar, he said, to the one that Gandhiji had used to print his newspaper, *Indian Opinion,* in South Africa. Details like that were invaluable when the moment came to begin producing our own *Satyagraha.*

A last and very valuable part of our visit to India was spent with the Khatikali Kalamandalum in the province of Kerala. The Khatikali is traditional song, dance and story-telling combined in one theatrical form. Kalamandalum actually means "school" or "institute." The institute was located in Churuturuty, a small town one hundred kilometers from the provincial capital of Kerala, Cochin. All the dramas presented were religious in nature, taken from the two great Hindu religious epics surviving from ancient times, the *Mahabharata* and the *Ramayana.* Gandhi had been particularly fond of the *Bhagavad-Gita* (translated as "Song of the Lord"), which is actually a relatively short excerpt from the *Mahabharata.* I had first seen the Khatikali in 1970 while visiting the American composer David Reck, who was studying Karnatic (South Indian) music in Madras. The visual effects of the theater, based on "realistic" renderings of the Hindu gods and kings, were particularly striking, and I was anxious for Israel and DeJong to see them, though at that moment there were no plans to incorporate any of these kinds of traditional materials into our work.

Besides making this tour in India, both of my collaborators had become familiar with Gandhi's writings, particularly the autobiographical books, such as *Satyagraha* itself. This year of preparation was invaluable, allowing us to work together toward a theatrical and, I feel, original approach to our subject. What we ended up with was something resembling an opera libretto—a staged telling of Gandhi's story divided into acts and scenes, complete with settings, action and vocal text.

I remember we began by listing what we considered the important events of Gandhi's South African years. That first list contained some twenty-one historic incidents. In itself, this is not an impossible amount. Brecht, for instance, used a similar number of scenes in two of his major works, *Galileo* and *Mother Courage.* It allowed him to develop his characters through many small moments covering an extended time period of twenty to thirty years.

The difficulty for me of using short scenes was that my music tends to have a greater emotional impact when it is allowed a longer sweep of time in which to develop. I wanted fewer scene changes, which would permit longer stretches of music. We cut our scenes to fifteen and then to eleven. I felt this was still too many and realized our "story" would have to be told in a somewhat different way. Finally, we arrived at a list of six scenes based on historic events. It seemed to me the minimum number necessary to indicate the major moments in the Satyagraha struggle. At this point, though, we were not really telling a story; our outline was more a series of moments in Gandhi's life. It would be like looking at a family photo album, viewing pictures taken over a span of years. The order in which you saw them might not even matter; it wouldn't prevent you from forming a picture of the family growing up, growing older together. In many ways, I found this somewhat more abstract story line closer to my way of thinking and closer to other work I had done in the theater.

There was one problem that continued to plague us: where to begin, or rather, *how* to begin, the opera. The best beginning would have been Gandhi's first important encounter with South African racial restrictions. He had boarded a train in Durban, armed with a first-class train ticket to Pretoria, but was asked to move to the third-class coach with the other "colored" passengers. When Gandhi refused, he was taken by the hand and pushed off the train. The night he spent shivering in the cold train station (his overcoat was in his luggage, which had been taken by the station authorities, and Gandhi was too afraid of more insults to ask for it) has been described by Gandhi in several places in his writings as representing a turning point in his life. You couldn't hope for a more dramatic or gripping scene than this, and some years later the Richard Attenborough film, *Gandhi,* began exactly in this way, and to wonderful effect.

My problem was this: *Einstein on the Beach* had also begun with a train scene. This really didn't matter at all, but I was very conscious that this, my second opera, would be scrutinized very closely, and I didn't want people to think I couldn't write an opera that didn't start with a train. Though this wasn't a *real* problem, it certainly bothered me at the time.

Finally Constance came up with an ingenious solution. She suggested we begin the opera in the mythical, historical setting of the *Bhagavad-Gita*. I saw immediately that the idea was perfect, from every point of view. In the *Gita,* Prince Arjuna stands poised, ready to go into battle. Looking at the approaching army, he sees friends, even relatives, armed against him. He hesitates, explaining his doubts to his companion, Lord Krishna. The next eighty or so pages, encompassing all of the *Gita,* is devoted to a dialogue between Lord Krishna and Prince Arjuna on the relative value of action and nonaction, and it remains to this day one of the most popular religious/philosophical works in India. It is a long, often eloquent, statement concluding that, though the methods of action and nonaction can each lead to liberation, action is superior. The appeal that this text must have had to the young Gandhi is obvious. Throughout his life, Gandhi would refer to the *Gita,* using it as a kind of moral yardstick against which he could measure his actions. He seems to have committed it to memory. He describes how he would paste small sections of it onto his mirror, so that he could study it while shaving in the mornings.

For our opera, the idea evolved that the first scene would begin at dawn. To the left and right we would see, lined up in the dim morning light, the two opposing armies. As the sun rises and the scene unfolds, we then would see that the two armies were not the mythological armies of the *Gita* but, on one side, Europeans and, on the other, the Indians of South Africa. In the beginning, in the still dark of predawn, our Gandhi would appear alone upstage. Soon he would be joined by Lord Krishna, transforming his opening solo into a duet. Now Prince Arjuna appears, and the duet becomes a trio. Finally, in the last moments of the first scene, the chorus (our two armies) joins the three soloists.

Israel presented the two figures from the *Gita* in the super-realistic style we had seen in South India. He had made a close study of the make-up and costumes and, aided by photographs, was able to render a likeness that, for our purposes, was very close to how they appear in the Khatikali theater. In addition, they arrived on stage in chariots, each drawn by attendants dressed as devils or monsters from some Hindu netherworld. This opening was a bold stroke, both in concept and design. It was one of those effects which can only be judged in the presence of a live audience, and we had to wait until opening night before we found out what a remarkable impression it would make.

We made an important series of decisions about the work during this period. The progression of scenes moved chronologically through the course of one day, with Act I containing, in their proper order, dawn, midmorning and late morning. The first scene of Act II began at noon, was followed by a scene in the afternoon and, finally, one in early evening. Act III became one long extended scene, the New Castle March, beginning at sunset and concluding at night.

In this way the ''time'' of the piece was expressed in two distinct ways: first, the historical events of Gandhi's Satyagraha movement spanning the years from 1893 to 1914 (though actually beginning with the mythological time of the *Gita*); and second, the dawn-to-night setting of the scenes as they would appear in order. An important final time sense was soon to appear.

It was my idea to have each act presided over by a historical figure connected with Gandhi. These would not actually be singing characters in the drama but, instead, would simply witness the action. Israel proposed placing them upstage on a small elevated platform overlooking the action. The stage action would then appear from two vantage points. The first was from that of the audience. The second, from that of each historical personage. As it turned out, this was a powerful visual device for the audience. Throughout the evening, their eyes constantly moved from the stage to the "witnesses" on high, and back again. This shifting of perspective added greatly to the dramatic effect of each scene.

For the three witnesses, I searched for characters who represented for Gandhi what, in India, is known as the "three times"—past, present and future.

For his past, there was Count Tolstoy. Though they never met in person, Gandhi and Tolstoy were in touch by letter until the death of the great Russian author in 1910. Some of Tolstoy's last letters were to the young Gandhi, and his ideas about spiritual values and communal life were truly inspiring to Gandhi. The second ashram Gandhi organized in South Africa was named "Tolstoy Farm." Their correspondence, copies of which we had brought back from India, makes movingly clear how alone Gandhi felt when first undertaking what would be his life's work. Tolstoy, on his side, seemed not to have had a very clear idea of what Gandhi was up to, though in other letters he refers to Gandhi as "our brother in the Transvaal." The correspondence is in English on both sides, a neighbor of Tolstoy's serving as translator and writer, while Tolstoy's name is affixed by himself at the end.

In our production, Tolstoy sits at his desk, looking down on the action below. It happened that a few years earlier, when passing through London on one of my Indian trips, I had seen an exhibit on Tolstoy at the British Museum. There, among photos and all sorts of memorabilia of the great writer, was a facsimile of his writing desk, complete with inkwells, pens, letters, etc., right down to his baby shoes cast in bronze. I described the desk from memory to Israel, and he included it in the opera.

Later, during the rehearsal period, I was discussing the desk with the prop man. This fellow was a specialist in odds and ends and would happily travel throughout Holland, poking into barns and flea markets, to meet whatever design needs the current opera might have. At the close of one day's run-through, I climbed a ladder to the platform to get a close look at how the desk was coming along, and there it all was, complete with baby shoes. I was, to say the least, surprised. I couldn't imagine how anyone in the theater could be aware of such detail. I thought our prop man had gone a little overboard, especially as the desk top was well above the heads of anyone sitting in the orchestra. A day later, during one of our dress rehearsals, I was sitting in the balcony in order to judge the balance between voices and orchestra. It was Act I, Tolstoy's act, and the person next to me lent me a pair of opera glasses. And there was Tolstoy's desk, clearly visible—pens, inkwells, shoes and all.

For Act II, I wanted the witness to be a contemporary of Gandhi and settled on Rabindranath Tagore, the great Bengali poet and playwright who won the Nobel Prize for literature in 1913. He had befriended Gandhi on the latter's return to India and, being something of an equal to Gandhi in terms of public renown, was able to become more of a real confidant than most of his associates. It was Tagore who first awarded him the title *Mahatma,* though it was a term Gandhi himself never used or even acknowledged.

I suppose Gandhi was one of those people who may be enlightening to read about, but must have been quite difficult to be with in the flesh. As husband and father, he appeared as something of a tyrant to his immediate family. He was extremely demanding of himself and routinely expected those around him to live by his own superhuman standards. But he would listen to Tagore, even allowing himself to be lectured by the poet about his arrogance. When, in later years, during his many confrontations with the British, Gandhi would take up one of his monumental fasts, the whole country would seem to stop in terror as he threatened to end his life. Then Tagore, it is reported, would don his black robes and travel the length of India to be with his friend. In our opera, Tagore sits beside a bird cage, a reference to his fondness for canaries (during his research, Israel had uncovered a photograph of Tagore with a bird).

For Act III, I wanted a figure from Gandhi's future. This could only be Martin Luther King, Jr. There is hardly a dissident political movement of contemporary times that doesn't make some use of Gandhiji's techniques of nonviolent civil disobedience, but no one has used them more in the spirit in which they were created than did King. I thought it important also that the last figure be a man of the West. Of course, Gandhi was a national hero for India, but his importance was international in scope. He is really a hero for everyone.

Of the three upstage figures, King is the only one who never faces the audience. We placed him at a lectern facing away from us, speaking, perhaps, to an unseen audience. Throughout Act III (the New Castle March) the chorus, Gandhi's Satyagraha army, are carried offstage one by one by policemen dressed as small-town Alabama cops or troopers. There was a large platform backstage that couldn't be seen by the audience, onto which the chorus then climbed. The drop for Act III was, like that for the other six scenes, a painting of the sky with clouds (later, stars appeared as night fell onstage); however, our Act III drop was actually a scrim, which has the very useful property of appearing opaque when lit from the front, but becoming transparent when lit from behind. During the last moments of the opera, the only figures left visible on stage are King at his lectern and Gandhi below. While Gandhi sings the last few notes of the opera, the lights on the scrim shift to the rear, and Gandhi's Satyagraha army appears as King's followers.

When the production came to New York the following year, Hans Nieuwenhvis, who had been David Pountney's assistant, restaged the opera from David's original direction and incorporated ideas of his own. One of the additions he made in the last scene was to have a man step out of the crowd of King's listeners (dressed as Indians) and act out, in slow motion, the murder of King, thereby linking both King's and Gandhi's assassinations from separate points in time. It was one of those moments in the theater which becomes almost unbearably real.

For almost all of their scenes, these witnesses were quite still. Pountney, though, gave them each one gesture to perform in their fifty-minute appearance. The gestures were very simple—standing up, opening a letter, or taking off a jacket—and were just sufficient to break a pattern of total immobility, thereby creating a different kind of tension and dramatic expectation in the audience.

The question of text was resolved during this period. I already knew that the story, such as it was, would not require a sung or spoken text to make itself clear to the audience. The action of each scene was so simple and self-explanatory that support by a text would have seemed redundant, even awkward. For example, in the last scene of Act II we see the members of the Satyagraha army step up, one by one, to a large cauldron and toss in their identity cards. (These cards were required to be carried by all of South Africa's "coloreds" and were symbols of their repression.) When all have stepped forward, the cards are ignited and burned. Action of this kind hardly needs further description. This being the case, I felt I was free to approach the use of language in an entirely different way. Instead of the text describing the action or, even worse, explaining the action, I thought of using it as a commentary on the action. Text thus became subtext to action.

The text I had in mind was the same one that had resolved one of our other problems, the *Bhagavad-Gita*. It became Constance's job to find passages from the *Gita* that would illuminate the thought behind Gandhi's plans and motives. Since Gandhi's actions were so tuned to the philosophy of the *Gita* to begin with, it wasn't a question of simply finding a suitable text but of finding one that was both appropriate and revealing.

That done, we had to tackle the problem of the actual language in which the opera would be sung. The *Gita* was written in Sanskrit, the classical language of ancient India. It is a language still used in ceremonial situations, as part of the vocal music of the classical tradition of South India, and even in some of the theaters of Kerala, where the Khatikali theater is found. However, it is not in everyday use any more than Latin is in modern western Europe. I was fairly sure that *Satyagraha*, in its first few years, would play in three countries: Holland (naturally), Germany and the U.S. My choices were therefore to translate the text into Dutch, German and English. Or leave it in the original language.

After much wrestling with the problem, I chose the original language, Sanskrit. At first the decision troubled me, but more and more, I found it appealing. I liked the idea of *further* separating the vocal text from the action. In this way, without an understandable text to contend with, the listener could let the words go altogether. The weight of "meaning" would then be thrown onto the music, the designs and the stage action. Secondly, since none of the national languages was going to be used, Sanskrit could serve as a kind of international language for this opera. It is common, after all, to present operas in their original languages. It seemed to me that audiences who are used to reading synopses of texts in their program notes and then hearing, say, *The Queen of Spades* in Russian, would find my approach really no different. To make that practical, I decided there had to be a translation of the text in the program notes in whatever country the opera would be performed, and this has been a requirement that, so far, all the producers of *Satyagraha* have willingly agreed to.

One of the most irresistible reasons to me for using Sanskrit was the sound of the language itself. I knew from the vocal music of South India, which I had frequently heard, how beautiful a vocal language it really is. Neither Dutch nor German nor English could compare to it. The closest contemporary language in sound, in my opinion, would be sung Italian, and it seemed pointless to translate from a superb vocal language into one far less beautiful when there seemed no compelling reason to do so.

Since singers could not be expected to possess the ability to read Sanskrit, it was necessary to make a phonetic transliteration of the text. Thus the Sanskrit text was translated phonetically into English, and I had to work from a transliteration. Later on, there were still problems of pronunciation to contend with and Constance, with the help of Sanskrit-speaking scholars, devised a pronunciation guide to aid singers in the correct sound of the language. The biggest problem, by far, came from a quite unexpected source, one I hadn't at all anticipated. Texts in foreign languages, especially exotic and unfamiliar ones, are far, far harder for singers to memorize than texts in their native languages. That has been a recurring problem with *Satyagraha*. It is a very difficult opera to learn—but, obviously, not an impossible one. At this writing it has been produced by four different companies in three different countries and recorded by yet another company.

By the time the first stage of our work had been completed, practically everything but the music for *Satyagraha* had been set. Besides the problems of structure, vocal content and characterization, many elements of the design were beginning to fall into place. Working closely with Israel and Riddell, we were able to integrate the design, lighting and my musical and dramatic ideas. For example, I wanted the scene changes to take place as quickly as possible so that in each act the music would flow from scene to scene without interruption. Israel's solution was to have the chorus and soloists pick up the built pieces—chairs, tables, even miniature replicas of buildings—and virtually change the scenes themselves. The "sky" drops could come in and out in seconds. It was visually interesting as well as rapid. This also meant I could keep my musical transitions between scenes very brief which, I think, added to the general flow of the work. In an opera of this kind that covers a period of over twenty years with little connective or motivational material between scenes, this consideration was highly important.

Our working method was certainly an aid to both Israel and Riddell, who were collaborating on the lighting while the design concepts were beginning to emerge. We had brought back from India actual photographs of Gandhi's European and Indian co-workers in South Africa, and some six of these became featured players in the opera. Though we hardly attempted to cast the parts by physical appearance, the style of dress and the general look of the times were important clues from which Israel and

Riddell could construct our visual representation of people of that particular time and place.

The material collected in India proved endlessly useful. One scene, "Rescue" (the first scene from Act II), was inspired by a newspaper account, in the *Durban Mercury,* that had been carefully saved by Gandhi. This report describes Gandhi's return from a visit to India. Briefly, he was met by a crowd of thugs who were giving him a very rough welcome. Mrs. Alexander, the wife of the local police chief, happened to pass by and, seeing the disturbance, stepped in, raised her umbrella over the helpless Gandhi, and swept him away from the crowd to safety.

David Pountney, using the journalist's description and working carefully with the performers, re-created the scene in detail. This moment in the performance has always given me an eerie feeling because, unlike most operatic scenes in which the true time-scale of events is distorted, what we see is literally a re-creation of events of more than eighty years ago, taking place in something like "real time." And at every performance, the scene is re-created anew.

This first working period completed, I turned my attention to the music.

By now, I was on the way to developing a working method for treating subjects in the theater. In many ways it was an extension of how I had worked earlier with the Mabou Mines company and, later, with Bob Wilson. When Mabou Mines needed music for a new production, I began by attending as many rehearsals as possible, trying to gain an impression of how the work was being created. This included watching lights being set and even costumes being fit. When working with Wilson, especially, there was no detail of a production with which I didn't try to acquaint myself. Working on *Satyagraha,* I extended this to the subject itself. During the year preceding the actual writing of the music, I had an insatiable appetite for any and all information about Gandhi, and this had been preceded by years of more casual reading on the subject. During this preparation period, I refrained from all work on the music. I didn't jot down themes or ideas. And I definitely did not wake up in the middle of the night with a major aria rattling around in my head. If anything, I held off, as long as possible, the moment when I began to work with the musical material.

When working this way, a moment comes when I feel I have formed a clear, if admittedly subjective and highly personal, image of the person I'm writing about. At that point, it becomes possible for me to write the music. This way of working began with *Einstein,* became fully crystallised with *Satyagraha,* and has been a reliable method for me ever since.

No doubt, writing this series of "portrait" operas—*Einstein on the Beach, Satyagraha* and *Akhnaten*—had a great deal to do with my developing this approach. In a very definite way, the personage about whom the work revolved replaced the traditional functions of story and character, interactions of which make up the subjects of most operas. The principal personage of each of my first three operas came to be far more important than the particular stage action that was devised to reveal him. Naturally, then, the musical ideas would derive more from my highly personal understanding of the character than in the stage action or story.

Seen from this point of view, it clearly is more important for me to make a firm connection between myself and the subject, in any way I can, than to spend my time constructing a story line. This is not to say that the dramatic shape of the work is unimportant. Subsequently, a good deal of effort must be spent, usually with the director, on the dramatic construction of the work. Nor can that be left to the last minute, another reason why, in the first work period while the work is being formed, I prefer, when possible, to have the director on hand. Still, the point for me is that the energy of the work comes from the subject himself.

This highly internal way of working can be risky. It requires complete confidence in my own ability to form an authentic bond between myself and the material. The benefit of this approach to opera is that it enables me to form a very clear emotional setting for the character. In this way, more than any other, I feel I've succeeded in the writing of these first three operatic works. In spite of whatever technical or dramatic flaws they might have, they seem to me emotionally clear, even accurate, in their musical settings. This is not the kind of thing that can be proven one way or the other, but it can perhaps be verified in performance: That is, its truthfulness can be felt by an audience.

It seems that the development of "docudrama" by the popular media has already begun to corrupt our notions of what is possible in the theater. I remember, after one performance of *Satyagraha,* one person complained that the "real life" Gandhi was not like the one portrayed on stage. I replied that I was well aware of that, and that the historical Gandhi, to begin with, couldn't have sung the part, a point that was not too obvious to make, it seemed to me. It had never been my intention to render a "real" likeness of Gandhi but, rather, an artist's vision of him. Let us not forget, after all, that theater (or opera) is a species of poetry. It is our confidence in the validity of artistic truths that gives courage to our efforts.

In any case, I expected, as I explained earlier, that the audience would further personalize the work. Whatever interpretations they brought to it, and how it became meaningful to them, was really not predictable by me, or even terribly important. The only thing I *could* do was to present the subject in as clear and powerful a setting as I could devise.

Because of the thoroughness of our preparation, and also undoubtedly because of my intense interest in the subject, when I began to write the music, it came quickly, even easily. As had by then become my custom, I began at the beginning and worked straight through to the end. Usually my writing day began early in the morning and lasted until early afternoon. By the end of August 1979 the music was completed. I composed directly into the orchestra score. A piano reduction (in which all the orchestra parts are reduced to a score playable on one keyboard) was prepared that fall so the chorus and singers could begin their work.

Our premiere was a year away, and now the practical matters of casting, completing the design and building the scenery came to the fore. The rehearsals were to begin the following summer in Holland, and there was much left to do.

At the beginning of our discussions, Hans and I talked about having the premiere under the musical direction of Dennis Russell Davies. Besides being an exciting conductor of new American music, Dennis had recently begun a successful career conducting opera in Europe, and I was looking forward to working with him. In the interim, though, he signed an extended contract to be music director of the Stuttgart State Opera and, though we were soon to have other discussions about opera, he was not available for our premiere in Holland.

It happened that Christopher Keene was available and interested. I had first met him in Spoleto, Italy, in 1972 where, though still a very young man, he was Music Director of the Spoleto Festival. I had been there with my Ensemble, performing in the Buckminster Fuller dome, and to this day I remember Christopher, with one of his sons on his shoulders, walking around during the concert and evidently enjoying the event very much. Perhaps I remember it all the more because there was a good deal of controversy about my appearance there. Some of the musicians had publicly boycotted me—Mr. Menotti even walked out during the performance. Since then, Christopher had become a principal conductor at the New York City Opera, and in him I found a conductor thoroughly seasoned and sympathetic to my music.

Just weeks before our rehearsals began, Christopher was hospitalized, seriously ill, and suddenly we were looking for yet another conductor. We showed the score to an up-and-coming young American,

Bruce Ferden, who until that moment didn't know a note of my music. His reaction to the score was spontaneous and enthusiastic. He quickly committed himself to the project and eventually led the chorus, singers and musicians through the rehearsals, premiere, and that first run of performances in Holland. In the end, though, all three of these men performed the work. Six months after the Dutch premiere, Dennis brought *Satyagraha* to Stuttgart in a new production by Achim Freyer (an East German designer/director with whom I would soon be involved on my next opera), and the following year, Christopher presided at the U.S. premiere in Artpark outside of Buffalo, New York, and soon after at BAM in New York. But all that came later. First we had our premiere to take care of.

Hans de Roo decided to audition the principal parts in New York. He intended having some Dutch singers in the production, but there was no tenor in his company at that moment who was suitable for the role of Gandhi. Since he would be casting the leading role from the U.S., he decided to audition several other principal parts in New York as well. I think one reason was that he hoped I might be able to work with some of the singers before we all arrived in Holland for the rehearsals, scheduled to begin in August 1980. Undoubtedly, a second reason was that American singers are among the best-trained and best-prepared in the world. You can find Americans working in opera houses all over Europe and the U.S.

At these auditions were Hans de Roo, Christopher Keene and myself, along with Constance DeJong and Bob Israel. David Pountney had not yet joined us. We found very good voices: Claudia Cummings, Bruce Hall, Richard Gill and Beverly Morgan. But we were having the devil of a time finding the right Gandhi. Almost the very last tenor we heard was Douglas Perry. Christopher had worked with him before and liked him. As was usual with me at these auditions, I found it difficult to form an idea of what a singer would sound like with my music when the audition material was really light years away from what I wanted to hear. As it turned out, Douglas was a superb Gandhi. He grew into the part so beautifully that for a long time I could imagine no one else singing it at all.

A few months before we were to begin rehearsals, we had the opportunity to run through the entire work with the principals and piano accompaniment. We were able to do this thanks to a workshop grant from the Rockefeller Foundation. (As mentioned before, Howard Klein was head of the arts division of the foundation and, from the beginning, had retained a keen interest in the progress of the work.) Grants of this kind, though perhaps not large, were timely, even crucial.

By then, David Pountney had begun working with us, and he attended the run-through in New York. For the singers and the designer and, to an extent, for David, it was indispensable to hear the work sung all the way through. It's important to remember that when a new work is being premiered, no one knows how the piece goes. You can't find it on records or even talk to anyone about it. This is *really* the first time. It was enormously helpful for so many who would be involved in the production to begin to get an idea of what *Satyagraha* was all about. I thought I knew what it would sound like, and I was confident that Christopher knew too. David could play the piano reduction himself (what a luxury to have a director who can actually *read* music!). But for the rest—including many of the singers—they wouldn't get to hear it until the actual rehearsals in Holland.

This was the first time I had encountered this problem. With *Einstein* it hadn't come up, since I had played at all the rehearsals myself and taught the music to our small chorus. Our brief workshop in New York had been an enormous help but not a real answer to the problem, and I determined that when the occasion again arose, I would find a better solution. It would take a few more years, with *Akhnaten,* for that to come about.

Meanwhile, during the spring of 1980 the sets were being built in the Netherlands Opera's own shops in Holland. Israel had turned in his designs the preceding December and, as with *Einstein,* we had seen a doll's-house version of all the visual elements. I invariably find this a thrilling moment in the creation of a work, and I'm always present at these showings. Since Israel had worked for a number of years with the shop people, he knew them well and had great confidence in them. Still, he made several trips to Holland during the spring and early summer to check on their progress.

In July, the company assembled in Rotterdam for the seven-week rehearsal period before our scheduled opening night on September 5, 1980. During those weeks Pountney set the stage action, and Bruce completed the music rehearsals. By the end of that time, the music had to be memorized by all the singers, including our chorus. I mentioned earlier that everyone had special problems memorizing an exotic language like Sanskrit, having to learn by rote sounds that, for them, had no connotative meaning. We had provided word-by-word translations, but the sheer *quantity* of text still made the memorizing process difficult.

For the chorus, this was especially difficult because of the large amount of singing they had to do. The chorus appears in four out of the seven scenes, making *Satyagraha* practically a choral opera. I was aware of the unusual demands I was making, but there seemed no other way to present our leading figure. After all, there has hardly been a more public leader than Gandhi; his entire life seemed to take place in the midst of crowds. It is partly this constant public nature of his actions that gives him his special character. So, a generous use of the chorus was appropriate.

Hans had a particularly shrewd and successful solution to the matter. Instead of using one of the professional choruses in Holland, which would have limited rehearsal time, he had engaged the chorus of the Rotterdam conservatory, who had started learning the music the winter before. Gandhi had a special appeal for them, as he will always have for young people, no doubt because of the fiery idealism which his life reflects. Our Rotterdam chorus brought an enthusiasm to the production that, I believe, no professional chorus could have matched.

There seemed to be no special vocal problems with the soloists. Once they learned their roles, they sang them admirably. The vocal parts in this, the first work I had intended for professional opera singers, were conservatively written. In later works, I have set some very demanding parts for singers, but in *Satyagraha* I suppose I must have been trying to minimize my problems. At least in this limited area, none arose.

A far more difficult matter was the question of acting style. David understood very well what was needed, but the singers had to discover a way of working with this material that made it real to themselves before they could appear convincing and natural on the stage. One of the singers presented the problem to me very clearly: "In this scene I don't *do* anything, so how can I create my character?"

What she was accustomed to was stage characterization based on plots, stories, dialogue, and so forth. I encouraged them to find out who their character *was* (they were historical people, after all) and to *be* the character. I gave them all books and photos and set them to studying their subject. The first several weeks were very difficult for them. Then, suddenly, these problems seemed to disappear almost overnight. As one person explained to me, they had to "get into it." I've noticed this process a number of times since then: A singer new to the music and the unfamiliar acting demands will often struggle for a time before becoming quite comfortable with his or her part. Two weeks seems to be the usual time it takes.

I was helped this first time by having Iris Hiskey in the cast. Iris had been cast as Mrs. Naidoo, one of Gandhi's supporters. She had sung with my Ensemble since the *Einstein* tour, replacing Joan LaBarbara when Joan went on to her own composing career. At least one singer, then, knew and understood the music.

I don't mean to understate the demands of the music. In *Satyagraha* the parts are long, sustained, and require special concentration. However, all that is really required are the tools necessary for any good musician—a good sense of rhythm and pitch, as well as good physical health and the ability to maintain a steady and concentrated attention. As I make that statement, I have to admit that these are abilities one doesn't find all that easily. But since when has new music (or any music, for that matter) been easy?

Bruce's work with the orchestra had been truly superb. For the same reasons the music was difficult for the singers to sing, it was difficult for the musicians to play. It is important to remember how very *new* this music was to the orchestra. At that time, the Netherlands Opera had no regular orchestra but engaged different Dutch orchestras for each production; for *Satyagraha* they were the members of the Utrecht Symphony and in the end they turned out a quite creditable performance. There was the usual grumbling which, I suppose, is the common reaction to *any* new piece, but the musicians definitely did not go on strike in protest (as a later unfounded rumor claimed they did). Bruce was tactful and patient and brought the music to performance even a little ahead of his allotted rehearsal time. The orchestra seemed to like him quite well and, I found out later, invited him to return to Holland the following year to lead them in a series of orchestra concerts.

All nine performances in Holland sold out. Hans told me later that the first day tickets went on sale, a line formed around the theater at 7:30 in the morning. The reception was a tremendous boost to the soloists. One of them admitted to me afterward that she had expected to sing to half-empty houses. It came as no surprise to see their enthusiasm for the work visibly increase night after night as they became aware of the appreciation of the audience. None of them, perhaps with the exception of Iris, had known what to expect.

Again, I saw an audience filled with young people, many of them obviously completely new to opera. The same kind of audience—made up mostly of young people but also with many middle-aged people, as well as some quite old—came to the performances in Stuttgart and New York. If there are no audiences for new operas, you certainly can't prove it by me.

THE STUTTGART PRODUCTION

The first problem a composer has with a new opera is getting a first production.

The second problem he has is getting a second production.

I decided to try solving both problems in the same year.

In Dennis Russell Davies I had an interested and willing music director. When he went to take up his new post in Stuttgart, he took several projects with him, and *Satyagraha* was one of them. Our discussions with Hans Peter Doll, the director, and dramaturg Peter Kehr, led eventually to a new commission as well. But more of that later.

It was decided that there would be a new production of *Satyagraha* in Stuttgart, led by Dennis with direction by Achim Freyer and scenery and costumes by Achim and his wife, Ilona. Achim was well known in Germany as a painter and theater designer. I had looked at samples of his paintings and design work, and had gone to see his production of Weber's *Der Freischütz*. I found his design highly expressive and as different as I could imagine from that of American designers I had worked with.

I agreed to what was sure to be a radically different version of *Satyagraha* for the following reasons:

I feel that only through reinterpretation of the standard repertory does a true understanding of a work emerge. Given this point of view, there is no final version of a work. Nor do the original authors necessarily have the final, or even the best, interpretations. Only through many productions of a work—*King Lear,* for example—can one begin to glimpse the real dimensions of the piece. I'm absolutely convinced of the validity of this point of view, though I know from personal experience that it can lead to very difficult experiences for the authors, should they allow this view to prevail.

Secondly, what I have seen of attempts on the part of authors, as well as publishers and heirs, to "protect" a work has led, more often than not, to the stifling of its potential life. Brecht's work in America is a good case in point. The publishers of the original translation successfully prevented any other translation of Brecht's work to appear for a long time. Since that translation was far from admired, his work, apart from *The Threepenny Opera,* was hardly known in the U.S. for years. It now seems to me doubtful that his writing will ever assume the importance in America that it has in Europe, in spite of the availability now of acceptable translations. (It took years of litigation to make them legally useable.)

I firmly believe that there is more to be gained by risking (within reason) new collaboration and interpretation than in sticking to what we know, what has already been done.

Achim saw the *Satyagraha* production in Holland. He assured me that his *Satyagraha* wouldn't "look" at all like ours. That much I took for granted. He wanted the freedom, he said, to reinterpret Gandhi for the German public. I told him that as long as he followed the settings in the libretto and his interpretation could be supported by the music, he was free to do as he liked. I knew that, as far as the music was concerned, I couldn't hope for a better interpreter than Dennis.

The Freyer production had its premiere in Stuttgart the following spring with the Stuttgart State Opera's own soloists. Gandhi, incidentally, was extremely well sung, again by an American, Leo Goeke. This production ran two years and was performed over thirty times. I saw it perhaps half a dozen times and, in the end, liked it very much. But the truth is that when I saw its premiere (I had stayed away from the rehearsals, not wanting to interfere), I was deeply surprised.

Achim had been as good as his word. At first this *Satyagraha* looked completely strange to me. In fact, apart from Gandhi himself, I hardly recognized anything in the opera except the music. And at that, there were three Gandhis instead of one (a dancing Gandhi, a singing Gandhi, an acting Gandhi). It was hard to miss images of modern-day Germany including police dogs, motorcycles roaring onto the stage with headlights aimed straight at the audience, a seminude female weightlifter and so on. One scene seemed to be set in an automobile junkyard.

The next day Achim and I met in the Opera House cafeteria. He got right to the point.

"Well, what did you think of my production?"

The fact was, I didn't know what to think. In principle, I believed that what he had done was artistically valid, but I actually didn't understand, at that moment, what he had really done at all.

"That was very interesting, Achim," I began. "But, tell me. Why did you do it that way?"

At first, he seemed surprised by my question. But he recovered quickly and said: "I did it just the way you wrote it!"

I thought about that for a long time.

THE MUSIC

When I embarked upon the writing of *Satyagraha* in 1978, my first concern was the orchestra. I had written quite a lot of orchestral music in my student days—symphonic works, concertos, pieces for strings, brass and so on—but the last time I had concentrated on orchestration had been more than fifteen years before when, as a young man on a Ford Foundation program, I had been writing music for the Pittsburgh public schools. In those days, I had been interested mainly in getting an orchestra to sound well. I can't say that my musical ideas at that time were so original that they needed new solutions in orchestral writing. Now the situation had become far different: I had my own ideas, and I knew an approach to orchestration was required that would effectively present those ideas through the medium of a modern-day opera orchestra.

By 1978 I had over ten years of work with my Ensemble behind me. The origin of the unique assortment of instruments that makes up my Ensemble (three electric keyboards, three saxophones doubling on flute and bass clarinet, one soprano voice) is a story in itself.

As I mentioned earlier, when I returned to New York in 1967, the only people willing to play my music were friends and acquaintances, some dating back to my days at Juilliard. I did not form an ensemble to fit an abstract concept of instrumental sound; instead, I began to write music to fit the musician friends I had at the time. Though the personnel shifted around somewhat in the early years, it finally stabilized into the

Philip Glass Ensemble. It featured a high incidence of keyboard players, and this led early on to the use of amplification and sound mixing. The problem with, say, three keyboard players is finding three pianos in the same room for rehearsal, not to mention performance. My solution was to use the small portable electric keyboards which were common in the world of pop music and rock-and-roll. I went through a number of different models, finally settling on a Farfisa mini-compact organ that, in 1968, was easy to find and quite inexpensive. (A used electric organ could be bought for $150.) The only problem with using electric keyboards was evident at our very first rehearsal: They easily overpowered any acoustic instrument. The only workable solution, then, was to amplify everything—flutes, violin, saxophones, whatever—and mix them together through a mixing board. Presto: an amplified ensemble!

Joan LaBarbara prompted the addition of a soprano voice. She was working in New York's downtown world of experimental music in those days, and suggested that I add a voice to the Ensemble. I took her up on her suggestion, and she sang with us for the next four years, leaving only when her own composing career began to take precedence. I've used a soprano with the Ensemble ever since.

With the Ensemble sound—finally a blend of amplified keyboards, winds and one singer—I had developed a unique and recognizable sound and, just as important, learned to bend it to my musical and expressive needs. In thinking about the orchestra for *Satyagraha*, I saw that the solution lay precisely in thinking of orchestral writing in the same way that I had thought of writing for my own Ensemble.

What I wanted to do was use "my" orchestra for my own musical purposes and, aside from the physical limits of the instruments and players, completely disregard past musical practices. The sound would be based on that of my own Ensemble, which was, up to that point, a sound I had made my own. What better model could I find than the one which had served my purposes so well until then? Using this sound as a guide, I began to make up my orchestra. The result was a score calling for triple winds (flutes, clarinets, oboes, bassoons, bass clarinet), using three players on a part (except the solo bass clarinet, which sometimes functions like a third bassoon) and a full complement of strings (first and second violins, violas, cellos and double basses).

That was it. No brass, no percussion. I asked for one electric organ to fill out the string parts and double the winds at those moments when, because of the lack of adequate resting places for breathing, their playing might become irregular. Even with three players on a part, this could become a problem, due to the repetitive structures and the rapidity of the music. This one electric organ also provides the reference to my own Ensemble, making the orchestra recognizable to me.

It further occurred to me that in choosing an orchestra of winds and strings, I was using instruments familiar to both East and West. This was not a crucial point for me, but it did make this particular orchestra seem appropriate for the occasion—an Indian subject presented within a Western cultural context.

I felt entirely comfortable about the choral writing. As a young man I had spent years singing choral music. I knew the standard oratorio literature fairly well and, better still, from the inside, as it were. As things turned out, there is quite a lot of choral music in *Satyagraha,* far more than one normally finds in opera. I must admit that, at the time, I didn't realize the special demands this would make on the resources of an opera house. The rehearsal time required to prepare a *Satyagraha* chorus is not impossible—after all, as I have said before, four different choruses have so far learned and performed it. However, the choral requirements are considerable, a consideration for anyone wanting to produce this work.

I treated the solo parts, at least in terms of their vocal ranges, rather conservatively. Though the amount of sustained singing is quite demanding, normal vocal limits, even as conservatively understood, are not challenged. With *Satyagraha* I began to use the human voice in a truly vocal way, whereas in the music for my Ensemble it has often been remarked, and quite correctly, that I use the voice as if it were just another instrument.

Treating a voice "vocally" means more than just knowing its natural range. Among many other items (color, diction, dynamics), perhaps the most important thing for a composer is learning how to *exercise* the voice. This means allowing the voice to use its full range without remaining too long in any one area. If the voice is judiciously exercised, it continues to sound fresh and does not tire too quickly. A good understanding of vocal technique takes years to acquire, and composers don't learn it in music school. You learn it from singers. If you remain available at rehearsals and make it clear that you are open to discussion, as I have made it a rule to be, singers will very quickly tell you what you did, and did not do, well for their voices. That is not the same as catering to specific needs, which can be a chore (and an unfulfilling chore at that, since the same singer seldom appears in all subsequent productions of an opera), but it does mean that when the voice is being used in an unusual way, you have the ability to adjust for it.

In other ways, I followed practices commonly employed in repertory opera regarding vocal usage. For example, I deliberately emphasized ensemble singing in *Satyagraha*. Arias, duets, trios, quartets, quintets and even a sextet can all be found in its pages. Furthermore, when writing *Satyagraha* I was well aware of the short supply (and expensive fees) of famous soloists, not to mention their reluctance to invest time in learning a role that ultimately would attract fewer paying engagements than yet another *La Bohème* or *Rigoletto*. Therefore, ensemble operas, as mine was turning out to be, are favored by many opera companies. I thought it not a bad idea to make this, my first ''real'' opera, more attractive to opera producers in this way.

Further, I knew that *Satyagraha* would appear highly unconventional to most opera companies, and I was not anxious to create unnecessary problems in the vocal parts. Frankly, I figured I would have enough problems, what with the use of Sanskrit, the unusual presentational style of the scenario, the extensive choral parts and the difficulties orchestra players were bound to have with such demanding and unfamiliar music. I hardly needed the extra burden of adding fresh problems by, say, inventing a new way of singing—if, indeed, such a thing would even be possible.

In *Einstein on the Beach* I had been looking for ways to combine harmonic and rhythmic structures, and a number of different solutions can be heard in that music. For *Satyagraha* I concentrated on only one such approach, using it in all seven scenes of the opera. Listeners familiar with Baroque music will recognize it as the chaconne, a form in which a harmonic pattern with changing rhythmic and melodic material is repeated throughout a piece, making it a specific kind of variation form. The fifth movement of Bach's D-minor partita for unaccompanied violin is an example that will be familiar to many people. In the first scene of Act I, the chaconne harmony is outlined in the low strings at the very beginning, as shown in Example A.

[EXAMPLE A]

An interesting feature of this progression is that it is the same as one often heard in flamenco guitar music. This particular form of Spanish folk music was introduced into Spain by gypsies who, it is believed, originated in India. There are very few harmonic practices shared by East and West since harmonic practice hardly ever turns up at all in Eastern music. This particular pattern is one of the few I know of that is common in the West and may have had its origin in the East. In this opening scene, the chaconne harmony goes through additive rhythmic variations while different vocal combinations—solo, duet, trio, full chorus—are sung over it.

Act II, scene 2 is a good example of how the rhythmic character of the chaconne can remain virtually unchanged, leaving all the variations to the vocal lines. The chaconne harmonies are shown in Example B, while Examples C and D show two different vocal duets written over the same harmony.

[EXAMPLE B]

[EXAMPLE C]

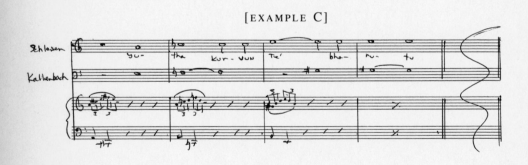

[EXAMPLE D]

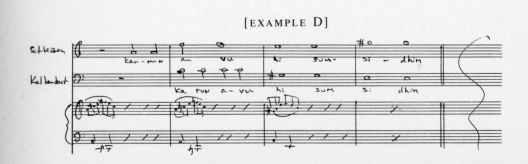

The most extended use of the chaconne technique takes place, somewhat paradoxically, over the briefest harmonic reiteration of two chords in the one extended scene of Act III, as shown in Example E. Here the emphasis is on rhythmic extensions of the chaconne harmony with little melodic development until Gandhi's entrance near the end of the scene.

[EXAMPLE E]

Another useful observation to make regarding the music in *Satyagraha* relates to thematic material common to all three operas in the trilogy. I took one of the main themes from *Einstein on the Beach* and then applied it in crucial places in the next two operas. This theme, heard in the first Knee Play as well as the other four Knee Plays, opens and closes *Einstein* (Example F). The chaconne harmonies of Act I, scene 2

[EXAMPLE F]

of *Satyagraha* actually constitute a harmonic extension of those opening notes. This becomes clear when they are heard together, as in Example G, though, in fact, they are never actually heard simultaneously in

[EXAMPLE G]

Satyagraha. One of the melodic elements which appears superimposed, sometimes alone but often together with other material, is heard in the flute (Example H). This forms the basis of the final moments of the opera, sung by Gandhi. It appears five times, each with a different melodic and rhythmic accompaniment, but still conforming to the harmonies of the trilogy theme.

[EXAMPLE H]

By using this material in Act I and later, in Act III, two otherwise distant moments in Gandhi's life—the establishment of his first ashram and his final days before leaving South Africa—are drawn together.

THE LIBRETTO

SATYAGRAHA
M.K. Gandhi in South Africa

An Opera in Three Acts
by
Philip Glass

MUSIC: Philip Glass

BOOK: Philip Glass and Constance DeJong

LYRICS: adapted from the *Bhagavad-Gita* by Constance DeJong

SINGING ROLES

Miss Schlesen, Gandhi's secretary	*(Soprano)*
Mrs. Naidoo, Indian co-worker	*(Soprano)*
Kasturbai, Gandhi's wife	*(Mezzo-Soprano)*
M.K. Gandhi	*(Tenor)*
Mr. Kallenbach, European co-worker	*(Baritone)*
Parsi Rustomji, Indian co-worker	*(Bass)*
Mrs. Alexander, European friend	*(Alto)*
Arjuna, mythological figure	*(Tenor)*
Krishna, mythological figure	*(Bass)*

NON-SINGING ROLES

Count Leo Tolstoy, historical figure	*(Act I)*
Rabindranath Tagore, historical figure	*(Act II)*
Martin Luther King, Jr., historical figure	*(Act III)*

ORCHESTRA

Woodwinds:	*Electric Organ*	*Strings:*
3 flutes	(or synthesizer)	strings I and II
3 oboes		violas
3 clarinets		cellos
1 bass clarinet		doublebasses
2 bassoons		

STAGING

On Stage Level: Satyagraha portrays the period from Gandhi's arrival in South Africa in 1893 to the New Castle March of 1913, the closing event of the Satyagraha movement in South Africa. These twenty-one years are set within the time frame of a single day—beginning at dawn's breaking in Scene 1, with subsequent scenes distributed over the daylight hours, and the final act occurring from dusk into the night. The participation of mythological characters at the outset and contemporary policemen at the end extends the historical narratives into a symbolic or epic time frame, from ancient to modern times.

Above Stage Level: Each of the opera's three acts has a figurative counterpart in the character of Count Leo Tolstoy, Rabindranath Tagore, and Martin Luther King, Jr. Their presence as witnesses on a level above establishes a temporal relationship with the staged events below and suggests the historical continuity of Satyagraha.

—Tolstoy (Act I) was an inspirational figure in forming Gandhi's ideas about nonviolence based on universal love. *The Kingdom of God Is Within You,* in particular, had made a deep impression and until Tolstoy's death in 1910, his letters to Gandhi were a source of support and guidance to the young Indian leader.

—Tagore (Act II) was Gandhi's contemporary, the poet and scholar who gave him advice and encouragement throughout his life. During their long and sometimes stormy friendship, Tagore remained the only living moral authority acknowledged by Gandhi.

—King (Act III) furthered the premise of nonviolence, when through him these ideas resurfaced again in the American civil rights movement.

Thus, in relation to the twenty-one-year struggle that took place in

Count Leo Tolstoy   *Rabindranath Tagore*   *Martin Luther King, Jr.*
(DRAWINGS BY ROBERT ISRAEL)

South Africa, these men individually are representatives of Satyagraha's past, present and future.

ACT I / SCENE 1 / THE KURU FIELD OF JUSTICE

Characters: Gandhi, Arjuna, Krishna, Duryodhana, Tolstoy*, members of two armies (52).

Setting: Dawn breaking (sky with clouds). Mythological Battlefield/ South African Plain.

Staging: Far upstage is a dawn sky backdrop in front of which is a truncated pyramid, twelve feet high, where Tolstoy is seated at his desk with all its papers, knickknacks, etc. From far upstage to the pit, the floor is covered with golden grass varying in height from knee-high to trampled. Two armies are situated stage right and stage left with an open area separating them. Center stage right and left (at the heads of the

---

*Tolstoy present at his desk throughout Act I.

armies) are Arjuna and Duryodhana in their chariots. Krishna stands downstage in the open area separating the armies. The armies are backlit, appearing in silhouette and as the scene progresses, lights come up on the armies to reveal them as Indians and Europeans respectively, also revealing their weapons as everyday objects.

Indian army, stage right, is wearing whites and light grays. European army, stage left, is wearing blacks, grays, beiges, off-whites. Krishna, Arjuna, and Duryodhana are in resplendent, full color. Gandhi in Satya-graha dress.

Gandhi appears upstage center and begins walking downstage between the two armies. After covering one-third of the distance, he starts his solo (5 minutes). Joined in duet by Arjuna (5 minutes). Joined in trio by Krishna (5 minutes). Followed by short chorus section, two armies singing. Ending with Gandhi in solo, downstage.

Synopsis: A great battle was impending between two royal families, the Kuruvas and the Pandavas. At a signal from the aged king, the trumpeter blew his conch, loosening the tempest in the waiting armies assembled on the sacred plain. From both sides, warriors and chieftains blew their battle shells announcing their readiness to fight with a din resounding between heaven and earth. And seeing the battle set, weapons unsheathing, bows drawn forth—Prince Arjuna spoke to Lord Krishna, wishing to look more closely at these men drawn up spoiling for the fight with whom he must do battle in the enterprise of war.

GANDHI

"I see them here assembled, ready to fight, seeking to please the king's sinful son by waging war." And thus addressed by Arjuna, Krishna brought that splendid chariot to a halt between the two armies. In front of Bhisma and Drona and all the rulers of the world, he said, "Behold Arjuna, these kinsmen assembled here." And the Prince marked on each hand relatives and friends in both armies. Seeing them, all his kinsmen, thus arrayed, Arjuna was filled with deep compassion and turned to Krishna.

ARJUNA

My very being is oppressed with compassion's harmful taunt. With mind perplexed concerning right and wrong I ask you which is the better course? Tell me and let your words be definite and clear. I am your pupil and put all my trust in you. So teach me.

KRISHNA

Be wise in the matters of death and duty. See in this war presented by pure chance a door to paradise. For sure is death to all that's born, sure is birth to all that dies and for this, you have no cause to grieve. Likewise, recognize this war as prescribed by duty. Hold pleasure and pain, profit and loss, victory and defeat to be the same: then brace yourself for the fight. So will you bring no evil on yourself.

CHORUS

To him thus in compassion plunged, to him desponding, Krishna spoke these words: "Whence comes this faintness on you now at this crisis hour? This ill beseems a noble, wins none a heavenly state, but brings dishonor, Arjuna. Give up this vile faint-heartedness. Stand up, chastiser of your foes!"

And so too, in view of the impending battle, Krishna's dialogue with Arjuna was echoed again.

GANDHI

Hold pleasure and pain, profit and loss, victory and defeat to be the same: then brace yourself for the fight. So will you bring no evil on yourself.

(Chapter 1, Verses 23–28; Chapter 2, Verses 7, 8;
Chapter 2, Verses 33, 37, 38; Chapter 2, Verses 1–3)

ACT I / SCENE 2 / TOLSTOY FARM (1910)

Characters: Gandhi, Kasturbai, Mr. Kallenbach, Miss Schlesen, Mrs. Naidoo, Indian workers (6).

Setting: Mid-morning (wispy clouds). An empty field in South Africa. Same grass as Scene 1.

Staging: Workers and principals building the settlement; primarily a clapboard facade shading from black to white as boards are successively added. Gandhi works alongside and oversees; consults with his co-workers. Indian workers carrying materials in and out, etc.

Begins with Gandhi in solo. Joined by women's trio. Joined by other male voice to end in quintet.

Synopsis: With only a handful of Satyagrahis pledged to resist the Europeans' racial discrimination, Gandhi initiated the first collective action among South Africa's Indian residents. No one knew how long the struggle would last, but with Tolstoy Farm, the Satyagrahis progressed toward securing an immediate goal. Here, all families would live in one place, becoming members of a cooperative commonwealth, where residents would be trained to live a new, simple life in harmony with each other. Everything from building to cooking to scavenging was to be done with their own hands. The building of the farm drew everyone into an active involvement with the Satyagraha ideal—"a fight on the behalf of Truth consisting chiefly of self-purification and self-reliance."

GANDHI

Between theory and practice, some talk as they were two—making a separation and a difference between them. Yet wise men know that both can be gained in applying oneself whole-heartedly to one. For the high estate attained by men of contemplative theory, that same state achieve the men of action. So act as the ancients of days old, performing works as spiritual exercise.

MISS SCHLESEN, KASTURBAI AND MRS. NAIDOO

Such a one is honorable who gives his mortal powers to worthy work not seeking gain. Do the allotted task for which one is fit, for work is more excellent than idleness and the body's life proceeds not, lacking work. Such an earthly task do free from desire, you will perform a high task.

KALLENBACH

When the motives and the fruits of a man's actions are freed from desire, his works are burned clean by wisdom's fire, the white fire of truth. When he casts off attachment to his deeds, a man embarks on his work ever content, on none dependent. With thought and self controlled, giving up all possessions, he cares for his bodily maintenance without excess; taking what chance may bring, surmounting all dualities, the same in success and failure.

(Chapter 5, Verses 4, 5; Chapter 3, Verses 8, 9;
Chapter 4, Verses 19–22)

ACT I / SCENE 3 / THE VOW (1906)

Characters: Parsi Rustomji, Miss Schlesen, Indian crowd (full chorus).

Setting: Noonday (bright clouds). Outdoor public meeting. Same grass as Scenes 1 and 2.

Staging: Miss Schlesen and Parsi Rustomji gather a crowd from passersby. Once assembled and seated on the ground, the audience is addressed by Parsi Rustomji, delivering his speech. At speech's end, Indians raise their hands, one by one, taking the Satyagraha vow. All end standing.
   Solo followed by chorus.

Synopsis: The British Government was proposing an amendment to institute an entire reregistration and fingerprinting of all Indians, men, women and children. Now they would be required to carry resident permits at all times, police could enter homes to inspect for certificates, and offenses were punishable by fines, jail, or deportation. The proposed Black Act became the occasion for a large rallying of the community around a specific issue. At a public meeting attended by over 3,000, a resolution was drawn up stating that all would resist the Act unto death. Suddenly, the Satyagrahis had come to a turning point. The life-and-death terms of the resolution called for a step beyond ordinary majority vote ratification and all in attendance listened to the speakers explain the solemn responsibility of taking individual pledges. For only a vow taken in the name of God would support an individual's observance of the resolution in the face of every conceivable hardship, even if he were the only one left.

PARSI RUSTOMJI

The world is not for the doubting man. Let a man by wisdom dispel his doubts. For nothing on earth resembles wisdom's power to purify and this a man may find in time within himself, when he is perfected in spiritual exercise. Then thoughts are steadied and come to rest allowing one to see the God in the individual. Knowing this, he stands still moving not an inch from reality. Standing firmly unmoved by any suffering, however grievous it may be.
   Whoever gives up a deed because it causes pain, or because he shrinks from bodily pain, follows the way of darkness, knowing nothing of self-surrender. But if a work is done because it should be done and is enjoined by Scripture and without thought for great benefits, then that

is surrender in Goodness. With doubt cut away, suffused with goodness, the self-surrendered man hates neither uncongenial work nor looks only for pleasant work.

FULL CHORUS

These works of sacrifice must be done. From old did the Lord of creatures say that in sacrifice you sustain the gods and the gods sustain you in return. So was the wheel set in motion and who here fails to match his turning living an evil life, the senses his pleasure ground, lives out his life in vain.

(Chapter 6, Verses 20–22; Chapter 18, Verses 8–10;
Chapter 3, Verses 10–16)

END OF ACT I

ACT II/SCENE 1/CONFRONTATION
AND RESCUE (1896)

Characters: Mrs. Alexander, Gandhi, Tagore,* European men (8).

Setting: 2 PM (stormy, black sky). The outskirts of a European settlement in South Africa. Upstage center, a road winds downstage left and off stage. Most of the buildings line the road, while a few are scattered in the landscape, the field of grass now blue in color. Two trees near one of the larger buildings, a clapboard Protestant church with a gold cross on its steeple. The others follow a severe Puritan-style architecture.

Staging: European men gathering together as Gandhi appears upstage on the road. While Gandhi makes his way down the road, the crowd becomes excited and begins to molest him—throwing rocks, pushing, etc. Mrs. Alexander appears carrying her umbrella under which she takes Gandhi, protecting him from the crowd and leading him on the road, offstage. Men follow them part way, still throwing things and abusing them verbally.

Small men's chorus with woman's solo.

Synopsis: Gandhi had spent a six-month sojourn in India acquainting the homeland with the settlers' conditions in South Africa. Thousands of Europeans had read of his speeches and meetings in somewhat exagger-

---

*Tagore present throughout Act II, on truncated pyramid, seated in his wicker chair with bird cage.

ated news accounts cabled by Reuters to the South African newspapers, and there was a great explosion of feeling when Gandhi set foot again in the Port of Durban. Already angered by his exposing events to the world, the Europeans were further inflamed by Gandhi's intention to bring back hundreds of Indian immigrants. If the Government would not prevent them from landing, then they would take the law into their own hands. Growing larger in numbers and more violent in actions, the excited crowd pursued Gandhi on the long walk through town. The wife of the superintendent of police was coming from the opposite direction and opening her umbrella for his protection, Mrs. Alexander began walking by Gandhi's side, leading him to safety.

MRS. ALEXANDER

The devilish folk, in them there is no purity, no morality, no truth. So they say the world has not a law, nor order, nor a lord. And thinking this, all those dark-minded ones of little wit, embark on cruel and violent deeds, the curses of their kind. Maddened by pride and hypocrisy, not caring right up to death, they have no other aim than to satisfy their pleasure, convinced that is all. So speak fools.

SMALL MEN'S CHORUS

"This I have gained today, this whim I'll satisfy; this wealth is mine and much more too will be mine as time goes on. He was an enemy of mine, I've killed him, and many another I'll kill. I'm master here. I take my pleasure as I will; I'm strong and happy and successful. I'm rich and of good family. Who else can match himself with me?"

(Chapter 16, Verses 7–11; Chapter 16, Verses 13–15)

ACT II / SCENE 2 / INDIAN OPINION (1906)

Characters: Gandhi, Miss Schlesen, Kasturbai, Mrs. Naidoo, Parsi Rustomji, Mr. Kallenbach, Indian residents (6).

Setting: 5 PM (orange burning sun). Part of communal residence that houses *Indian Opinion*. Large, working press sits center stage. Blue grass field.

Staging: Farm residents set up, issue and distribute *Indian Opinion*. Gandhi appearing late in the scene, inspects their activity in the printing process. All exit, leaving press to run alone during three-minute orchestra tutti.

Kallenbach and Miss Schlesen, joined by principals.

Synopsis: Central to the movement's activities was the weekly publication of *Indian Opinion*. Every aspect of production was considered in light of the struggle and the paper progressively reflected the growth of Satyagraha principles. The decision to refuse all advertisements freed the publication of any outside influence and made its very existence the mutual responsibility of those working on the paper and those readers whose subscriptions now supplied the only source of financial support. In policy, *Indian Opinion* openly diagnosed movement weaknesses as a means for eradicating them. Though this kept their adversaries well informed, it more importantly pursued the goal of real strength. Setting a standard with a strong internal policy, *Indian Opinion* could with ease and success inform the local and world community, and thus develop a powerful weapon for the struggle. At its height, there was an estimated readership of 20,000 in South Africa alone.

KALLENBACH AND MISS SCHLESEN

With senses freed, the wise man should act, longing to bring about the welfare and coherence of the world. Therefore, perform unceasingly the works that must be done, for the man detached who labors on to the highest must win through. This is how the saints attained success. Moreover, you should embrace action for the upholding, the welfare of your own kind. Whatever the noblest does, that too will others do: the standard that he sets all the world will follow.

KASTURBAI, MRS. NAIDOO AND PARSI RUSTOMJI

Act as God does, for the sake of others: "In the three worlds there is nothing I need do, nor anything unattained that I need to gain, yet action is the element in which I move. If I were not tirelessly to busy Myself with works, then would men everywhere follow in my footsteps, sinking back. If I were not to do my work these worlds would fall to ruin and I would be a worker in confusion."

(Chapter 3, Verses 25, 19, 20, 21; Chapter 3, Verses 22–24)

ACT II / SCENE 3 / PROTEST (1908)

Characters: Gandhi and Indian crowd (full chorus).

Setting: Twilight (evening stars). Empty outdoor field. Same blue grass as Scenes 1 and 2. Church and trees from Act II, Scene 1, now smaller and far upstage.

Staging: As crowd gathers around Gandhi, he begins a prayer meeting. Crowd joins in vocally. Cauldron on tripod brought in, center stage. Chorus passes in front of cauldron, dropping in their registration cards— chorus having all eventually moved across stage from left to right. Indian from crowd sets fire to cards.

Solo followed by full chorus.

Synopsis: Movement leaders were sentenced to jail for disobeying an order to leave South Africa, issued on their failure to satisfy the Magistrate that they were lawful holders of certificates of registration. The community resolved to fill up the jail, and courting all kinds of arrest, the number of Satyagrahi prisoners rose to 150 by the week's end. The Government proposed a settlement: if the majority of Indians underwent voluntary registration, Government would repeal the Black Act. But the community was stunned to learn that after fulfilling their part of the bargain, the Black Act was to be carried through legislation. Ready to resume the struggle, Satyagrahis issued their own ultimatum: If a repeal was not forthcoming, certificates would be collected by the Indians, burned, and they would humbly but firmly accept the consequences. On the day of the ultimatum's expiration, the Government's refusal was sent to the site where Gandhi conducted a prayer meeting before the burning of the registration cards. These were all thrown into the cauldron, set ablaze, and the assembly rose to its feet making the whole place resound with their cheers—even greater than the commencement of the movement, Satyagraha now had had its baptism of fire.

GANDHI'S PRAYER

The Lord said:

Let a man feel hatred for no being, let him be friendly, compassionate; done with thoughts of "I" and "mine," the same in pleasure as in pain, long suffering.

His self restrained, his purpose firm, let his mind and soul be steeped in Me, let him worship Me with love; then will I love him in return.

That man I love from whom the people do not shrink and who does not shrink from them, who is free from exaltation, fear, impatience, and excitement.

I love the man who has no expectation, is pure and skilled, indifferent, who has no worries and gives up all selfish enterprise, loyal-and-devoted to Me.

I love the man who hates not nor exults, who mourns not nor desires, who puts away both pleasant and unpleasant things, who is loyal-devoted-and-devout.

I love the man who is the same to friend and foe, the same whether he be respected or despised, the same in heat and cold, in pleasure as in pain, who has put away attachment and remains unmoved by praise or blame, who is taciturn, content with whatever comes his way, having no home, of steady mind, but loyal-devoted-and-devout.

But as for those who reverence these deathless words of righteousness which I have just now spoken, putting their faith in them, making Me their goal my loving devotees, these do I love exceedingly.

(Chapter 12, Verses 13–20)

END OF ACT II

ACT III/NEW CASTLE MARCH (1913)

Characters: Full chorus, principals (6), contemporary policemen (2), King.*

Setting: Dusk to night (starry sky). Mythological Battlefield/South African Plain. Golden grass from Act I.

Staging: Chorus is heard singing offstage as Kasturbai and Mrs. Naidoo enter. During their short duet, Gandhi, Kallenbach, Parsi Rustomji, and Miss Schlesen enter and join them in a brief sextet. The army slowly enters, singing, while Gandhi reviews them. Contemporary police enter and slowly escort the army offstage, several at a time, while Gandhi instructs them in nonviolent resistance. Finally, he is left with principals on stage. They settle for the night as darkness descends. Gandhi lights his lantern and inspects his sleeping comrades. After his five-minute solo Gandhi, standing down stage, turns, looking toward platform where King reappears and a moment later Satyagraha army appears behind him, up

*King appears throughout Act III, on truncated pyramid, in shirtsleeves at a podium with microphones.

in the starry, night sky. Their image is seen for ten to fifteen seconds in silence, then fades out.

Synopsis: With two overt racially discriminatory laws, the Government was effectively controlling the influx of new Indian settlers and keeping the old class of indentured laborers under its thumb. A "color bar" restricted the immigration of even those applicants who could pass an educational test, and a special tax was levied against those workers who chose to remain after their seven years, binding them to pay annually the equivalent of six months salary for each family member. Both the Three Pound Tax and the Asiatic Immigration Law were in effect when the great Indian leader, Shree Gokhale, made a tour of South Africa and secured from the Government a public promise for their repeal. The Government's breach of promise gave Satyagraha an opportunity to include new objectives within its scope as a fight for truth and, in turn, to increase its strength in numbers. The miners in New Castle were selected to be the first drawn into the expanding struggle and a deputation of Satyagraha women traveled there, organizing a strike in sympathy with the movement. It was further decided that striking miners and their families should leave the homes provided by mine owners, and with only their clothes and blankets, join the Satyagraha army. Led by Gandhi, who would likewise attend to their provisions, they would march the thirty-six miles to the Transvaal border. If arrested at this registration check point, the army of 5,000 would flood the jails, incurring heavy expenses and difficulties for the Government. If allowed to proceed to Tolstoy Farm, they would prolong the strike, conceivably drawing all of the 60,000 laborers affected by the tax law into the struggle. And in either event, they were bringing strong pressure for repeal, all within the dictates of Satyagraha. Thus the army was instructed to stand any test without opposition and their movements were openly announced to their adversaries—"as an effective protest against the Minister's breach of pledge and as a pure demonstration of our distress at the loss of self-respect."

KASTURBAI AND MRS. NAIDOO
(Joined by principals)

In what for others is night, therein is the man of self-restraint wide awake. He roves through the world separate from passion and hate, self-possessed and drawing near to calm serenity. This is the athlete of the spirit, whose ground remains unmoved, whose soul stands firmly on it. This is the fixed, still state which sustains even at the time of death the athletes of the spirit, who even then set forth, some to return, some never to return. Outstanding is he whose soul views in the selfsame way comrades and enemies, loving all alike.

GANDHI

The Lord said, I have passed through many a birth and many have you. I know them all but you do not. Yet by my creative energy, I consort with Nature and come to be in time. For whenever the law of righteousness withers away and lawlessness arises, then do I generate myself on earth. I come into being age after age and take a visible shape and move a man with men for the protection of good, thrusting the evil back and setting virtue on her seat again.

*(Chapter 6, Verses 8–10; Chapter 2, Verses 62–69;
Chapter 8, Verse 23; Chapter 5, Verse 18; Chapter 4, Verses 5–8)*

END

AKHNATEN

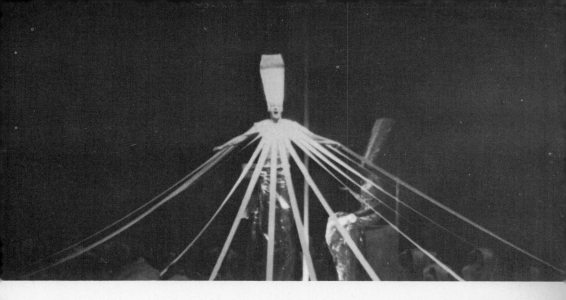

In the summer of 1979 I visited Dennis Russell Davies at his summer home in Vermont. He was about to take up his post as music director of the Stuttgart State Opera and, though unable to lead *Satyagraha*'s world premiere in Rotterdam, was very interested in conducting its German premiere. The main purpose of my visit was to go over the newly completed score with him. On our first day together we had a piano-four-hands play-through of *Satyagraha*. I especially appreciated that because it was the first time I actually heard most of the parts played together.

As director of the St. Paul Chamber Orchestra, Dennis already had an established reputation as a champion of American music, and though that was not what brought him to Stuttgart (probably his work with the German composer Hans Werner Henze, as well as his conducting appearances in Berlin and Bayreuth, had brought him to the notice of the Stuttgart State Opera), it was more or less expected that he would be doing some American opera during his tenure. Over the next few days, Dennis told me some of his plans for Stuttgart. Since his initial contract was for five years (later extended another two), he had an opportunity for genuinely long-range planning. Included in these plans were a number of "American" projects.

We got along extremely well in those initial meetings, partly because, I suppose, of our similar backgrounds. Dennis had been a Juilliard student a few years after me and had studied with the formidable French conductor Jean Morel. Morel did not have a remarkable international career, but he impressed those who had the good luck to work with him by the clarity of his musical thinking and the high standards he brought to the performance of orchestral music of all periods. His influence extended well beyond his conducting students, to the young players in his orchestra at Juilliard. My first lessons in orchestration really were from Morel when, as a young man, I spent many hours following his morning orchestra rehearsals with a score.

I found in Dennis something that composers encounter all too rarely: an irrepressible curiosity and enthusiasm for new music. Even better, not only does Dennis love new music, he is prepared to do something about it. In my case, that meant presenting *Satyagraha* in Germany. And by the end of our first day together, we were talking about doing another new opera in Stuttgart as well.

The idea of an operatic trilogy was born at this meeting. Dennis suggested that Stuttgart might commission a new opera, and I instantly saw that if such an opera were linked to *Satyagraha* and *Einstein on the Beach,* the company might be persuaded to do all three. At that moment, I didn't even have a subject for this third opera, but I promised Dennis I would start thinking about one, and that when I came up with a subject, it would certainly be related to the first two. I figured that if an operatic trilogy could happen anywhere, it would be in Germany, where opera projects of this size were not new and where the public was known for its capacity to absorb new work. I felt confident about the project from the beginning. Dennis agreed to take the proposal to Stuttgart and let me know the official reaction as soon as possible. After all, it was one thing to present a new opera—even commissioning a new work would be an accomplishment—but to go to Stuttgart with a proposal for an entire trilogy (and by an American composer) was unheard of.

Not the least of our obstacles, we suspected, would be the complications arising from the normal administration of a German opera house. Approval would have to filter down through various departmental levels and, since the opera company is funded through the government, approval becomes almost a matter of regional cultural policy.

I heard from Dennis again in the spring of 1980. Our proposal was being discussed very seriously, and it was time for me to come over and meet the people who were going to make it possible. Dennis sounded very excited on the phone. I was elated by the news and within weeks was in Stuttgart for the first of our meetings.

Meanwhile, I was thinking about my third subject. What I wanted was a historical figure of the same stature as Einstein and Gandhi. Other than that, I had no clear idea of what I was really looking for, but I trusted I would recognize it when it appeared. At the outset, my approach was anything but systematic. Looking back, it's startling how soon this problem was solved, for my candidate appeared quickly and was accepted readily.

Perhaps I should explain that I am a very general and casual reader of everything from fiction to history and science. One writer in whom I had taken an interest was Immanuel Velikovsky, an extremely controversial theorist who applied himself to subjects as diverse as geology, astrophysics and history. He matched a powerful imagination with detailed, concrete knowledge of his subjects. However, his disregard for the usual rules of inductive reasoning, sacrosanct to the scientific method, earned him a large number of enemies in the academic community.

For me, though, Velikovsky was a lively, interesting and provocative writer. *Earth in Upheaval* and *Worlds in Collision*—books in which he used folk legends and Biblical accounts of cataclysms to stimulate some truly radical theories of planetary catastrophes involving our own planet—brought to life subjects that seemed arcane to me and would have, I suspect, to most general readers.

About this time I came across a work by this author that was new to me: *Oedipus and Akhnaten*. It is a concise and scholarly work in which Velikovsky attempts to trace the origin of the Oedipus legend to the period of Akhnaten, the Eighteenth Dynasty Egyptian pharaoh who, in modern times, is looked upon as the first monotheist. Like everything else about Akhnaten, though, this one-word description hides more than it reveals.

Velikovsky's contention was that all the events in the fictional life of Oedipus—the tragic figure of Greek myth who unknowingly murdered his father, married his mother and, discovering the truth of his actions, blinded himself—had actually occurred in the life of Akhnaten hundreds of years before. I suspect that, of all of Velikovsky's works, this book ranks among his most speculative, but I must say he makes an extremely persuasive case for it.

However, historical validity hardly mattered to me at all. Practically from the moment I saw Velikovsky's title page, I knew I had found the subject for my third opera, one that could stand up to the scale of music theater. I was happy to let others squabble over the possible or impossible historical connection between Oedipus and Akhnaten. Theatrically speaking, I knew it made perfect sense. I had hoped to work with Velikovsky on the libretto and had found a mutual friend in Princeton, New Jersey, where Velikovsky was living at the time. My friend promised to arrange a meeting, but Velikovsky died in November 1979, before our meeting could take place.

Akhnaten completed the trilogy in many satisfying ways. First of all, Akhnaten, like Einstein and Gandhi, had changed forever the world into which he was born. In the case of Akhnaten, it was through the imposition of a radical new state religion upon fifteenth-century BC Egypt. His idea of a single, universal deity for all mankind was not warmly accepted by the people of his time (to say the least), and his brief seventeen-year reign—the pharaohs normally ruled for a lifetime—ended when both he and his religion were overthrown and replaced by the former, more traditional, state religion.

His ideas were not lost, though. It is currently argued that Akhnaten's monotheism was preserved by the Hebrews of his time and became the basis of the Judeo-Christian tradition of the West. This is an extremely complicated and interesting issue, but the main point for me was that Akhnaten had changed his (and our) world through the *force of his ideas* and not through the *force of arms*. This is not to say that Akhnaten was a pacifist, though some have described him that way, probably incorrectly. It is important to remember that in Akhnaten's day, Egypt was *the* military power in the world, with all the cruelty and ruthlessness such a role required, though Akhnaten himself may have refrained from taking part in the military exercises that must have been routine. It was in the realm of ideas and theology, however, that Akhnaten clearly distinguished himself, and it is that legacy of his—not the military force of ancient Egypt—that has come down to us today.

It was at this point that I became aware that social issues could play an important part in my choice of subject matter. To put it another way, subject or content in music theater could remain neither passive nor accidental, so that what an opera was "about" began to emerge for me as a major issue. After all, putting on opera is a tremendous enterprise involving literally hundreds of people—orchestra, chorus, soloists, sometimes dancers, all the backstage people, designers, builders, fitters—the list goes on and on. At some point it must occur to the authors that involvement of so many people in so many diverse creative levels should be justified by the seriousness of the subject.

That isn't to say that the piece cannot be entertaining as well. In fact, for it to work for the audience requires attention to its entertainment value. Add to this the fact that an opera project can easily occupy me for three years. This means that when I choose a subject, it will be with me a long time, another reason why it must function for me on several levels of interest. One of these levels, that of social issues, has become particularly meaningful for me.

This was certainly true of *Satyagraha,* for Gandhi represents one of the great moral and political consciousnesses of our time. My relation to that aspect of *Satyagraha* had been almost instinctive. It was the power of Gandhi's personality that drew me to him, not his ideas. But by the time I was working on *Akhnaten,* I saw that ideas (social, political, religious) could be central to the work. Though this may not have been seen as such by other people, for me it was a fundamental reorientation of my thinking about my relation to theater.

In a number of ways, my choice of Akhnaten as a subject accorded with my thinking in general. In this way, particularly, I could relate Akhnaten to Einstein and Gandhi. The key is that we know Akhnaten as a man of ideas and, to me, the entire history of humanity is a history of ideas, of culture. When I think of ancient Greece, Rome, France, China, or wherever, what comes to my mind are poets, painters, writers, musicians, philosophers. I never think of the generals and politicians. Except, perhaps, for Alexander the Great or Napoleon, that part of history is a story of faceless violence which, though it may be exciting to read about, adds little or nothing to the sum total of our humanity. And yet we often act as if the opposite were true, naming airports, highways and other public places after warriors and politicians who are barely remembered, and sometimes totally forgotten, by the next generation. It is a brand of silliness more embarrassing than damaging to us as a civilization. For example, Europe has a Leonardo da Vinci Airport (in Rome) and countless public areas named after Goethe, Mozart, Rembrandt, Verdi and many other creative geniuses, but in my own native land, the United States, the thought of a Jackson Pollock Airport, a Charles Ives Square, a Walt Whitman Stadium is still—sadly—unthinkable.

Akhnaten, at any rate, took his place easily and naturally with Einstein and Gandhi. I saw that if Einstein epitomized the man of Science, and Gandhi the man of Politics, then Akhnaten would be the man of Religion. Each of these men was more complex than this implies, and each included elements of the other two, but the idea of Politics, Science and Religion as the overview from which each of the works could be considered a part appealed to me very strongly.

I think the final element that made Akhnaten so right for me was that he was not another contemporary person. I didn't think of my three subjects as confined or even defined by contemporary times. By reaching back to the ancient world for Akhnaten, I felt I could emphasize the historical perspective of the Trilogy.

These reflections on Akhnaten did not come to me immediately. But soon after my first meeting with Dennis in Vermont, I had seized upon Akhnaten as the central character of my third opera, and it became the focus for ideas that unfolded over the next three years.

In the spring of 1980 I arrived in Stuttgart with the first draft of a scenario for *Akhnaten* that I had written. My initial idea had been to follow the outline of Velikovsky's book; accordingly, I had transported a double subject to the stage, both Oedipus and Akhnaten.

In this first version, the audience would have seen two operas going on at the same time. Upstage and on a slightly higher level would be the Akhnaten story. Downstage, closer to the audience, would be the Oedipus legend. In this way, their historical relationship could be reflected in their physical distancing from the viewer. As in Velikovsky's theory, the two plots would be similar, though I had arranged that the intermission for each story would occur at different times so the overall stage action would be continuous. I already had begun to work out the coordination of two different musical elements, one for the Egyptian story and another for the Greek.

Ultimately, this first concept failed to survive. It definitely was an interesting approach for me, and as I write about it now, it still seems so. The problem was simply this: The more involved I became with Akhnaten and the Egyptian aspects of the story, the less interesting the Oedipus side seemed to me. Finally I realized that Oedipus was becoming a burden to the Akhnaten story, and I dropped him entirely.

All that, though, was still in the future. At the moment, I was in Stuttgart in pursuit of a new commission. I met Herr Doll, the overall financial manager of the company; Dr. Schwinger, the general director; and Peter Kehr, the dramaturg. They all greeted me very cordially and were eager to talk about the new project. Dr. Schwinger, it seemed to me, took a particular interest. However, it was really Peter Kehr, the dramaturg, who championed the new work and with whom I worked over the next five years.

Americans are generally unfamiliar with the idea of a dramaturg. Though virtually unknown in the U.S., the dramaturg plays a key role in a German opera house. Technically he serves as a liaison between the different artistic elements in an opera production. For example, he might be instrumental in choosing a choreographer if one is needed. He would also be the one to resolve any problems that arise between the music director and the stage director. In the case of a new work, he certainly would be consulted as the libretto is completed. He can perform very useful services when the composer and the director begin to discuss the interpretation of a work. His voice is also heard when the schedule of performances is drawn up. Finally, as if he hasn't enough to do, he is responsible for the program booklet which is made available to the public at performances. An American might begin by asking what the dramaturg does and end up realizing the amount of work he is required to do borders on the incredible. In the case of Stuttgart, which has a company performing about twenty productions a year (not all of them new, admittedly), one dramaturg and his assistant oversee the whole season.

I consider myself extremely fortunate to have had Peter Kehr as dramaturg in Stuttgart. Though the other officials were certainly helpful and willing, Peter was the one I worked with, and he was my main access to the opera company. From the very beginning, he was open to the idea of a new commission but, more important, it was he who began planning the presentation of all three operas as a Trilogy. In terms of the opera house schedule, this meant thinking a number of years into the future. At these initial meetings, little more was determined than our overall intentions. However, since *Satyagraha* was to be done in the spring of 1981, I came back to Stuttgart quite a few times over the next year, and gradually an overall plan for the Trilogy came together.

One of the first points on which Stuttgart insisted was that all three works have a unified style and look. To achieve general cohesiveness, Peter and Dr. Schwinger proposed that Achim Freyer undertake the overall direction and design of the Trilogy. They felt that with Achim committed to the whole project, there was every chance it could go through. Though I had not yet seen Achim's *Satyagraha*, by then I did know his other theater work and had met with him a number of times. I liked their proposal and agreed.

However, the big question was: How were they to do *Einstein on the Beach*? After all, no one had ever re-created a Robert Wilson work. As a practical problem, this took years to resolve, and it raised questions about authenticity and interpretation that everyone in the theater eventually has to face. But in 1980 they were new to me.

As I wrote in an earlier chapter, my instincts have been that, in the long run, fresh interpretations can only strengthen a work. Wilson and I had many discussions about that, discovering that we were in basic agreement on this point. Exactly *how* such a work as *Einstein on the Beach* could be reinterpreted, though, was not at all clear. The fundamental problem lay in Wilson's unique approach to theater. He had combined the elements of story, libretto, design and direction into something very new. A Bob Wilson "libretto," for example, might have no words at all, only pictures. Therefore, to redesign a work (or redirect it, for that matter) could mean to change its basic vocabulary. And in that case, what would be left of the original idea?

This question prompted yet another, one with which Wilson, as well as many others working in the "new theater," were concerned: How would it be possible for these works, which, from their very inception, were so strongly linked with design and directorial concepts, to survive their creators? These are not easy questions, and they are ones to which members of my generation of theater people are, even now, only beginning to address themselves.

One solution has been to film completed works. Libraries of film and video of contemporary theater have already begun to appear—a solution to the problem of preservation, but this doesn't solve the problem of reinterpretation of new works. Though I run the risk of repeating myself, it is in this area of interpretation and re-creation that fresh insights can be brought to completed works, thereby renewing them in other productions. This is, of course, how our literature has come down to us in the theater, so I am hardly suggesting anything new. What I'm really arguing for is the integration of a newer tradition with the received one.

Wilson and I discussed these issues on and off over the next several years and, finally, at least with regard to *Einstein on the Beach,* resolved it in the following way: Before a new *Einstein* would be done, we would remount the first production, which would, in effect, be a revival of the original production. The score had been committed to paper years before and was unlikely to change further but, for technical reasons, the first production of *Einstein* had never been adequately documented. This was partly due to the fact that there was no money to spend on documentation, and also because, in 1976, video could hardly be done without special lighting, which we didn't have. There were a few fairly dark-looking tapes floating around, but we considered them inadequate for even basic reference purposes. Therefore, at this revival, we would make a complete video record of the staging and design.

Once we had documented the original, we would then make *two* versions of *Einstein on the Beach* available for production. The first would be an "original version" that would have to be based on the video tape and would be obliged to faithfully reproduce the lights, images and movements. We would also allow another version to be done. This need not follow the original design concepts but would still adhere to the structure of the work as it appears in the music and with the prescribed divisions into acts and scenes. It would, further, follow the general out-

▲ Philip Glass with JoAnne Akalaitis
in Spain, summer of 1964. (JOANNE AK-
ALAITIS) ▶ Philip Glass in Paris in
1965. (JOANNE AKALAITIS) ▼ Nadia
Boulanger. (FREDERICK PLAUT)

Alla Rakha and Ravi Shankar in performance. (MASON-RELKIN CO.)

▲ The Philip Glass Ensemble performing at New York University on February 4, 1971. From the top, left to right: Arthur Murphy, Steve Chambers, Barbara Benary, Dickie Landry, Jon Gibson and Philip Glass. (TINA GIRUARD)

▼ Ellen Stewart of La Mama, 1973. (LA MAMA)

▲ A scene from JoAnne Akalaitis's *Dressed Like an Egg*, produced at Joseph Papp's Public Theater by Mabou Mines. (DICKIE LANDRY)

▶ Philip Glass and Bob Wilson taking a break during *Einstein on the Beach* rehearsals, 1975. (photography by BETTY FREEMAN)

▲ The original title page drawing by Robert Wilson for *Einstein on the Beach*.
(© ROBERT WILSON)

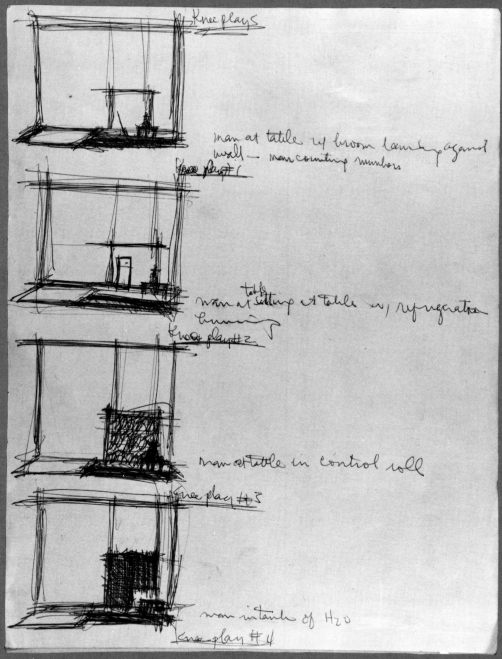

▲ The Knee Play organization.

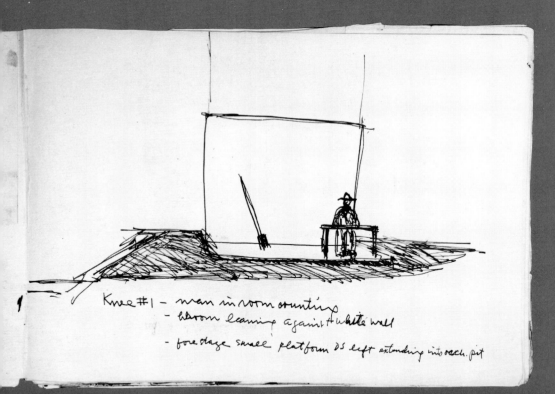

Knee #1 – man in room counting
- broom leaning against white wall
- fore stage small platform DS left extending into orch. pit

Knee play # 4
· man in tank of H_2O

▲ Original Knee Plays #1 and #4.

ACT I Section I

▲ Act I, Scene 1.

▲ Act II, Scene 1—Field/Spaceship.   ▼ Act IV, Scene 1—The Building.

▲ The Bus at night, which would become Knee Play #5.

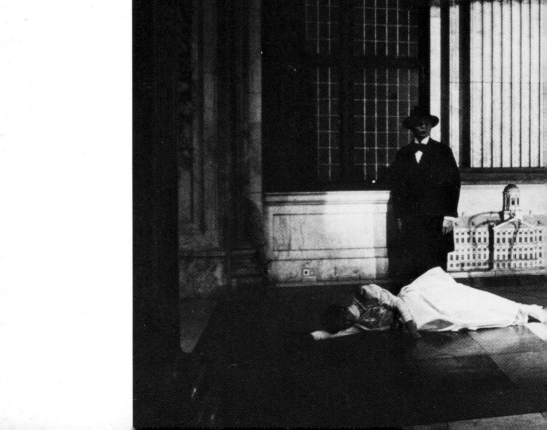

◀ ''The Grid'' from Godfrey Reggio's 1983 film *Koyaanisqatsi*. (GODFREY REGGIO)

▼ Act IV of the original production of Rob Malasch's *The Photographer*, presented by the Holland Festival in the Royal Palace, Amsterdam, June 1982. (CBS INC.)

the CIVIL warS (Rome Section) Prologue: Abraham Lincoln and the Snow Owl, 1984. (TOM BRAZIL)

line of the original sequence of Train, Trial, and Dance sections. This approach provides both a reference point to the original version and a departure point for new interpretations.

Peter Kehr and Achim Freyer readily agreed to our proposal, though by the time we had resolved it Achim was well into his production of *Akhnaten*. In effect, Stuttgart had, in principle, agreed to produce the Trilogy before the details relating to *Einstein on the Beach* had actually been resolved. Eventually, in December 1984, Harvey Lichtenstein, a long-time supporter and presenter of Wilson's and my work, staged the revived *Einstein* at BAM (Brooklyn Academy of Music). The video documentation was completed at the same time, and the way was cleared for Achim's future Stuttgart production.

When discussions with Stuttgart on the Trilogy began in 1980, these problems still lay before us. Peter Kehr, though, was unperturbed and went ahead, calmly planning despite whatever problems arose along the way. It wasn't long before we had set an opening date in March 1984 for *Akhnaten*. With *Satyagraha* behind me, and the new date scarcely three years away, I was already beginning to feel time growing very short.

The general plan, set quite early, was to start the Stuttgart Trilogy by presenting *Satyagraha* in 1981. It would run in repertory through the 1983 season and then, with the premiere of *Akhnaten* in 1984, would be temporarily retired while *Akhnaten* ran in repertory through 1986. In October 1988, *Einstein* would be ready, and in January 1989, *Satyagraha* would be brought back into the repertory. In January 1990, all three operas would be presented together on consecutive nights. At this writing (spring of 1987) the idea is to present the Trilogy for three successive nights.

So far, the schedule is holding up extremely well, largely, I think, due to Peter Kehr's decisiveness and careful planning. It was important to me, while writing *Akhnaten,* to know that a full production of the Trilogy was being planned, for that greatly affected my writing of the Egyptian opera. Taking a long view of the project, I began to think in terms of the rehearsal schedules required to bring all three works to performance at virtually the same time. A repertory opera house like Stuttgart arranges its schedule with the orchestra and chorus in terms of "services"—three-hour blocks of working time, whether they be rehearsal or performance. It becomes very difficult to stretch the limits of such a house beyond its normal capacities, though in the case of a special project like the Trilogy, *some* stretching would be expected.

With *Einstein* and *Satyagraha* completed, this definitely became a factor in my choice of voices, the kind of choral writing I included in the new work and even decisions about its orchestration. For example, there is quite a lot of choral singing in *Satyagraha* but only a chamber choir in *Einstein*. In *Akhnaten*, I ended up with several large choral numbers but none of them of any great length. In a similar way the orchestras used in all three works are somewhat different but, in a way, complement each other. There were also other factors that entered into the *Akhnaten* orchestration that had to do with the conception of the work vocally as well as the size of the orchestra pit.

To explain, the year that *Akhnaten* was scheduled to open, the main opera house would be closed for renovation, and that season's opera performances would take place in the neighboring Playhouse which, though similar to the opera house, has a somewhat smaller orchestra pit. So this too became a factor in planning *Akhnaten*. During one of my visits to Stuttgart, the orchestra manager and I set up the chairs, music stands and percussion instruments in the Playhouse pit so I could have a precise idea of what would fit.

With Stuttgart committed to *Akhnaten*, and plans for the complete Trilogy in the works, I left Germany, anxious to start the next stage of writing, shaping and fitting this new work to what had come before. And, as with *Satyagraha*, I began looking around for another opera house to mount a second, different, production the same year.

David Gockley at the Houston Grand Opera had been interested in my work for some time. His opera workshop was already preparing a chamber work of mine—*A Madrigal Opera*—in a staging by the German designer/director Manuel Luetgenhorst, with musical direction by Houston's John De Main. Gockley also was very interested in doing the American premiere of *Akhnaten*. At the same time, Beverly Sills at the New York City Opera wanted to present the piece with her company, and with Christopher Keene there as music director, I felt I had a strong supporter. Ultimately, Margaret Wood was able to work out a coproduction agreement between Houston and New York.

The plan was to build, rehearse and premiere *Akhnaten* in Houston in November 1984, six months after Stuttgart. It would then come to New York several weeks later. There was yet another presenter who ultimately played an important part in the second *Akhnaten*, and that was the English National Opera in London. Margaret had been meeting with Lord Harewood, then its director, off and on for a number of years, talking about different possibilities of presenting my work in London, and at one point I remember *Satyagraha* was under discussion. Lord Harewood liked the *Akhnaten* project even more, came to Houston for the premiere and finally brought it to London the next spring, thereby introducing a third stage in its presentation (after Houston and New York) where some unresolved problems in the production were finally worked out. At the time we didn't realize it, but in its own way the English National Opera would play an important role in the development of the second *Akhnaten* production.

With all these administrative details falling into place—it actually took several years for it to really jell—I could get into the real work of making the opera. Achim, with his wife, Ilona, would design and direct the premiere in Germany, and we would consult with them whenever necessary or possible.

That settled, I began to put together the American team. I was anxious to continue the very successful collaboration with Israel and Riddell that had begun with *Satyagraha,* and on *Akhnaten* they would be sharing the design functions for the American production. As for the scenario, I felt we needed someone who was knowledgeable about the period and could bring a scholarly expertise to bear on our efforts. In Shalom Goldman we found just that person.

Shalom was a specialist, at New York University, in studies relating to the ancient Near East. Besides being fluent in the reading of hieroglyphics, he also could read a number of languages contemporary to that time, including ancient Hebrew, Aramaic, and the cuneiform script of Akkadian, the ancient language of Babylonia. Just as important for us, he was one of those people for whom their work is completely alive. When I heard Shalom talking about Akhnaten and the people of his time, I could almost believe the events were happening that day, right around me, and not in a dim and remote past. For our theater work this was ideal.

From the end of 1981 through much of 1982, Israel and Riddell traveled back and forth from California, where they were based, to New York, and together with Shalom we began to develop the libretto for *Akhnaten*. Shalom supplied us with reading lists on our subject, and what began almost as a small seminar on *Akhnaten* ended up as a working team in producing the libretto.

As usual with me, I composed no music during that period, giving myself over entirely to the "literary" construction of the work. Also during this time I met with Peter Kehr and Achim to keep them up to date on the progress of the libretto—after all, the premiere was to be in Stuttgart, and the commission itself had come from the Stuttgart State Opera. I suppose this was a somewhat peculiar situation, but it was not uncomfortable for anyone.

Another sometime participant in our New York meetings was Jerome Robbins. It turned out that Jerry knew quite a lot about Akhnaten, Ancient Egypt having been something of a hobby of his. Mostly he just listened to our discussions, which he seemed to enjoy, and his occasional advice always revealed the depth of his understanding of the theater. It was through that association with Jerry that *Glass Pieces,* his ballet for the New York City Ballet, came about. He took two earlier works of mine—*Rubric* and *Facades* from my *Glassworks* record—and added to them a third piece, the funeral music from Act I of *Akhnaten,* to make a musical suite on which to set his dances. I had hoped that in the end Jerry would become our American director, but his duties and commitment to the New York City Ballet made that impossible.

In fact, we were still looking for a director to complete our production team. Bob Wilson was in Germany and very involved in his own work, and David Pountney had taken up duties as artistic director of the English National Opera, which gave me another friend there but didn't help solve the current problem.

David Gockley suggested I meet the young Australian director David Freeman. For some years Freeman had been working out of Geneva with his own company, The Opera Factory, and also with the English National Opera in London. He was considered a brilliant director, sometimes radical in his approach and not afraid to be shocking. We met in San Francisco while I was on one of my Ensemble tours. David, having flown in for the meeting, suggested we take a stroll, and we spent the day walking back and forth over the Golden Gate Bridge, talking about ourselves, about theater, about opera. By the end of our second round trip (it's a *very* long bridge), everything was decided. He still had to meet Israel, Riddell and Goldman, but I felt that would all work out.

So we had a director. Once again, design concepts had begun to take form before the director was there to take part in the meetings. But there was still time for discussion, for adjustment, for change.

As part of the first stage of work on *Akhnaten,* I went to Egypt and spent some time in Luxor, the present-day site of Egypt's ancient capital, Karnak. I also visited Cairo and Akhetaten, the site of Akhnaten's own city, whose ruins are located near the modern village of Tell El-Amarna. This visit made a great impression on me and had a marked effect on the outcome of the opera. Eventually all the members of our team made the trip, though not at the same time since scheduling problems made it impossible for us to go together. Still, though not together, we experienced Egypt in surprisingly similar ways, and it really became a kind of shared experience for us.

One of the most striking experiences for me was visiting the Cairo Museum. At first sight, this appears to be one of the most hysterically disorganized museums you could ever find. The initial impression is one of huge, gloomy hallways literally crammed with statuary and relics. With a little time, this gives way to a sense that there is, in fact, a kind of order to the exhibits. The building is basically a U-shaped hallway with small rooms off to the sides. You enter at one end, proceed around the bend and then out the other leg.

The Amarna room (Akhnaten's period is named after the present-day site) is situated right at the bend of the U. It's also the only room with large, high windows, giving it a feeling of air and light. After you round the bend, the light is behind you until you actually leave the building. This museum arrangement turns out to be a surprisingly accurate metaphor for Akhnaten's place in Egyptian history. As you make your way to the Amarna room, you pass hundreds of faceless, cold pharaohs. Then it suddenly changes as you come into the sunlit room and see the first large bust of Akhnaten himself—strange, to be sure, but definitely a very human face.

For an Egyptian pharaoh, Akhnaten seems to have been a relatively peaceful man, but his ideas, or at any rate the ideas he wished to impose on the world he lived in, seemed to the people of his time to do such violence to their customs and sense of order that there appears to have been a monumental effort to blot out all traces of him after his death. His temples were taken apart, his name removed from the list of kings and erased from monuments wherever it appeared. Only a few vague references to "the Great Criminal" remained. In fact, until the end of the nineteenth century, Egyptologists hardly suspected Akhnaten even existed. We might well wonder what kind of man this had been, and how powerful was the personality that could have inspired, immediately after his death, such strong reactions by those who knew him: revulsion, horror, finally a total cultural amnesia.

As it turned out, the amnesia was not permanent, though that was the intention. Akhnaten's ideas remained, out of sight, resurfacing only decades later and (though this is speculation) becoming part of the monotheism of the Judeo-Christian tradition. By the early twentieth century, through improved scholarship and the discovery of new tombs in the Valley of the Kings in Karnak as well as excavations near the town of Tell El-Amarna, at least part of Akhnaten's story was discovered. But it is important to remember that it is still fragmentary. The complete story of Akhnaten's rise and fall will never, in all likelihood, be fully known.

Still, enough has been discovered to inspire a number of contemporary writers, including Freud (*Moses and Monotheism*) and Velikovsky (the already mentioned *Oedipus and Akhnaten*), to explore the Akhnaten mystery. In recent decades there have been plays, novels and movies, all inspired by Akhnaten's life. In my few years work on the subject, I have personally met any number of scholarly and not-so-scholarly types working in this field. The attraction Akhnaten still exerts, even at the distance of 3,500 years, is astonishing. A final irony, perhaps, is that despite the efforts to forget him, he is today one of the few, out of literally hundreds of pharaohs, whose name is known outside academic circles. Ask anyone, and if they know the names of any pharaoh at all, it will be Tutankhamen first, Akhnaten second. (Ironically, Tutankhamen was young and ineffectual; he died at seventeen and never made any mark at all on his country, but he did have the good luck to be buried in a spectacular, gold-filled tomb.)

The known facts are few and can be summarized quickly. Akhnaten lived in what we call the Eighteenth Dynasty. His dates are, with a little guessing, 1385 to 1357 BC. His father was Amenhotep III, his mother was Queen Tye, and his wife was Nefertiti, famous for her statue in the Berlin Museum, probably one of the best-known works of art of all time. Akhnaten had six daughters, and we know all their names. Tutankhamen—the famous "King Tut"—was either his half-brother or nephew and was married to the third of these six daughters. Akhnaten's reign lasted seventeen brief but obviously dramatic years. We don't know how, when or where he died. His burial place, if he had one, has never been discovered.

On becoming Pharaoh of Upper and Lower Egypt (as the Egyptians described it in his day), he declared a new religion based upon Aten, associated with the sun but not actually the sun itself, a very important point theologically. His new god was supreme and alone, making Akhnaten the first declared monotheist in recorded history. Just as important, Akhnaten's god was a universal god transcending locale, another first. Finally, by not completely identifying his god with the physical sun but emphasizing his independent nature, Akhnaten's god is the first truly abstract godhead we know. The Amon priests, who until then upheld the accepted pantheistic religion of the Egyptians, were given second place and finally banned altogether. Wherever possible, Akhnaten had Amon's name removed from public monuments.

Reflect a moment on what this must have meant to the people of

Akhnaten's time. Before Akhnaten, there are perhaps another 1,500 years of recorded history, and in the Nile Valley perhaps another unrecorded 2,000 years before that. There probably has never been a more conservative society in the history of humankind than that of the ancient Egyptians. By that, I mean change came slowly and, for long periods, not at all. Violent changes of power were few, and the dynasties sometimes represent hundreds of years of peaceful transition of power. Violence was regularly exerted on their neighbors, often in barbaric ways, but the people who lived in the Valley of the Nile actually saw little of it. So, not only were Akhnaten's ideas unorthodox, but his way of imposing them—as the "Son of Aten" he would himself have been treated as a god—must have been deeply offensive to the society at large.

I dwell on this because it gives an idea of how my thinking about the opera developed. These elements—on the one hand, Akhnaten as a radical peremptorily upsetting time-honored customs; on the other, what must have been a profound revulsion on the part of his people to his ideas and manner—became central features to my portrayal of the characters in the opera. Of course, this is guesswork (intelligent guesswork, I hope), since the facts are slim and few.

Still, there are many things we can be fairly certain about, how Akhnaten *looked*, for example. The art of the Amarna period may be the first period of conscious naturalism in the history of art. One of Akhnaten's dictums was "living in truth," and presumably he chose to be portrayed as he really appeared, not in the formal, idealized style of the pharaohs who preceded him. If this is true, then he certainly must have been an odd-looking character: swollen thighs, enlarged hips, breasts almost pendulous. At first glance he appears almost hermaphroditic. Medical analysis is not conclusive. Akhnaten's appearance could have been genetic in origin, or it may have been the result of disease. In any case, he was biologically male and capable of fathering children.

The art of the Amarna period dwells on nature, representing birds, flowers, animals, etc., in a lovely lyrical style. Another innovation, perhaps related to this, was the introduction of the colloquial language— the language of everyday Egypt—into religious practice. Interestingly enough, this is the only innovation of Akhnaten's that was allowed to remain after he disappeared from history.

As our team began to absorb all this diverse information with the help of Shalom, our resident scholar and guide, we began to form a picture of who Akhnaten might have been. Certainly we were equipped to present, if not a complete account of this odd pharaoh, at least a reasonable picture of him for the musical stage. And if, as I have already admitted, some guessing was involved, at least nothing we showed in the end could be proven untrue.

Still, the mode of presentation was not clear to me for a time. It is common in the fiction and even in some of the scholarship surrounding Akhnaten to simply fill in parts of the missing story. For instance, little is known about his childhood, a fact that offers a free field for an inventive mind. Nor has anyone been able to discover exactly how he died, though this has not prevented the appearance of some surprisingly assured fictional accounts of his demise. In general, I shied away from such inventions. It seemed to me that they could only belittle our subject. To me, the mystery of not knowing began to have a certain attraction of its own.

I found the central solution of the scenario problem back in the Cairo Museum, which had already contributed so much to my ability to envision Akhnaten. In the Amarna room I wandered from case to case of tablets, jewelry, fragments of various sorts. From two corners of the room two huge busts of Akhnaten, his deformed body looking curiously Asiatic in profile, preside over the visitors. The chronology of the material is vague; the connections seem to be one of style. And yet, after a time, the fragments begin to tell their story. If parts of the story are missing, it serves to add poignancy rather than make it any less real. It occurred to me that in the same way that this room, in relation to its place in the museum, served as a metaphor for Akhnaten's place in Egypt's history, the contents of the room itself—only fragments, beautiful and obscure—could be a metaphor for the opera. It seemed to me, at that moment, that we needed no more story than was already there, that the missing pieces, far from needing to be filled in or explained, actually added to the mystery and beauty of our subject. A theatrical approach, to be sure, but theater was what we were making.

Back in New York, I explained my idea to Shalom: an opera about Akhnaten based upon fragments with the missing bits intact, as it were. His face lit up, and at the end he exclaimed, "Ah! Singing archaeology!"

Ultimately, that became our compass, guiding us, if sometimes erratically, through to the discovery and completion of our libretto. I still think it a fairly accurate description of what we tried to do.

Our first job was to locate texts or pictures about Akhnaten, or at least from Akhnaten's time. They added up to mere bits and pieces.

We had to examine these fragments to see what we really had on which to base the opera. Shalom was responsible for collecting, sometimes translating, material for us to pore over and try to arrange. Often, however, it would work the other way around: We would want a specific kind of text, then go looking for it. If the scenic idea came first, then the appropriate text had to be discovered. We knew, for instance, that there must have been a coronation, and we needed a text to be sung at our re-creation of it. What we decided to use was the list of names and titles Akhnaten assumed on becoming pharaoh.

Akhnaten, like *Satyagraha,* would be in three acts. I like the rhythm of a two-intermission evening. Since we were trying to make the opera fit into one "service" (three hours in the U.S., a little longer in Europe), this meant each act would run forty-five to fifty minutes. These considerations are important for me when I compose, for they tell me what kind of time scale I can realistically think in, and this in turn affects the scale and arrangement of scenes within each act. In a general way the three acts would comprise the rise, reign and fall of Akhnaten. That really is all the story there is. Besides having the advantage of being a natural organic sequence, it would seem the only way it could have happened, historically speaking.

With that as a starting point, the scenes fell into place very easily. We devised them either from an available text, from visual evidence or from what we knew must have taken place. The funeral of Akhnaten's father, and also Akhnaten's coronation in Act I, fall into the last category. On the other hand, the family scene in Act II is based entirely on a well-known relief of Akhnaten sitting with his six daughters and Nefertiti. Of course, all the scenes are imaginary, but some, admittedly, are more imaginary than others.

For example, in Act II we have a duet between Akhnaten and Nefertiti. From the way Nefertiti appears in paintings, we know that Akhnaten thought very highly of her, elevating her to a place equal to his own, and this was highly unusual even in the royal families of Egypt. It is easy to imagine a tender romantic connection between these two. If this is so, then Akhnaten and Nefertiti are among the earliest, if not *the* earliest romantic couple in recorded history, predating Antony and Cleopatra by many hundreds of years. It seemed, then, that we should at least given them a scene to themselves in the opera. Besides, who could resist writing a love duet for such a pair?

Shalom uncovered a beautiful love poem that had been found in a royal sarcophagus of the Amarna period. It may even have been written by Nefertiti herself. Like many love poems from the ancient world, it is somewhat ambiguous and can be read two ways: as if addressed to a god, or to a person. In my setting, I used it both ways, first in its religious sense and then as if the lovers had addressed it to each other.

Another scene grew out of my visit to the site of Akhnaten's own city, Akhetaten. These ruins near the present-day town of Tell El-Amarna are still virtually buried in the sand, but excavations have unearthed the floor plans of palaces and official buildings. It seems that, with Akhnaten's death, or at least disappearance, the city was simply abandoned. I knew that there had been markers, or stelae, erected to mark the limits of the royal city, and I wanted to see one of them for myself.

After some fairly aimless driving around in a jeep with a guide, we spotted what looked like a large fragment of a wall cut into one of the cliffs surrounding this part of the valley. The driver left the jeep there, and we trudged through the sand for half a mile to the stele.

It was quite large, maybe fifteen feet high, and carved into the rock was a, by now, familiar Akhnaten scene: the hands of the sun (the Aten) reaching down from the heavens to touch his son, Akhnaten. The ceremonial fanfare that concludes the declaimed text and introduces the City/Dance scene in Act II of the opera derives directly from that moment, when I first stood in front of this monument that was virtually lost in the desert but seemingly unchanged for all its 3,500 years.

These kinds of experiences, reflections and discussions allowed our creative team to form a highly personal vision of our subject and his time. Of course, this was crucial if we were to portray material as exotic as that of Ancient Egypt with any kind of conviction. I believe this approach was, indeed, the key to our dramatization of Akhnaten. Often we found ourselves deep in discussions that became richly speculative about what life in Akhnaten's time was really like.

One of the most striking things I became aware of in our studies was the sharp contrast between the sophisticated and refined life of upper-class Egyptians, as shown in tomb paintings, and the militaristic and primitive manner in which Egypt treated its neighbors. It was common throughout Egypt's long history for pharaohs to regularly lead their armies into the neighboring countryside to subdue their vassal princes, who seem to have been in a constant state of near-rebellion. These forays could be quite extensive since Egypt controlled what in those days was a world empire extending into Asia Minor in the East, and Nubia (Africa) in the South.

These military activities were a normal part of Egyptian life. It is reported that when Akhnaten's great-grandfather, Thutmos III, led his army into battle (the pharaohs, after all, were considered gods and therefore immortal, so personally leading their armies may have been common), his face and demeanor were so frightening that, at the mere sight of him, enemies would drop their swords and run! The Egyptians habitually chopped off the left hands of their dead enemies and left them in piles so they could count their numbers more easily. It was common for ships returning up the Nile from some recent conquest to display the heads of the conquered kings and princes on poles at the bow of the ship. This practice of regular invasion seems to have been dropped, or at least substantially curtailed, by Akhnaten and his father (a fact that became an important part of our story).

To me, this was also part of Akhnaten's Egypt, along with the impressive buildings, statues, paintings and jewelry, and this cruel and barbaric side of Egyptian life made me speculate on what a royal Egyptian funeral may have sounded like. Musically speaking I was clearly on my own, since the only hints we have of how Egyptian music sounded comes from pictures of flutes, lyres and so forth found in tombs. To judge from that evidence, Egyptian music was soft, lyrical stuff. About funeral music, no mention is made at all. Thus the music I designed for the funeral of Amenhotep III in the opening scene of the opera does not resemble any funeral music I have ever heard before. The drumming that begins it, the flourishes for brass and winds and the emphatic entrance of the singing, give it a raw, primitive, quasi-military sound.

In this music, coming as it does right after the prelude to Act I, my idea was to give an unmistakable and clear image of how, at least in part, "our" Egypt would be portrayed. By vividly portraying that world through the music, I hoped to set off the idealism of Akhnaten even more strongly. The blaring brass and pounding drums introduce the world into which Akhnaten was born.

By contrast, the "Hymn to the Sun"—the only text we had which may have been written by Akhnaten himself—occurs at the end of Act II and portrays, both musically and emotionally, the opposite end of the spectrum. Here Akhnaten, alone in the desert, sings a hymn to his god in words startlingly similar to the psalms of the Old Testament.

Death, of course, is the great subject of Egyptian culture, and this obsession made it seem all the more fitting to begin *Akhnaten* with a funeral. Probably no culture or society has been so death-conscious as the Egyptians'. They seem hardly ever to have stopped thinking about it. The first order of business for the pharaoh was to begin his funeral preparations, and building his tomb was usually a lifetime activity. In the period known as the Old Kingdom, the huge pyramids seem to be almost a physical attempt to overcome death with sheer size and grandeur. Certainly any depiction of Ancient Egypt must include a large measure of this death anxiety.

One aspect of this death thinking especially fascinated me. In reading the funeral texts—I didn't confine myself to the Amarna period but drew from the older dynasties as well, including the collection of chants, charms and prescriptions known as *The Egyptian Book of the Dead*—I learned that when the pharaoh dies and begins his journey to the heavenly kingdom of Ra, he is urged to employ various strategies to ensure that the gods will *notice* what is happening. Of course, as son of Ra, he is entitled to a place beside his heavenly father, but what should happen, the texts seem to ask, if for some reason the gods do not notice the pharaoh's passing and are not prepared to assist him in finding his way to them and to welcome him? With that in mind, I strove to make my funeral music capable of drawing attention to itself in every way possible. If any gods in the heavenly land of Ra were dozing, I was determined that my music would wake them up.

The more involved I became with the material, the more I began to see the funeral as an overall "image" for the work. In fact, though there is actually only one funeral scene, the libretto specifies that we see the funeral of Amenhotep III three more times, once in each act. The accompanying music, though not a reprise of the first act's funeral music, is meant to be heard in conjunction with these later visions of the funeral cortege. At the end of Act I, Akhnaten silently gazes at the distant funeral cortege floating on barques across a mythical river to the Land of the Dead. Midway through Act II, after the Akhnaten/Nefertiti duet and just before the City/Dance, we see the procession again, this time borne aloft on the wings of giant birds to the heavenly land of Ra. Finally, in the last moments of the opera, the funeral procession is joined by the now-dead Akhnaten who, presumably, was deprived of his own proper funeral. In this way the action of the opera becomes enclosed, as it were, in the image of the funeral which we, like our Egyptians on stage, never quite have out of our minds.

One aspect of the opera continued to trouble me for some time. I was aware of the fact that Akhnaten as a stage work must inevitably be seen as a period piece. Of course, this is a theater convention that has been hallowed and dignified by countless works for the dramatic and musical stage. Still, to present it as such without some acknowledgment of the special "unreality" of period pieces seemed to me a little negligent. I wanted to somehow underscore the fact that although we twentieth-century people were looking at an imaginary version of Egypt in

1400 BC, the very real ruins of that Egypt exist today. Therefore I decided to create an Epilogue set in the present.

This radical shift of viewpoint comes at the very end, just before we leave the theater, as we see what is now a twentieth-century ruin with our twentieth-century eyes. I think this could provide a richly speculative moment for future designers and directors. In the final scene, we have the remains of Akhnaten's pillaged temple before us. The transition from that to a scene showing the present-day ruins of Akhetaten, Akhnaten's city, can be a most moving and natural one.

The main characters of the work are all drawn from those immediately around Akhnaten during his lifetime, all historical persons whose names and titles are known to us. The chorus represents not only the society in which Akhnaten's revolution occurred, but also the two priestly factions that were pitted against each other: the older order of Amon priests and Akhnaten's priests who served the new religion of Aten.

The figure of Akhnaten himself required special care. This was a man so unusual, even unique, as to be virtually unprecedented in Egyptian, and therefore human, history. The problem for a theater composer is that the time we have on stage is very limited, and one cannot convey everything necessary to illustrate a subject. I thought a long while about how to present our title character. After all, you could use up the better part of Act I just indicating, in various ways, how extremely peculiar Akhnaten really was.

There simply was no stage time for that. To demonstrate his strangeness with costuming could work, but that was risky because it left a crucial noninterpretative matter in the hands of people over whom, in future productions, I would have no control. More and more it seemed to me that the problem was best solved musically, and my solution was to make Akhnaten a countertenor. For those to whom this is new, a countertenor is often described, somewhat incorrectly, as a male alto. Incorrectly, since the countertenor voice, though it can sail high above any other male voice, does not comfortably reach the high range of the normal (female) alto. Countertenors were quite common in Renaissance and Baroque music. Late Renaissance and Baroque operas routinely used this type of voice to sing female parts. Along the same musical lines were the famous castrati, men who had been castrated as boys so that they could retain the sweetness and strength of their boyish voices while adding the physical force of a mature male physique. This practice continued into this century, the last castrato of note being the Italian Alessandro Moreschi (admiring Italians called him ''The Angel of Rome''), a soprano castrato who lived long enough to make a number of recordings that are the only surviving examples of castrato vocalism. (Moreschi died in 1922 at the age of sixty-four.) The last thirty or forty years have seen a renewed interest in music from earlier times, and this has brought about a resulting emergence of the modern countertenor who, through rigorous training of the falsetto part of his voice, can achieve impressive and beautiful vocal results. There are, however, few modern works written for this type of voice.

The attraction for me in using a countertenor for Akhnaten must, by now, be obvious. The effect of hearing a high, beautiful voice coming from the lips of a full-grown man can at first be very startling. In one stroke, Akhnaten would be separated from everyone around him. It was a way of musically and dramatically indicating in the simplest possible way that here was a man unlike any who had come before.

I heightened the effect of hearing that first note sung by Akhnaten by delaying his vocal entrance as long as possible. He is not heard in the prologue, of course, nor does he sing in the first-scene funeral music. We see him all through his coronation, including the preparations leading up to it, but still we do not hear his voice. Finally, some thirty-five minutes into Act I, in the third scene—named The Window of Appearances (a lovely double-entendre title taken from the Egyptian)—where he greets his subjects as the new pharaoh, we hear him for the first time as he is joined in duet by Nefertiti, a mezzo-soprano. This becomes a trio when his mother, Queen Tye, a soprano, joins them. Normally the younger woman, in this case Akhnaten's wife, Nefertiti, would sing the higher part, but for musical reasons, I wanted the voices in the Act II duet between Akhnaten and Nefertiti to be as close as possible to the same range, to create a more intimate effect in their vocal intermingling.

Decisions of this kind can often lead to unexpected results and therefore new solutions. In Act II when Akhnaten leads, with Queen Tye, an attack on the Amon temple, the queen (a high soprano with, hopefully, dramatic thrust) can be more clearly heard above the full orchestra than Akhnaten himself. From this it can be seen that casting the voices—that is, assigning the type of voice for each major character—is something that must be done with a great deal of care, keeping in mind all manner of musical and dramatic needs. But, even so, there can be surprises.

In that first year of working together, we functioned as a team on all these considerations of form, dramatic structure and outline, character and design concepts. At the same time, working with us, Shalom was locating the texts I would need to set, and two interesting points emerged. First, all but one of the texts came from Akhnaten's time. The sole exception was a Fifth Dynasty pyramid text used during the funeral scene of Act I. Second, almost all the texts were taken from monuments of one kind or another. With a little reflection, the reason for that is obvious: Inscriptions carved in stone had a far greater chance of surviving. We have much less of the everyday kinds of communications, for they were in the form of papyrus.

We used two texts not taken from monuments. The first was the love poem actually surviving on gold leaf, no doubt because it had been buried with a royal mummy which had only recently been discovered. The second was from the famous "Amarna letters." These were "letters" from some of Akhnaten's vassal princes, written in cuneiform in Akkadian, the ancient language of Babylonia (Akkadian served as the diplomatic language of the time), and was inscribed on small clay tablets. These texts, also recently discovered, comprise some forty or fifty surviving tablets and are, perhaps, the best picture we have of the court politics of the Amarna period. Thus we had texts in two languages: the hieroglyphs of ancient Egypt, and Akkadian from Babylonia. To these two languages we added two more.

The first was English (or whatever language would be understood by the specific audience). In the Epilogue, when a group of tourists visits the ruins of Akhnaten's city, I selected a page of Fodor's *Guide to Egypt* to be spoken by the Tour Guide. This is a very straightforward, somewhat quaint, description of what the modern site of Akhetaten looks like and was used to shock the audience back into a "present" viewpoint. English was also used in a second way, but more of that shortly.

The final language we used was ancient Hebrew for the offstage chorus that closes Act II following Akhnaten's "Hymn to the Sun." The intent here was to underline the connection of Akhnaten's ideas with those of our own time and culture. This connection, of course, is only theory, but it is supported by modern scholarship and, indeed, by the texts themselves. When the "Hymn to the Sun" is set side by side with Psalm 104—the one sung by the chorus—the parallels are more than striking. The Hebrew can easily be seen as an adaptation, if not in places an actual translation, of the Egyptian. There seems little doubt that the Old Testament, at least in the Psalms, had Egyptian sources. For me, there were no theological problems in making these connections explicit in the opera; to add another level of historical interest enriched it even further.

The question remained, in what language was the opera to be sung? Anyone who has read this far will not be surprised to learn that, as far as the sung text was concerned, I used the original languages, phonetically transliterated for the singers. This turned out not to be so difficult as it might at first appear. There has been quite a lot of scholarly work on the sound of these languages. Coptic, still spoken in the Middle East, is thought to be the modern-day survivor of ancient Egyptian. Working backwards from this as a source, and remembering that ancient Egyptian was related to the Semitic language group, has given us a fair idea of how it must have sounded. Working with Shalom, we strove for authenticity as far as possible in matters like these. It is my feeling that this kind of detail invariably merges powerfully into the work, rendering it that much more convincing. In *Akhnaten*'s case, a lot of trouble was taken to get the text to sound as "right" as possible.

The one exception occurs when Akhnaten sings his "Hymn to the Sun." Here he sings in the language of the audience, English or German in the case of those first two productions. In the other scenes, I was quite willing to retain the original languages since they served to heighten the "archaeological" and exotic aspects of the opera. The actual content of the text was conveyed to the audience in another way, which I will come to presently. However, when Akhnaten sings his Hymn, I wanted it to affect the listener in a special way. The Hymn contains the kernels of Akhnaten's thought and appears as a highly personal statement. By the end of Act II the audience has been listening to more than one and one-half hours of singing which, though accompanied by explicit action requiring little explanation, they can hardly be expected to understand. Suddenly, with the Hymn, the words are intelligible. I wanted at that moment to create the effect of entering into Akhnaten's mind, sharing his thoughts, and in this way making the moment highly intimate, a direct communication between Akhnaten and ourselves. It can be a very dramatic effect, achieved by the direct presentation of the text itself.

However, I was not willing to let the rest of our hard-won libretto pass by the audience without being understood. For this reason, I introduced the role of a narrator into the opera. Throughout the work he delivers, in the language of the audience, the text either just before or soon after it is sung. Thus, at one point or another, the entire text is heard spoken over music. The words were not keyed to the rhythm of the music but were left to the narrator to "fit" into extended passages. (In one scene, just before the City/Dance in Act II, he is left to speak alone without any musical accompaniment at all.) In a real way, I was returning to a technique Bob Wilson and I had employed with *Einstein on the Beach:* spoken words and music. The technique continues to interest me, and I have developed it further since this first Trilogy.

The narrator plays the part of the Scribe, the natural role he would assume in the society of Ancient Egypt. In the Epilogue, however, when the ruins are invaded by tourists, he reappears, this time as a Tour Guide. In London, when *Akhnaten* was done at the English National Opera, the Tour Guide part was prerecorded on tape by Lord Harewood. His voice was well-known through radio and TV appearances, and the audience recognized it immediately and almost cackled with delight. As this was his last production before retiring, it also provided a special, and touching, farewell to his—and our—audience.

The period I spent with Goldman, Riddell, Israel and, at the end, David Freeman was extensive and, as can be imagined, intense. Our subject and libretto emerged very thoroughly worked out. The designs were underway, and composition of the music had begun even as the last pieces and ideas were coming together. Achim Freyer and Peter Kehr were kept up to date on all developments, and I knew that Achim was already at work and, I was sure, adding concepts of his own to our vision of the work.

In the summer of 1982, I was back in Nova Scotia, eager to start writing the music. Shalom had promised to send me the funeral text, which had been difficult to find and still was not in hand. As usual, I was prepared to start at the beginning and write straight through to the end, and the delay was making me jumpy. To fill in the waiting time, which turned out to be two weeks, I wrote a prelude to the opera. Until then, a prelude had not been planned, but it turned out to be a striking beginning. And since no libretto or action existed for it, it became a director's piece, a point where he is free to do anything, or nothing at all, to create a beginning.

I had no special problem writing the music, except for the counter-tenor part itself. Here I was working with a voice that was unfamiliar to me. What I knew of the sound I had learned from recordings and a very few live performances. Until then, I had never met anyone who actually possessed such a voice. Eventually I did meet with Paul Esswood, who would be singing the part at the premiere in Stuttgart, though that meeting came almost one and one-half years later during Christmas of 1983, just months before our first night. He was in New York to sing Baroque Christmas oratorios, and we met one afternoon in the coffee shop of his hotel. There he very kindly and carefully looked over his part, making comments and suggesting changes to make my musical ideas singable for his voice. Moments like these are invaluable for a composer. I've learned much more about music theater from conductors and singers than I ever did from the standard opera repertory.

With the score completed, there was still a fair amount of time before rehearsals would actually begin and everyone concerned could hear the music for the first time. The question now arose as to how they would hear it during the prerehearsal learning period. With repertory operas there is, of course, no problem. A director doing, say, *Cosi fan Tutte* need only go to a record store, pick any of a number of recordings and listen away to his heart's content. For a score still in the leaf, as it were, it is a different story. Few designers, directors and choreographers read music well enough to get an idea of how a new work will actually sound. Usually a piano version of the orchestral score is available but, again, one has to be able to read music and play the piano for this to be useful.

Being able to hear a new work is really crucial for the director, since total familiarity gained over repeated listening sessions is the only way to gauge the dramatic sense of a piece. Without that, a director cannot prepare himself for the rehearsal period with the singers and chorus. In the case of *Satyagraha* I had been quite lucky. David Pountney reads and plays music and could bang through the score on the piano as well as I could, if not actually better. He is a rare find. But I still wanted to find a solution to the problem.

What we finally did was simply record the whole opera. Since I had Michael Riesman and Kurt Munkacsi on hand, it was a relatively easy thing to do. We had a studio full of synthesizers as part of my Ensemble equipment and, by carefully programming them, Michael achieved a fairly good facsimile of an orchestra. Kurt handled the multitrack recording and mixing. Initially, with the assistance of composer Richard Einhorn, we entered the parts one by one into a computer-based sequencer, but this proved cumbersome, and Michael ended up playing all the parts directly onto tape. The result was that a full year before our opening night in Stuttgart we had a complete synthesized orchestral version of *Akhnaten*. In this first work tape, we did not have the vocal parts (this approach was completely new and we were still experimenting), but in subsequent work tapes, we have recorded the voices as well.

These work tapes have turned out to be an extremely valuable tool for developing a new work for production, removing a great deal of uncertainty from the learning and rehearsal period. When the real orchestra finally plays the music, it does, of course, sound far better. Work tapes, though "correct," always sound emotionally flat, with little of the dynamic range and expressivity of a live performance. But what an advantage for the production team to actually hear the piece!

Though I had kept in touch with Achim, he and his wife, Ilona, were really very much on their own when it came to the realization of *Akhnaten*. I think neither Achim nor I were unhappy about that, for I know he prefers to work that way. *Satyagraha* was still in production in Stuttgart, right through 1983, and I often came back to see it and discuss it with Peter and Achim when he was there (he lives in Berlin). I had grown to like his *Satyagraha* and had come a long way in understanding his way of working in the theater. Besides, I couldn't help but notice that, no matter when I saw *Satyagraha,* the house was invariably full. He once told me that he knew his public, and I had every reason to believe him. Not that his work was in any way "easy." Far from it. But he works in a theatrical language and symbols that are clearly meaningful, if somewhat disturbing, to his particular audience. And finally, we had an understanding about the work. He took great care to comprehend the music and my dramatic intentions. After that, he would do the piece "just the way I wrote it."

Actually, I've come to see that working with a director like Achim, who is both faithful to a work and irreverent of it, can be exhilarating. David Freeman is much the same way, in fact, though the results could not be more different. Achim's realization of *Akhnaten* was powerful in terms of images, and it was a piece of highly technical theater involving elaborate lighting, costumes and props. I was in Stuttgart for the final weeks of rehearsal and could at least watch those last days of preparation.

Even then, though, I was present only part of the time. At exactly the same time, a new work I had just completed with Bob Wilson—the Rome section of his mammoth, multinational *CIVIL warS* project, which had been planned for the Los Angeles Olympics Arts Festival in 1984, though never presented there in full—was in rehearsal. This section was a work commissioned by the Rome Opera for chorus, soloists and orchestra and, by sheer accident, was receiving its premiere at the same time as the Stuttgart *Akhnaten*. In fact, the premieres of the two operas were only one day apart: the Stuttgart *Akhnaten* on March 24, and the Rome *CIVIL warS* on March 25. What with the awkward flight connections between Rome and Stuttgart, I was having real problems.

The staging of both works was proceeding very well, though in Rome we were faced almost daily with strikes and "work stoppages," apparently not unusual there. These were directed at the management for all sorts of petty, and some not so petty, grievances. My problem was that the music was entirely new to the Italian musicians. We had an excellent leader in the conductor Marcello Panni who delivered a spirited and convincing performance. But it was clearly one of those situations where a composer, just by his presence and encouragement, can be helpful.

So, during my few weeks in Stuttgart, I seemed to be constantly running off to Rome to help things along. The schedule was so tight that I found I couldn't physically be at the dress rehearsal of each opera. I went to the *CIVIL warS* dress rehearsal and then to the *Akhnaten* premiere in Stuttgart the next night. At this distance in time, it doesn't seem so bad, but at the time it was, to say the least, quite draining. I recall getting to the Rome airport for my dash to Stuttgart for the premiere and running into the music press corps that had come from the U.S. to cover both events. Double premieres are about as common in the world of opera as double sunrises, and this was something of a story. Anyway, there were Alan Rich from *Newsweek,* Mike Walsh from *Time,* and John Rockwell of the *New York Times,* all sitting together and looking none too happy for being up at that early hour. For some unaccountable reason, it struck me as extremely funny. I suppose we composers have all too few moments of revenge on the critics.

For all these reasons, when I finally saw the completed *Akhnaten* at the Stuttgart premiere, it was very fresh, and I saw it without the disadvantage of having had weeks of rehearsal behind me. It was, as I had come to expect from Achim, a highly dramatic and compelling vision of Ancient Egypt with a good bit of the twentieth century thrown in. He had used the prelude to show in pantomime the young Akhnaten growing up. Velikovsky's Oedipus was not missing, either. He certainly got the militaristic side of it too, and from a number of centuries and different political viewpoints. In fact, the first image of a fierce, military totem is likely to stay for quite a long time in the memories of all who saw it. Paul Esswood was not made up to look like the "deformed" Akhnaten of our American/English production. Instead, he played Akhnaten straight on, and with regal dignity. It all made a great impression on the first-night audience, as it has continued to do in the following seasons in repertory in Stuttgart.

When the curtain came down, I joined the company on stage with Achim, his wife and Dennis Russell Davies. The audience was cheering and booing. This went on for quite a time. I think they actually were booing and cheering at each other, and I distinctly saw one fellow vigorously clapping and loudly booing at the same time. Dennis and Achim seemed very pleased with the uproar. When I pointed out the opposition in the audience, Dennis smiled broadly and said to me (we were still taking our bows on the stage), "Yeah, it's kind of like a sport over here."

Achim wagged his finger approvingly at the boos and said solemnly, "Very important!"

And in fact, everyone *did* look like they were having a wonderful time.

Achim's production emphasized the social side of Akhnaten's rebellion as well as the military, power-conscious side of the Egyptian rulers. The funeral and death image was not carried through as much as I would have liked, though he did give Amenhotep III quite a splendid funeral in Act I. There were some other things I didn't anticipate, though not all of them were off the mark, only a little unexpected. The narrator was played by a large, deep-voiced woman who was also an excellent actress. Actually, Peter and I had discussed that a year before, and I had agreed that it would be workable, though the Egyptian scribes were always male.

Achim had "choreographed" the dance in Act II himself—for actors, not dancers—and it came out very well. On the whole, the truth is that Achim's *Akhnaten* was more faithful to the libretto than our second production, which opened in Houston. This is definitely not meant as a relative judgment of the two productions, since there are many other values besides "correctness" that come across in a work.

Still, it is important to me, even more so now that I'm often not involved in all the productions of theater works containing my music. I suppose what I've come to look for is faithfulness to intention as well as a largeness of interpretation—obviously, some ambivalence here! But I can't say that these tensions and conflicts, which in effect are structural and thereby unavoidable, have been bad for me.

At this point, I've seen two-thirds of the Trilogy as realized by Achim Freyer. Both operas received individual and remarkable interpretations. What his *Einstein on the Beach* will be like (surely he will take the second option of a "new" *Einstein*), only time will tell. But I have confidence that it will be well worth waiting for.

The Freeman production (for the U.S. and England) proceeded in a very different way. In fact, David's way of working could not have been more different from Achim's. To date his version has been presented in three opera houses, first at the Houston Grand Opera, next at the New York City Opera, finally at the English National Opera in London. In the last venue it finally took on the character and look that he had been seeking, and it enjoyed a great success there and was brought back two years later for seven additional performances (which played to 107 percent capacity!). I mention this because, before it reached London, David's production was not always treated kindly by critics. But for those of us who have been involved with the whole work process, it has been extremely interesting and, for me personally, rewarding.

Of course, from the beginning it looked nothing like the German *Echnaton* (as the title was spelled in Germany). This was due to several very early design choices that David made with Bob Israel and Richard Riddell. David wanted to emphasize the sun, sand and river motifs that he had brought back with him from *his* Egyptian visit, which he had made shortly after my own. Therefore he required very few built pieces, and his stage was always open, light and airy. Another important decision concerned the look of Akhnaten himself. He wanted the audience to actually *see* the physically deformed, weird-looking individual who so totally overturned the world he lived in.

Christopher Robson, the countertenor for David's production, is a younger man than Paul Esswood (he trained with Esswood at one point) and has a quite beautiful voice. In addition, he is a perfectly normal, in fact rather nice-looking fellow, in his real-life persona. Israel, though, had designed a body-suit that our American/English Akhnaten had to wear, and it was so complicated that it took almost three hours to do Akhnaten's make-up and costume. Christopher had to get to the theater about 3:00 PM for an evening curtain and 9:00 AM for a matinee.

In an early scene Akhnaten is being dressed for his coronation and appears absolutely naked on stage. What we actually saw was Christopher in the body-suit. Israel's design was complete in every anatomical detail and convincing to such a high degree that many in the audience thought they were looking at the real Christopher when they saw this poor, misshapen, hermaphroditic Akhnaten. One can easily imagine that, along with the expected musical and acting problems, there must be some major psychological difficulties involved in rendering such a character! Christopher never complained, and I think actually began to enjoy these nightly transformations. Once in his Akhnaten suit, though, he couldn't see to his normal bodily needs, and he once complained to me that, starting the evening before a performance, he couldn't drink liquids of any kind.

At any rate, both the visual and vocal impression Christopher made as Akhnaten was decidedly startling, especially when Akhnaten sings for the first time at the end of Act I. A number of people in our audiences were quite upset by Christopher's appearance on the stage. One very famous musician, a man who had spent his life in the theater and might have been expected to be aware of the wonders achieved by make-up artists, expressed genuine sorrow that we had not been able to engage a less grotesque-looking singer for our title role! Near the end of the New York City Opera run, we received a letter denouncing us for (1) having found some poor hermaphrodite; (2) forcing him to display his deformities in public; and (3) making him sing my music!

David wanted to make several deletions and additions to the text. Since I already had one *Akhnaten* in Germany, and since David had missed many of the early meetings with our team of collaborators, thereby depriving him of the opportunity to make his own contributions early on, I agreed, and he had a fairly free hand with the material. In retrospect I see that, on the one hand, that is the way David probably works best. On the other hand, during the early stages of the production, and before his work finally matured in London, I had some serious doubts as to what kind of *Akhnaten* was being presented.

For one thing, the Dance in Act II was cut for the simple reason that David didn't want to do the choreography. Bringing in a choreographer, which is how I had expected this would be solved (exactly what Wilson and I did in the Rome *CIVIL warS*), went against the grain for him. I often joked to David that he made me feel like a real opera composer because, as with composers of the past, the first thing opera companies did was cut the ballet. I've come to think of the Dance at this point as not really indispensable to the drama though, when possible, I definitely would prefer to have it included.

David made several additions that were not included in the text but come under the heading of "director's prerogative." David wanted to show the particular kind of centuries-old continuity one becomes aware of in countries like Egypt that haven't fully experienced the effects of twentieth-century technology on a nationwide scale. When you leave the cities for the countryside, you feel you are going back in time, so little changed are the daily activities of the ordinary peasants. Great men and events come and go, and they hardly touch society at this level at all.

To show this, David had a brickmaker downstage making bricks out of mud throughout the entire evening. On the other side of the stage a man and his wife ceaselessly tossed wheat into the air so that the wind could separate the chaff from the grain. A third element he introduced was the idea of the ceaseless struggle and violence that have been a part of that region of the world since ancient times, reaching into the present. This was represented by a group of eight wrestlers, dressed only in loin cloths, who performed a very slow-motion, dancelike, fighting scene. This was used to great effect when, in Act III, they slowly moved from upstage left into the center to surround and carry off Akhnaten. The libretto does not specify exactly how it is to happen, but in this act, during the destruction of his temple by the resurgent Amon priests, Akhnaten is carried off. (We never actually see his death.)

Akhnaten opened in Houston in November 1984, with John De Main conducting. The Houston Grand Opera had been very supportive throughout the long seven-week rehearsal period. It was clearly a work they liked and were proud of, and this feeling extended to the first-night audience as well. In fact, for a time it seemed the whole city had gone *Akhnaten*-crazy. Some downtown department stores even had their windows dressed with Egyptian mannequins. Jones Hall was still in use then—a three-thousand seater that is always hard to fill—but all through its run, *Akhnaten* drew extremely well. This was especially true of its nonsubscription nights (when people who don't have season tickets can buy seats for a single performance) which is always a good sign and one that pleased David Gockley, the Houston Grand Opera's director, very much.

The transferral of the production to New York did not go smoothly, though we had the same principals for the leading parts and, with Christopher Keene conducting, we had an excellent, committed music director. The problem was simply one of moving into a very busy repertory house. In Houston we could plan a schedule in terms of weeks and days. In New York, with some twenty or so productions in a six-month period, one makes up a schedule in terms of hours and minutes. What it comes down to is less rehearsal time, less set-up time, even less sand on the stage. (The sand was very dear to David. He wanted literally tons of it, and he finally got just that in London. In spades.)

However, the New York City Opera is not short on enthusiasm and vitality. I have always felt that, even with the very heavy schedule of the house, Beverly Sills was truly proud to present *Akhnaten* and took a special interest in it. At the same time, David's approach continued to evolve in New York, with innumerable small changes and refinements.

For financial reasons, the American sets did not go to London for the premiere in June 1985, and of the original company only Christopher Robson and Marie Angel, the Queen Tye, were present. With a whole new company and rehearsal period, David's approach remained basically the same, but in actual realization it was considerably revised. A long-time associate of his, David Rogers, produced new designs. Though based on concepts originated by Riddell and Israel, they were considerably altered and, it must be admitted, better suited to David's interpretation. Our young English conductor, Paul Daniels, seemed to have an immediate affinity for the score and led the orchestra, chorus and principals in an inspiring series of performances. The English audience seemed to like *Akhnaten* particularly well, and I wonder whether their historical connection to, and interest in, Egypt may have had something to do with it.

In a general way, while Achim's *Akhnaten* emphasized the play of power and society, David's portrayal leaned toward the intimate and personal. Starting from the same libretto, the productions had gone in almost opposite directions. I'm always asked which I preferred, notwithstanding the fact that I was involved in the development of one of them. First of all, that is hardly the point for me since, had I been seeking a definitive *Akhnaten,* I wouldn't have set about having two versions in the first place. In all honesty, there are elements of each production I liked enormously. I also had reservations, sometimes serious ones, about each. The "funeral image," for example, did not appear in either production to the extent I would have liked.

This business about authenticity versus freedom of interpretation is very tricky, and I continue to struggle with it, as other theater authors have done most of their lives. It looks to me that a lifetime of experiment and experience is needed, and even then there are questions which may never be finally settled. At the moment, I am leaning in the direction that Wilson and I have taken with *Einstein* where, basically, there are two possible ways of approaching a work. One is the original version as conceived by the authors. The other is a redesigned version, possibly quite unlike the original.

At this writing a new production of *Akhnaten* is being planned for Holland. I was asked what role I wished to play in the work, and I chose to be "artistic consultant." I did not want to be either a director or a codirector, but rather to function as an artistic supervisor to the production. This would allow designers, directors and others a good measure of artistic freedom while retaining an original-version concept of the piece. In other productions, as with that of Achim Freyer, I might not be involved at all. These would be interpretative versions.

As an interesting postscript to the two *Akhnaten* productions, I should mention Michael Blackwood's documentary film entitled *A Composer's Notes: Philip Glass and the Making of an Opera.* Very early in the planning stages of *Akhnaten,* Blackwood, a maker of documentary films, heard of the project and approached me about filming the entire process. This meant having a film crew around us, off and on, for the entire three-year period, including my excursions into Egypt and India.

To his credit, Michael and his crew—cinematographer Mead Hunt and editor Peter Geisman—insinuated themselves into our lives so discreetly that, after a time, we more or less forgot they were there. The resulting film amounts to a continuous record of the creation of the opera from the first meetings in 1981 to the first two productions in 1984.

In those two productions, Freeman and Freyer produced drastically different interpretative versions, and neither could be accused of being overly faithful to "the original." David encountered what seems to me to have been an unfair amount of problems, and it took a lengthy evolution to work them out, but in London the production finally came into its own. Despite our problems and all the reservations on all sides, in the end there were two extremely different and original productions of *Akhnaten,* and both were successful. I was not at all unhappy about how it all came out.

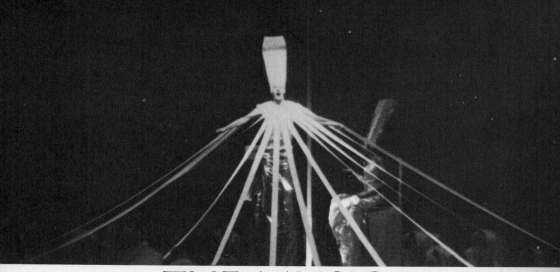

THE MUSIC

Having established a comfortable working relationship with the orchestra in *Satyagraha,* I found myself working under sharp orchestral restrictions in *Akhnaten.* Because the Stuttgart opera house was closed for renovations and the smaller Playhouse was being used for the premiere, I would have an orchestra pit of limited size, necessitating a commensurate reduction in the number of players. Nevertheless, the music I was going to write would be ceremonial in many places, militaristic in others, and I needed a full complement of brass and wind players. At least, however, I was willing to cut back from the tripled winds of the *Satyagraha* score to the more usual complement of double winds. This would mean careful writing to ensure that the players would have adequate breathing and resting places.

With the percussion, there would also be severe limitations of space. I elected to use three percussionists and then began to consider what they would play. Timpani were out (though they would have been useful), since they alone can take up as much room as four string players. Instead of timpani, I used bass drum, snare drum, and an array of hand-held instruments; for the Coronation scene I also called for tubular bells.

The only place to cut further was in the strings. Instead of going with reduced players in all sections, which would have made balancing with full brass and wind sections tricky at best, I chose to eliminate the violins altogether. This left me with all the low strings—violas, cellos and basses—in full strength, giving the orchestra a low, dark sound that came to characterize the piece and suited the subject very well. At this point I was certainly thinking of *Akhnaten* as the "tragic" opera of the trilogy. By contrast, *Einstein,* with its amplification, seemed filled with a high explosive energy, and *Satyagraha,* with its long vocal lines set against winds and strings, was more the lyrical opera. Besides complementing the other two nicely, this tragic quality of *Akhnaten* was easy to see in the material. By articulating it in the music, I felt that any director trying to realize this work in a production would take the music as a guide and present its basic overall character.

This decision regarding the strings fit very well with others I had already made about the voice. With Akhnaten cast as a countertenor, my three main leading voices were all high. I knew there would be frequent ensembles in the opera: duets and trios with Akhnaten; his mother, Queen Tye, sung by a soprano; and his wife, Nefertiti, sung by a mezzo-soprano. (The score calls for a contralto, but true contraltos are rarely found.) By using the middle to upper ranges of the mezzo-soprano and countertenor voices with the lower and middle range of that of the soprano, voice crossing (where lower voices sing above higher voices, and vice versa) also could happen easily. In the final libretto, we stayed away from the Oedipus theme, since the text already seemed fully freighted with abundant social, religious and philosophical issues. However, a veiled reference to the ambiguous sexual relationship of the three principals does remain in this aspect of the vocal writing. Especially when they are heard together for the first time, in the final scene of Act I (The Window of Appearances), the voice crossings produce a purposely confusing effect, making it sometimes difficult for the listener to follow the separate parts. The setting of the voices against the low strings proved highly effective, giving a somber backdrop to the higher, lyrical vocal writing.

Again, partly for considerations of space, I had wanted to have some musicians on the stage itself. I had liked the placement of the *Einstein* violinist midway between the orchestra and stage, and I again wanted to introduce musicians, even if in a limited way, to a more vital part of the stage action. The libretto calls for this in two places.

First, the drums in the Funeral March are meant to be on stage. This would require them to be placed downstage near the conductor for purposes of musical coordination; with thoughtful staging, however, that should be no real problem.

Secondly, I wanted to have a variety of hand-held instruments— wood block, tambourine, triangle—played on stage for the City/Dance in Act II. In both cases I expected the musicians to be costumed and appear as part of the stage action. This stage direction has been omitted in both of the first two *Akhnaten* productions—regretably, from my point of view, since I feel in both cases it would enliven the stage action by introducing a new and spectacular visual element.

The orchestration in general took on quite a different character from the previous operas, in which the instrumental parts played a somewhat less assertive role. This change resulted in no small measure from separate discussions I had with Christopher Keene and Dennis Russell Davies. After *Satyagraha* had opened in both Stuttgart and New York, I asked them to look over the score with me and offer their comments. Both men were strong supporters of the work and understood the basis on which I had approached the use of the orchestra. They each, in different ways, argued for a more "orchestral" approach, one in which individual instruments and sections had a more "soloistic" sound. These discussions were very detailed and the arguments persuasive. In *Akhnaten,* I had wanted to implement these suggestions in terms of what they would mean to my own music. And I think the results are clearly discernible in this generally more colorful score, its overriding darkness and somber quality notwithstanding.

One particular device was useful in depicting Akhnaten himself. When he sings, he is invariably accompanied by a solo trumpet. This is used dramaturgically in the opera, since Akhnaten's every appearance, whether vocal or merely visual, is heralded by the solo trumpet in the orchestra. There was another reason for this: Since Akhnaten's part is often quite prominent, and I didn't want to tire the voice, I gave the countertenor a sort of orchestral "partner" with whom Akhnaten could share the burden of the vocal line. The trumpet, when softly and lyrically played in its lower middle range, is a good match for the countertenor voice, and this device worked extremely well. There are moments in the "Hymn to the Sun" at the end of Act III where the countertenor and trumpet perform a kind of parallel duet. When the voice seems to reach for a higher note than is in its range, the trumpet crosses the vocal line to pick up the high note. When done well, the change of parts is barely noticeable, apparently adding an extra third to the top range of the voice.

Though the relationship of harmonic and rhythmic structures had formed the musical subject of the first two operas, and though I continued to use some of these devices in *Akhnaten,* in this third work I began to think about musical material in a different way, exploring key relationships in terms of the overall piece. I also used thematic devices which could be identified with persons or actions and could be carried through and developed throughout the rest of the work. This has turned out to be a subject of such absorbing interest to me that I have continued to explore it through three subsequent operas: *the CIVIL warS, The Juniper Tree* and *The Making of the Representative for Planet 8*.

In the case of *Akhnaten,* the musical themes and their key relationships form a changing mosaic throughout the opera, reaching a specific musical resolution in the very last moments. It is impossible in a few words to describe in detail a process that takes place over the course of a more than three-hour piece; briefly, however, I designed the Epilogue to form a kind of restatement of all the important materials, this time forming a new, compressed series of musical events. The series repeats four times with a final resolution at the end.

The first part of the Epilogue sequence is made up of the Trilogy theme in a simple harmonic form (Ex. A). In its third and fourth recurrence, the opening notes of *Einstein* are heard under this harmony. Earlier in the opera, the Trilogy theme had been used, first in the opening of the Coronation scene (Act II, scene 2). Here, it is in the altered melodic form (Ex. B) found also in the fourth and fifth Knee Plays of *Einstein*. It recurs again in almost exactly the same way at the opening of Akhnaten's Hymn in Act II, scene 4, and again as an interlude later in the same scene. This Trilogy theme, linked as it is to scenes in which essential aspects of Akhnaten's character are revealed, is strongly associated with *Akhnaten* himself.

[EXAMPLE A]

[EXAMPLE B]

This is precisely how the Trilogy theme is used in *Satyagraha* and *Einstein* as well. In *Satyagraha,* it appears in the second scene when the young Gandhi embarks upon his life's work, and again in the final scene at the penultimate moment of his political victory. The Trilogy theme occurs in all five Knee Plays of *Einstein,* scenes which represent the more intimate portraits of Einstein.

The next theme in the Epilogue sequence is shown in Example C. Its most distinctive feature is the bass line (Ex. D), which ascends and then abruptly drops an octave. This first appears in the Prelude and gives it its ominous quality. Again, we hear it in the City/Dance, this time accompanied in unison by the flutes. Finally, it forms the concluding phrases of Act III, scene 2 (Attack and Fall), in which Akhnaten's temple, and finally the pharaoh himself, are destroyed. For me, this music is synonymous with the downfall of Akhnaten. In the fourth measure of Example C, there is a curious play between B♭ Major and minor, this major/minor coincidence creating an uneasy harmonic ambiguity, which also occurs in its earlier appearances (in the Prelude, City/Dance, and Destruction of the Temple). It is easy to see this as a musical metaphor for that part of Akhnaten's character that was so unusual and unsettling to the people of his time.

[EXAMPLE C]

[EXAMPLE D]

The next section of the Epilogue sequence, shown in Example E, has been heard in both scenes of the opera that feature violence and destruction (Act II, scene 1, The Temple; and again in Act III, scene 2, Attack and Fall). In the Epilogue it has taken on a lyrical, almost distant, quality, as if death and the passage of centuries (the Epilogue is set in the present) have softened the violence of those moments, making them almost beautiful. The concluding phrase of the Epilogue sequence is a passing reference to Akhnaten's Hymn from Act II (seen in Example F) and is used in the same way at the end of each verse of the Hymn.

[EXAMPLE E]

[EXAMPLE F]

Finally, at the very end of the Epilogue, we have the music shown in Example G. This has appeared as an "ending" motif for several important moments of the opera—before Akhnaten's Coronation in Act I, preceding the Hymn, and at the conclusion of the Hymn. The important aspect of this theme, which rocks back and forth between the upper note A and the lower note E, is how it relates to the key of A minor that begins and ends the opera. Leighton Kerner (music critic of the *Village Voice*) remarked that the key of A minor envelops the opera like a shroud, a description I find both poetic and accurate.

[EXAMPLE G]

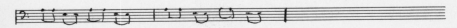

When Example G appears earlier in the opera, the note E is the lower note, this being an inverted position of the chord, since A, the key note, is not in the lowest, or bass, position. (Inverted chords never have the feeling of conclusiveness; even when they are in the key of the piece, there is always something unsettled about them.) In the final moments of the opera, it finally assumes the root position with the A below the E, achieved through a final appearance of the Trilogy theme heard in the upper parts of Example H. The Trilogy theme becomes the key that turns the lock, setting the ending firmly in A minor, the "relative minor" of C Major, the key in which *Einstein* began.

[EXAMPLE H]

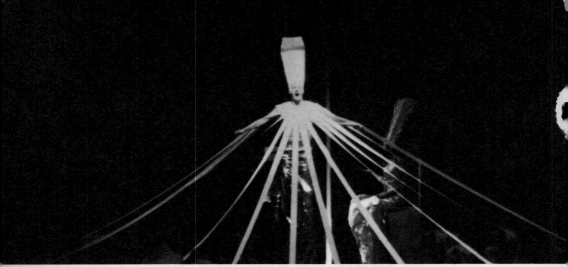

THE LIBRETTO

AKHNATEN

An Opera in Three Acts
by
Philip Glass

Libretto by Philip Glass in association with
Shalom Goldman, Robert Israel, Richard Riddell

————

Vocal text derived from original sources
by Shalom Goldman

SINGING ROLES

Akhnaten	*(Countertenor)*
Nefertiti, wife of Akhnaten	*(Alto)*
Queen Tye, mother of Akhnaten	*(Soprano)*
Horemhab, General and future Pharaoh	*(Baritone)*
Aye, father of Nefertiti and advisor to the Pharaoh	*(Bass)*
Amon High Priest	*(Tenor)*
Six Daughters	*(Women's Voices)*
Funeral Party	*(8 Men's Voices)*
Large Chorus	*(Mixed Voices)*

SPEAKING ROLE

Amenhotep, son of Hapu, the scribe   *(Male Speaker)*

ORCHESTRA

Woodwinds:
2 flutes (doubling piccolos)
2 oboes (doubling oboes d'amore)
2 B♭ clarinets
1 B♭ bass clarinet
2 bassoons

Brass:
2 trumpets
2 horns
2 trombones
tuba

Strings:
violas
cellos
doublebasses

Percussion:
4 tom-toms (2 players)
snare drum
bass drum
cymbal
finger cymbals

tubular bells
wood block
tambourine
celeste

Synthesizer

ACT I / YEAR 1 / THEBES / PRELUDE

The opera begins with an orchestral Prelude. The curtain rises toward the end of the Prelude, revealing the narrator in the funeral setting. He delivers the *first speech* (through verse 2 of the Pyramid Texts) as the Prelude is completed. In the moments of silence before the funeral begins, he continues his speech through verse 3.

Spoken Text: —(from the Pyramid Texts of the Old Kingdom)

Refrain:

Opened are the double doors of the horizon
Unlocked are its bolts

Verse 1:

Clouds darken the sky
The stars rain down
The Constellations stagger
The bones of the hell hounds tremble
The porters are silent

When they see this king
Dawning as a soul

Refrain:

(repeat above)

Verse 2:

Men fall
Their name is not
Seize thou this king by his arm
Take this king to the sky
That he not die on earth
Among men

Refrain:

(repeat above)

Verse 3:

He flies who flies
This king flies away from you
Ye mortals
He is not of the earth
He is of the sky

He flaps his wings like a
      zeret bird
He goes to the sky
He goes to the sky
On the wind
On the wind

ACT I / SCENE 1 / FUNERAL OF AMENHOTEP III

The scene presents the funeral of Akhnaten's father, Amenhotep III. As
the starting point of the opera, it represents the historical moment immediately before the Amarna period, or the reign of Akhnaten, and depicts the society in which the reforms of Akhnaten (reforms which appeared so extreme that they can be called revolutionary) took place. The

action of the scene centers on the traditional funeral rites of the New Empire of the Eighteenth Dynasty. It is dominated by the Amon Priests and appears as ritual of extraordinary traditional character drawn from *The Egyptian Book of the Dead*.

The funeral cortege enters downstage led by two drummers and followed by a small body of Amon Priests who are in turn led by Aye (father of Nefertiti and an advisor to the recently dead pharaoh and the pharaoh-to-be).

Vocal Text (Sung in Egyptian): —Small men's chorus (from *The Egyptian Book of the Dead*, Budge, intro. p. ivii)

> *Ankh ankh, en mitak*
> *Yuk er heh en heh*
> *ahau en heh*

(English translation)

Live life, thou shalt not die
Thou shalt exist for millions
 of millions of years
For millions of millions of years

As the music goes to the cellos alone, the deceased Amenhotep III enters behind the procession. He appears to be headless, and is holding his head in his hands.

The music for orchestra, small chorus and solo bass voice (Aye) resumes.

During the next section for orchestra alone, the funeral cortege (Amon Priests and Amenhotep III) moves upstage. Akhnaten and the people of Thebes join Aye downstage.

In the final section of the funeral, the people of Thebes and Aye join the orchestra in a last salute to the departing Amenhotep III.

Vocal Texts (Sung in Egyptian):— Large mixed chorus (from *The Egyptian Book of the Dead*, Budge, pp. 85–86)

> *I, inen mekhent ent Ra,*
> *rud akawik em mehit*

em khentik er she neserser
em kheret netcher

(English translation)

Hail, bringer of the boat of Ra
Strong are thy sails in the wind
As thou sailest over the Lake of Fire
In the Underworld.

ACT I / SCENE 2 / THE CORONATION OF AKHNATEN

The short opening to the next scene shows Akhnaten alone as the Scribe, Aye and the people of Thebes leave and the funeral cortege departs. Akhnaten's attendants appear and, by changing his costume, prepare him to receive the double crown of Upper and Lower Egypt. There is no singing or narration in this scene.

The next section for orchestra accompanies the appearance of the Scribe, the Amon High Priest, Aye and Horemhab as well as the people of Thebes. Akhnaten has remained with his attendants.

The following section includes the trio of Amon High Priest, Aye and Horemhab with orchestra. The dramatic intent of this moment is to prepare Akhnaten for receiving the double crown.

The opening music of the scene reoccurs as the Scribe announces the name and titles of the new pharaoh. During this speech Akhnaten receives the double crown from the High Priest assisted by Aye and Horemhab.

The music returns to that of the second section of this scene as the people of Thebes greet their new pharaoh.

Vocal Text (Sung in Egyptian):— Amon High Priest, Horemhab, Aye and large chorus (from *An Egyptian Reading Book,* Budge)

Ye-nedj hrak yemi em hetepu
Neb aut yeb sekhem kha-u
Neb wereret ka shuti
Nefer seshed ka hedjet
Mertu netcheru maanek
sekhti men em wept-ek

(English translation)

Hail to thee, thou who art in peace
Lord of Joy, Crowned Form
Lord of the Wereret Crown, Exalted of Plumes
Beautiful of Diadem, Exalted of the White Crown
The gods love to look upon thee
The double crown is established upon thy brow

Spoken Text:— (from a list of Akhnaten's titles)

Live the Horus, Strong-Bull Appearing as Justice;
He of the Two Ladies, Establishing Laws-and Causing
    the Two-Lands-to-be Pacified;
Horus of Gold, Mighty-of-Arm-when-He-Smites-the
    Asiatics;
King of Upper and Lower Egypt, Nefer Kheperu Re Wa en Re,
    son of Neb-maet-Re
    (Lord of the Truth like Ra)
Son of Re, Amon-Hotep (Amon-is-pleased)
Hek Wase (Ruler of Thebes) Given Life.

Mighty Bull, Lofty of Plumes; Favorite
    of the Two Goddesses, Great in Kingship in Karnak;
Golden Hawk, Wearer of Diadems in the Southern Heliopolis;
King of Upper and Lower Egypt
Beautiful-Is-the-Being of Ra, the Only-One-of-Ra
Son of the Sun, Peace-of-Amon, Divine Ruler of Thebes;
Great in Duration, Living-for-Ever and Ever, Beloved of
Amon-Ra, Lord of Heaven

ACT I / SCENE 3 / THE WINDOW OF APPEARANCES

A windowed balcony of the palace, in which the king and queen appear
in state.

    The music from the opening of the Coronation scene reappears,
played on large bells and providing a musical and dramatic transition to
what follows.

    Akhnaten is joined by Nefertiti and his mother, Queen Tye. They
approach the Window of Appearances and sing (first a solo, then duet,

then trio) through the Window. It is a hymn of acceptance and resolve and, in spirit, announces a new era.

Vocal Text (Sung in Egyptian):— Akhnaten, Queen Tye, and Nefertiti (from *The Gods of the Egyptians,* Budge)

Tut wu-a yeri enti
Wa-a Wa-u yeri wenenet
Perer en rem em yertif
Kheper Netcheru tep ref
Yeri semu se-ankh menmen
Khet en ankhu en henmemet
Yeri ankh-ti remu en yetru
Apdu genekh pet
Redi nefu en enti em suhet
Se-ankh apnentu yeri; ankhti khenus
Djedfet puyu mitet yeri
Yeri Kherti penu em babasen
Se ankh puyu em khet nebet
Ye-nedj hrak yeri
Enen er a-u

(English translation)

Oh, One creator of all things
Oh, One maker of all existences
Men came forth from his two eyes
The gods sprang into existence at the utterances of his mouth
He maketh the green herbs to make cattle live
And the staff of life for the use of man
He maketh the fish to live in the rivers, the winged fowl in
   the sky
He giveth the breath of life to the egg
He maketh birds of all kinds to live
And likewise the reptiles that creep and fly
He causeth the rats to live in their holes
And the birds that are on every green thing
Hail to thee maker of all these things
Thou only one.

The singing of the previous scene stops, and the music for this short ending continues the preceding material, this time for full orchestra. Tye and Nefertiti leave Akhnaten alone. He stands gazing at the distant funeral cortege floating on barques across a mythical river to the Land of the Dead.

END ACT I

ACT II / SCENE 1 / THE TEMPLE

The scene begins with a short introduction for orchestra. We then see an Amon temple and a small group of Amon priests led by their High Priest. They sing a hymn to Amon (at that time the principal deity of the Egyptian pantheon) and enter the Temple.

The following orchestral section introduces Akhnaten, Queen Tye and a small party of followers (Aten priests, soldiers, etc.) of the new order.

After surrounding the Temple, the Atenists, led by Akhnaten and Queen Tye, attack the Temple. Here we see Akhnaten for the first time as the rebel he was, venting his hatred of the old order on the Amon Temple. Their attack is complete, and the roof of the Temple is pulled off as the light of "the Aten" pours into what once was the "holy of holies." The attackers sing a vocalise, no words being necessary here.

Vocal Text:— Amon High Priests and Amon Priests

(Sung in Egyptian)

Amen men khet nebet
Ya-u-nek em em djed
Sen er ayu
Nek henu-nek
en wered ek imen

(English translation)

Oh Amon, creator of all things
All people say
We adore you
In jubilation
For resting among us.

ACT II / SCENE 2 / AKHNATEN AND NEFERTITI

An orchestral transition prepares for the next scene, devoted entirely to a duet between Akhnaten and Nefertiti.

With the introduction of the solo trombone, the Scribe begins reciting a poem. This first time we hear the poem it is as if addressed to a god.

With the entrance of the strings, the poem is heard again, this time spoken as an exchange between two lovers. During this second reading, Akhnaten and Nefertiti appear. There follows the duet between the two, now alone together. The vocal text is the same poem sung in Egyptian.

Near the end of the duet the music returns to the orchestra alone. There is a brief pause, and Akhnaten and Nefertiti resume singing, while behind them is seen the funeral cortege in a later stage of its journey, this time ascending on wings of large birds to the heavenly land of Ra.

Spoken Text: —A love poem found in a royal mummy of the Amarna period (from *Journal of Egyptian Archeology,* vol. 43 [1957], Sir Alan Gardiner, tr.)

> I breathe the sweet breath which comes forth
> from thy mouth. I behold thy beauty every day.
> It is my desire that I may be rejuvenated with
> life through love of thee. Give me thy hands,
> holding thy spirit, that I may receive it and
> may live by it. Call thou upon my name unto
> eternity, and it shall never fail.

Vocal Text (Sung in Egyptian):— Akhnaten and Nefertiti

> *Sensenet neftu nedjem*
> *per em rek*
> *Peteri nefruk em menet*
> *Ta-i nehet sedjemi*
> *Kheruk nedjem en mehit*
> *Renpu ha-i em ankh*
> *en mertuk*
> *Di-ek eni awik kher ka-ek*
> *Shesepi su ankhi yeme*

I ashek reni er heh
ben hehif em rek

ACT II / SCENE 3 / THE CITY / DANCE

The Scribe speaks the first part of this scene alone, without musical accompaniment. His speech is taken from the boundary markers (or stelae) of Akhnaten's new city, Akhetaten ("the Horizon of the Aten"). During his speech, Akhetaten appears behind him, a new city of light and open spaces that represents architecturally and visually the spirit of the epoch of Akhnaten.

The dance which immediately follows the brass fanfare contrasts with the heavy traditional ritual of the Temple scene which opened this act. Musicians (with triangle, wood block and tambourine) appear onstage with dancers, as well as Akhnaten and principal members of his entourage, in a dance that marks the celebration and inauguration of the city of Akhetaten.

Spoken Text—: (from the boundary markers found in the valley at Tell El-Amarna)

Stela 1:

And his majesty said unto them, "Ye behold the City of the Horizon of the Aten, which the Aten has desired me to make for him as a monument in the great name of my majesty forever. For it was the Aten, my Father, that brought me to this City of the Horizon. There was not a noble who directed me to it; there was not any man in the whole land who led me to it, saying 'It is fitting for his majesty that he make a City of the Horizon of Aten in this place.' Nay, but it was the Aten, my Father, that directed me to make it for him." Behold the pharaoh found that this site belonged not to a god, nor to a goddess, it belonged not to a prince nor to a princess. There was no right for any man to act as owner of it.

Stela 2:

I will make the City of the Horizon of Aten for the Aten, my Father, in this place. I will not make the city south of it, north

185

of it, west of it or east of it. I will not pass beyond the southern boundary stone southward, neither will I pass beyond the northern boundary stone northward to make for him a City of the Horizon there; neither will I make for him a city on the western side. Nay, but I will make the City of the Horizon for the Aten, my Father, upon the east side, the place for which he did enclose for his own self with cliffs, and made a plain in the midst of it that I might sacrifice to him thereon: This is it.

Neither shall the queen say unto me, "Behold there is a goodly place for the City of the Horizon in another place," and I harken unto her. Neither shall any noble nor any man in the whole land say unto me, "Behold there is a goodly place for the City of the Horizon in another place," and I harken unto them. Whether it be downstream or southward or westward or eastward I will not say, "I will abandon this City of the Horizon."

ACT II / SCENE 4

The music that follows the dance is taken from the orchestral introduction to the Coronation scene and serves as preparation for Akhnaten's "Hymn to the Sun." At its conclusion, Akhnaten is left alone.

The "Hymn to the Sun" is a central moment of the opera. In it, Akhnaten espouses, in his own words, the inspiration for his religious and social reforms. The Hymn is sung in the language of the audience.

At the close of the Hymn, Akhnaten leaves the stage deserted, and the act ends with an offstage chorus singing, in Hebrew, Psalm 104 from the Old Testament.

Vocal Text: —Akhnaten's "Hymn to the Sun" (from *Documents from Old Testament Times,* 1958, Winton Thomas)

(English translation)

Thou dost appear beautiful on the horizon of heaven
Oh, living Aten he who was the first to live
When thou has risen on the eastern horizon

Thou has filled every land with thy beauty
Thou art fair, dazzling, high above every land
   to the very end of all thou has made
All the beasts are satisfied with their pasture
Trees and plants are verdant
Birds fly from their nests, wings spread
Flocks skip with their feet
All that fly and alight live when thou has arisen
How manifold is that which thou has made
Thou sole God there is no other like thee
Thou didst create the earth according to thy will,
Being alone, everything on earth which walks and flies on high
Thy rays nourish the fields when thou dost rise
They live and thrive for thee
Thou makest the seasons to nourish all thou hast made
The winter to cool them
The heat that they may taste thee
There is no other that knows thee save thy son, Akhnaten
For thou has made him skilled in thy plans and thy might
Thou dost rise them up for thy son who comes forth from
   thyself

Vocal Text (Sung in Hebrew): —Offstage Chorus (Psalm 104, Old
Testament)

     ma ra-bu ma-a-se-kha ha-shem
     ku-lam be-khokh-ma a-sita
     ma-la-a ha-a-rets kin-ya-ne-kha

     o-te or ka-sal-ma
     no-te sha-ma-yim ka-yi-ri-a

     ta shet kho-shekh vi-hi lie-la
     bo tir-mos kol khay-to ya-ar

     (English translation—King James version)

Oh Lord, how manifold are Thy works
In wisdom hast Thou made them all
The earth is full of Thy riches

Who coverest Thyself with light as with a garment

Who stretchest out the heavens like a curtain
Thou makest darkness and it is night
Wherein all the beasts of the forest do creep forth
   (repeat first three lines here)

END ACT II

ACT III

Year 17 and the Present—Akhetaten

ACT III / SCENE 1 / THE FAMILY

The stage is divided, one side showing a room in the palace in which can be seen Akhnaten, Nefertiti and their six daughters. Outside the palace, on the other side of the stage, are the people of Egypt, soldiers and the outlawed priests of Amon and the Scribe. The opening of the scene depicts Akhnaten and his family in a moment of intimacy, oblivious to the crowd outside. As they sing to each other a sweet, wordless song, it is apparent that in their closeness they have become isolated from the outside world.

The focus shifts to the people outside the palace. The Scribe (drawing on letters from Syrian princes to Akhnaten from the "Amarna letters") begins to incite the crowd, which presses toward the palace and becomes increasingly restless.

The scene shifts back to the palace. This time Akhnaten is alone with his two eldest daughters. They continue to sing, appearing more withdrawn and isolated from the events outside.

Spoken Text: —(from the "Amarna letters")

LETTER NO. 1 I have written repeatedly for troops, but they were not given and the king did not listen to the work of his servant. And I sent my messenger to the palace, but he returned empty-handed—he brought no troops. And when the people of my house saw this, they ridiculed me like the governors, my brethren, and despised me.

LETTER NO. 2 The king's whole land, which has begun hostilities with me, will be lost. Behold the territory of Seir, as far as Carmel, its princes are wholly lost; and hostilities prevail against me. As long as ships were upon the sea the strong arm of the king occupied Naharin and Kash, but now the 'Apiru are occupying the king's cities. There remains not one prince to my lord, the king; every one is ruined. Let the king take care of his land and let him send troops. For if no troops come in this year, the whole territory of my lord, the king, will perish. If there are no troops in this year, let the king send his officer to fetch me and his brothers, that we may die with our lord, the king.

LETTER NO. 3 Verily, thy father did not march forth, nor inspect the lands of the vassal-princes. And when thou ascended the throne of thy father's house, Abdashirta's sons took the king's lands for themselves. Creatures of the king of Mittani are they, and of the king of Babylon and of the king of the Hittites.

LETTER NO. 4 Who formerly could have plundered Tunip without being plundered by Thutmos III? The gods of the king of Egypt, my lord dwell in Tunip. May my lord ask his old men if this not be so. Now, however, we belong no more to our lord, the king of Egypt. And now, Tunip, thy city, weeps and her tears are flowing and there is no help for us. For twenty years we have been sending to our lord, the king, the king of Egypt, but there has not come to us a word—no, not one.

ACT III / SCENE 2 / ATTACK AND FALL

Horemhab, Aye and the Amon High Priest push to the front of the crowd and also begin to rouse the people (large chorus). The principals and chorus sing a text taken from the "Amarna letters." Soon the palace is surrounded.

Finally, the mob bursts through the palace doors and windows in a wave of shouts, overwhelming Akhnaten and his remaining family and carrying them off.

Vocal Text (Sung in Akkadian):— Horemhab, Aye, Amon High Priest and Chorus (from *The Tell El-Amarna Tablets,* S. Mercer, Toronto, 1939)

> *Lim-lik-mi sha-ri a-na ma-ti-shu*
> *Khal-kat mat sha-ri. Ga-ba-sha*

tsa-ba-ta-ni; nu-kur-tu a-na ya-shi
A-di ma-ta-ti She-eri Gin-Ti-kir-mil
shal-mu a-na gab-bi kha-zi-a-nu-ti
u nu-kur-tu a-na ya-shi.
Ip-sha-ti e-nu-ma a-mel a-mi-ri
u-la a-man i-na sha-ri be-li-ya;
ki nu-kur-tu
a-na mukh-khi-ya shak-na-ti
e-nu-ma e-lip-pa i-na lib-bi tam-ti
kat shar-ri dan-na-tu
Ti-lik-ki Nakh-ri-ma u kapa-si
u i-nan-na a-la-ni sha-ri
Ti-li-ki-u Kha-bi-ru
Ya-nu-mi ish-ten kha-zi-a-nu
a-na shar-ri be-li-ya; khal-ku gab-bu

(English translation)

Let the king care for his land
The land of the king will be lost
All of it will be taken from me
There is hostility to me.
As far as the lands of Seir even to Carmel,
   there is peace to all the regents.
But to me there is hostility.
Although a man sees the facts
Yet the two eyes of the king, my lord, do not see
For hostility is firm against me.
As sure as there is a ship in the midst of the sea
The mighty arm of the king will seize Nahrima
   and Kapasi.
But now the 'Apiru are taking the cities of
   the king.
No regent is left to the king, my lord,
All are lost.

In the silence at the close of this scene, the Scribe appears out of the chaos to announce the end of Akhnaten's reign.

Spoken Text: —(from Aye's Tomb)

> The sun of him who knew thee not
> Has set, O Amon.
> But, as for him who knows thee,
> He shines.
> The temple of him who assailed
> Thee is in darkness,
> While the whole earth is in
> Sunlight.
> Who so puts thee in his heart,
> O Amon,
> Lo, his sun hath risen.

The next section for orchestra and narrator (the Scribe) is a reprise, in shortened form, of the opening Prelude. It serves as a transition to the present day and is divided as follows:

The Scribe describes the rebuilding of the Amon temples after the fall of Akhnaten.

Spoken Text: —(from Tutankhamen's Tomb)

> The new ruler, performing benefactions for his father Amon and all the gods, has made what was ruined to endure as a monument for the ages of eternity, and he has expelled the great criminal and justice was established. He surpassed what had been done previously. He fashioned his father Amon upon thirteen carrying poles, his holy image being of fine gold, lapis lazuli, and every august costly stone, whereas the majesty of this august god had been upon eleven carrying poles.
>
> All the property of the temples has been doubled and tripled and quadrupled in silver, gold, lapis lazuli, every kind of august costly stone, royal linen, white linen, fine linen, olive oil, gum, fat, incense, myrrh, without limit to any good thing. His majesty (Life! Prosperity! Health!) has built their barques upon the river of new cedar from the terraces. They make the river shine.

The orchestral music becomes very full and no action is indicated. Finally the city Akhetaten appears as it exists in the present: a ruined city, recently excavated, the walls barely three feet high at most.

Several groups of tourists wander through the ruins taking photos, exploring, looking about.

Spoken Text: —the Tour Guide (from *Frommer's Guide to Egypt* and *Fodor's Guide to Egypt*)

> To reach Tell El-Amarna, drive eight miles south of Mallawi to the point where you cross the Nile. On the east side of the Nile the distance is less than a mile and can be covered on foot or on donkey.
>
> Behind the present village, at the ancient site of Tell El-Amarna, the ruins known as the palace of Nefertiti are among the very few remnants from the Akhnaten period. Tablets in cuneiform writing, which contain correspondence between Egypt and Syria, were found here and are now in the Cairo Museum. (To see any sights on the Eastern bank of the River you must cross by ferry which carries cars along with the usual donkey carts and local traffic. The ferry docking station is located at the southern end of the town. You should arrive there at least one half hour before the 6:00 AM crossing. The ferry does a brisk business and you will need every available second for sight seeing.)
>
> There is nothing left of this glorious city of temples and palaces. The mud-brick buildings have long since crumbled and little remains of the immense stone temples but the outlines of their floor plans.
>
> In addition to the tombs and ruins of the city, there are several stelae scattered around the plain which mark the limits of the land belonging to the city. Most of them are too widely scattered to visit and are also in bad condition.

ACT III / SCENE 4 / EPILOGUE

All the tourists have left. The ruined city is empty. The ghosts of Akhnaten and the other principals appear moving about their now-dead city. Singing parts are taken by Akhnaten, Nefertiti and Queen Tye, but they sing no words. At first they seem not to know that they and their city all are dead and now a part of the past. They become aware of the funeral cortege of Akhnaten's father (Amenhotep III) moving across the background. They form a procession of their own, and as the opera ends, can be seen moving off toward the first funeral group still on its journey to the heavenly land of Ra.

END OF THE OPERA

SOME OTHER MUSIC

D eveloping the synthesizer work tapes for *Akhnaten* had presented no special problem, since by that time the recording studio was a familiar and comfortable workplace for me. Michael and Kurt had become an excellent music director-producer team, and we had been making records together since the *Music in Twelve Parts (Part 1 & 2)* recording in 1977. During the Trilogy period, I had signed a CBS Masterworks recording contract and, besides the theater work I had been doing, had had the opportunity to do several projects specifically tailored to a studio situation.

The first of these was *Glassworks,* my debut record on CBS. This was music written for the recording studio, though a number of the pieces soon found their way into the Ensemble's repertory. A six-"movement" work, *Glassworks* was intended to introduce my music to a more general audience than had been familiar with it up to then. My overall plan with Joe Dash of CBS Masterworks was to alternate one-record releases with larger opera projects. At this writing, some five years after our program was undertaken, *Einstein* has been reissued, *Satyagraha* (with the original soloists and Christopher Keene conducting the New York City Opera chorus and orchestra) has been released, and in 1987 *Akhnaten* will be released (performed by the Stuttgart company and conducted by Dennis Russell Davies). In between these releases, the albums *The Photographer, Songs from Liquid Days* and *Dance Pieces* have all appeared. But these plans were still very much in the future when *Glassworks* was recorded, and the first thing that had to be established was that there in fact existed a real public for this music.

The *Glassworks* record begins with a solo piano piece, "Opening," written for Michael Riesman, that was meant to create an intimate atmosphere at the very start. The four pieces that follow are written for a mix of my Ensemble plus additional strings and brass. There is a final reprise of the piano in "Closing," this time joined by the other instruments. When some of these pieces became part of the Ensemble repertory, I wrote an additional vocal part for Dora Ohrenstein, who at this writing has been with the Ensemble five years, giving her the distinction of being the vocalist with the longest history of singing my music. As my vocal writing evolved, she was often the first singer who "tested" new material and whose insights and comments could be most helpful. A vocal presence in performances of *Glassworks,* though absent from the recording, has given the music a new and lively quality.

This was our first digitally mixed record. As usual, Kurt and Michael had been very much on top of this new development in recording technology and were ready and eager to implement it in this, our first release on an international label. Since then, digital recording has been an important part of our recording process. When compact discs became a real option in the early 1980s, we were very well placed technically to take advantage of this new technology. Kurt introduced another innovation which, in retrospect, seems more like a novelty, but was very interesting at the time. He made a special "Walkman" mix of *Glassworks,* intended to be heard on small, portable cassette players. This was no gimmick but a truly different mix made with headphones plugged directly into the mixing board, and it is an example of the innovative thinking that Michael and Kurt bring to the recording studio and that has made our work together exciting and continually new. Such thinking, at present, extends to uses of new computer technology for producing work tapes, performing mixes, and programming click tracks, for example, as well as employing the new generation of "sampling" instruments which store and make available an increasingly wide variety of natural and electronic sounds on floppy disks. This has meant that each new recording project has become an opportunity to improve the recorded presentation of the music. The recording of *The Photographer* represented such a new approach.

The Photographer, conceived by Rob Malasch, is a music theater work that falls into no particular category. Rob's idea was to base the work on the life of the nineteenth-century English/American photographer Eadweard Muybridge, who not only was an important pioneer in photography but also murdered his wife's lover and was acquitted after a sensational trial. The story was presented in three different ways in each of three acts. The first act told the story as a play with music. The second act was done as a concert with a slide show of Muybridge's photographs, and Act III was presented as a dance piece. In addition, the photography theme was carried out in another way. In Act I, photographs were made of the stage action; during Act II they were "developed," and in Act III they were projected during the dance.

The Holland Festival first presented *The Photographer* in June 1982 before Queen Beatrix and an invited audience at the royal place in Amsterdam. That premiere was followed by a run at the Carré Theater. *The Photographer* was next seen in New York, at BAM's Next Wave Festival in the fall of 1983, this time directed by JoAnne Akalaitis with a new text by Robert Coe and choreography by David Gordon. This production then had a limited American tour during the winter of 1983–1984.

It was during this period that our newest Ensemble member, Martin Goldray, joined us, becoming our second keyboard player, after Michael. At that point I became third keyboard player, taking the smaller incidental keyboard parts for myself, leaving me more time for composing, since I would require less time for practicing. With two first-rate keyboardists, we entered a new period with the Ensemble music where, with the aid of the new synthesizers, the transcriptions from the operas could take on a more "symphonic" sound.

Our recorded version of *The Photographer* included the important musical portions of the stage work, though several short minor pieces from Act I were omitted in order to keep the project to a single record. Of particular interest to us was a full use of overdubbing techniques, used to a certain degree in *Glassworks* but greatly extended with *The Photographer*. We began by recording, one part at a time, the original orchestra for which *The Photographer* was written. By recording each part on a separate track of our twenty-four available tracks, we ensured the greatest possible flexibility when it came time to mix all the parts together in the final stage of the recording process. After the original orchestra was recorded, additional parts were added, or doubled, onto the original ones. These were synthesized sounds, electronically generated, used to enhance and extend the original instruments. A trombone part, for example, might have an electronic part added to it an octave below what was originally played. On the final mix of the record, instead of hearing a trombone, the listener is hearing something more like a super-trombone. Applied to the whole orchestra, the result is a sound beyond anything an orchestra could play live.

All this is in keeping with our attitude toward recording in general. We have never attempted to make what Kurt calls an "aural photograph" of a piece. In other words, it never occurred to us to simply hang a mike over our performing Ensemble and go for a "live" recording. It seems to us that a record is an altogether different matter and need not follow the practice of live performance at all. What we look for is the best possible presentation of the music on a record (or a tape) that we can musically and technically manage. To merely reproduce a live performance on record is simply not good enough.

Some people have objected that this approach risks losing a live "feeling" or the excitement of a performance. Ten years ago, we were concerned about that too, and in some early recordings we even attempted to integrate live performance with multitrack overdubbing. But an interesting thing has happened in the last ten or fifteen years and has made that no longer necessary: Musicians have become increasingly comfortable working in recording studios, and they have learned how to *perform* in this new situation. In our recording of *Satyagraha,* for example, Douglas Perry recorded a vocal line over and over until he was satisfied, all the orchestra parts having been recorded at earlier sessions. This allowed him and us to work toward an almost ideal performance of his role.

In some of our recording projects, musical problems took precedence over technical considerations. In *Songs from Liquid Days,* for example, I addressed myself to the use of English for the first time, my previous vocal settings having been in such languages as Sanskrit, Hopi, Egyptian, Hebrew, and Akkadian; other texts, such as solfège and numbers, were not "languages" at all. Like many another listener, I had long noticed how difficult it is to understand the English sung in opera houses and concert halls, and often the words in the musical sections of Broadway-type musicals as well. The struggle to understand what is being sung in our own language can be a distracting part of an audience's experience. *Songs from Liquid Days* was, like *Glassworks,* a project designed for the recording studio and one where I felt I could focus on this problem.

Also, I was about to begin work with the writer Doris Lessing on an opera based on her book *The Making of the Representative for Planet 8.* This would be my second opera completely in English (*The Juniper Tree* was the first), and my main concern was to set the text in a way that would allow the audience to understand the words as fully as possible. Mrs. Lessing, after all, is one of our most important living writers, and it seemed hardly worth the trouble to involve a talent of her magnitude if her words would not be understood.

On the other hand, I realized that the words of most pop and rock songs come across fairly clearly. I may not get 100 percent, but I do understand most of them, probably because singers of this kind of music, being amplified, produce a far lower level of volume than "legitimate" singers and thus can form vowels and consonants with greater clarity. I found this difference between opera and pop music very striking, and I wanted to take a closer look at it. I thought that perhaps songwriters might know something about setting text that was worth learning about. Again, it occurred to me that singers outside of the opera world, focusing on different situations and expressive needs, must be approaching their vocal texts quite differently. Therefore, in *Songs from Liquid Days* I decided to choose my collaborators from the world of popular music, expecting that in this way I would learn more about setting text, as well as things about writing for the singing voice that I had not thus far picked up working in opera houses. In many ways this project was successful, for it did bring me to think about singing in another way. Not only was the project extremely interesting in itself, but when I began work on *The Representative,* I was able to bring to it another point of view.

For example, I had learned how much comprehension of a phrase or word is affected by where it lies in the vocal range. Quite simply, the higher the voice, the more difficult it is to understand. On the other hand, the closer the sung part is to a normal speaking range, the easier it is to hear the words. There are other similar observations that can be made about phrasing or grouping of words. None of these thoughts are new or very startling, and I suppose if one were to just think about it, it would become obvious. However, as is usual with me, the work process is my best learning method. Having acquired a skill or an idea this way, it becomes part of my technique and therefore increasingly useful to me.

At any rate, in 1985 I set about writing a "song cycle." That's how I thought of this song record project. In keeping with my idea, I asked songwriters I knew (Paul Simon, David Byrne, Laurie Anderson and Suzanne Vega) to contribute texts. Laurie and Suzanne gave me finished pieces. Paul's text, on the other hand, continued to evolve as I wrote the music; as he heard the music in various stages of evolution, he would adjust phrasing and change words. This was the kind of collaboration I had been looking for, and it was extremely interesting for me. Paul was still changing the title as we went into print, and his final choice ("Song with Refrigerator in It") did not make it before the print deadline. Watching Paul so closely, I learned an enormous amount about the craft and care that goes into his own work. This kind of contact with other artists makes collaboration a very inspiring way of working.

To an extent, this was true with David Byrne as well, though his comments to me, like his text, could be fairly elusive, even cryptic. Once, when I was working with David, he gave me several unnumbered pages of verse grouped irregularly into two-, three- and four-line stanzas. Furthermore, each group was written in a different color of ink. He watched me calmly while I began assembling the text from the puzzle he had presented me. When I finished, I asked him if my arrangement would be acceptable. "That's just how I thought it would work," he said.

Finding the right singer for each song was a process that took us over six months. Kurt and Michael had already recorded the basic tracks—in this case, most of the orchestra parts—and were leaving the vocal parts until last. We began to hear singers in the studio, and I was frankly astonished at the degree to which different singers, merely through voice quality and phrasing, can affect the interpretation of a song. In opera, a role comes as a "given" for a singer, and though there can be a great range in how the part is played, it will always be limited to an "interpretation" of that particular character.

But when a song does not present a specific character or situation, a singer must invent more, bring more to the work. As I went through the process of "casting" the songs, hoping to find the "right" singer for each, my respect for singers increased. In retrospect, I see now that I could have begun the whole process by choosing the singer first, then selecting texts, and finally writing the music, but I'm not at all unhappy with the results of this, my first time out with a song record. In this case, starting with the texts, I did have the opportunity to arrange them into a coherent thematic order. I began with the abstract ideas of sound in Paul's song, moved to the more intimate, romantic, sometimes loony and occasionally even religious middle songs of Suzanne and David, and concluded with Laurie's song about memory, thus returning to a more abstract idea at the end. In this way, *Songs from Liquid Days* resembles a traditional symphonic song cycle more than it does a collection of unrelated pop songs. Songs, after all, belong to all music practices, whether they be classical concert songs, pop, folk or rock. In undertaking a record of songs, a composer may be saying a lot about where he thinks his music may fit in. If it is *still* harder to fit the music into one tradition, or one practice, than another, so be it.

My increasing experience in collaborative work proved useful when

I began working with Godfrey Reggio on his nonnarrative film *Koyaan-isqatsi* in 1981. The film is a reflection on nature, technology and contemporary life, and it uses only images and music, no spoken dialogue, story line or even actors. The result was remarkable, and it was achieved without the use of the abstractness that such an approach might imply. In many ways, working with Godfrey resembled the give-and-take process to which I had become accustomed in the theater. When I began working on this project, Godfrey, cinematographer Ron Fricke and principal editor Alton Walpole had already spent years on it with Godfrey's own organization (the Institute for Regional Education), shooting and collecting footage and assembling this material into thematic groups.

Over the next three years I regularly visited Godfrey's studio in Venice, California, where he and his team were happily trying to figure out how to make this mass of stuff into a movie. Borrowing from work methods learned in the theater, I gave my score to Kurt and Michael who made it into a work tape, to which Godfrey cut his film. There were countless revisions of both music and film. On occasion, Godfrey would even shoot new material to go with music I had written. Finally, in 1983, the film was completed. The close match between film and music in *Koyaanisqatsi,* which so many people have commented on, was achieved through this kind of intense, protracted collaboration.

The following year, I was able to apply this method to my work with Paul Schrader for his film *Mishima,* though my role in this was more in line with that of a traditional film composer. However, there were also important differences.

For one thing, after my first discussions with Paul—almost a year before the film was shot and at a point before his script had even been completed—I immersed myself in the writings of this remarkable modern Japanese writer, Yukio Mishima. In a substantial way, this approach resembled my method in working on my portrait operas. I first sought to establish for myself a clear, personal picture of Mishima the man and author. Later, when I was involved in the actual composition of the score, this became a primary source fueling my musical imagination. Once the script was completed we carefully went over it together, and Paul encouraged me to determine for myself places in the film where there would be music. In the end, more than an hour of music was recorded, much more than what is normally found in a narrative film. As with *Koyaanisqatsi,* I provided Paul with a work tape to which the film could be cut.

In effect, I had written the music to the script and not to the picture. This meant that after the film had been edited to my work tape, with its very approximate timings, many of the musical segments were either too long or too short, and I had to refit the music to its new and final timings. This meant that I had to make an extensive revision of the score, and I eventually found that I had completely written the score *twice*. This, obviously, is the reason film composers do not normally work this way.

Paul's film was structurally quite complex, being divided into four "chapters," each chapter containing three distinct narrative modes. Paul needed music that would reflect and reinforce this structure, and I don't know any other way by which we could have arrived at a successful resolution of these problems without thoroughly working through the film together.

Besides film and record projects, I have continued to work in the theater. Nearly ten years had passed between the time I began work with Robert Wilson on *Einstein on the Beach* and the premiere of *Akhnaten* in Stuttgart in March of 1984. When the complete Trilogy of operas is produced in the 1989–1990 season, it will have taken almost fifteen years for the entire work to be seen as an entity. During the decade in which these works were being written and presented individually, I also completed a number of other stage projects.

The first of these was *Attacca—A Madrigal Opera* which, like *The Photographer*, was coauthored with the Dutch designer/director Rob Malasch. *A Madrigal Opera* is a vocal work for six voices, violin and viola, and it could be classified as a chamber opera with an unspecified story line. My idea was to write a musical/dramatic work that could, with different direction, be realized with different narrative content. In this way, I was following a common practice in the dance world, where choreographers routinely adapt music written for another purpose to their own dramatic needs. In this case, a new writer can be brought in to complete the work for each new production. This can lead to occasional confusion, since *A Madrigal Opera* can appear with different titles preceding it; at this writing, there already have been three completely different interpretations. The first, written with Malasch, was presented at the Carré Theater in Amsterdam in 1980. The second was designed and directed by Manuel Luetgenhorst, who used Rilke's poem *The Panther* as his starting point; it was presented under that name at La Mama in New York, and with the Houston Grand Opera. The work was next produced at the Mark Taper Forum in Los Angeles in 1985 and called simply *A Madrigal Opera*. Here it had a libretto by the playwright Len Jenkins and was directed by Bob Woodward.

After 1984, immediately following the completion of *Akhnaten*, I continued my work in music theater with four evening-length works. The first was with Robert Wilson on the Rome section of *the CIVIL warS,* already mentioned as appearing at the same time as the Stuttgart *Akhnaten.* The complete *CIVIL warS,* a ten-hour epic, was being built in five different cities prior to its planned assembly in Los Angeles, where it was to have been part of the 1984 Olympics Arts Festival. Unfortunately, it has never been produced in its entirety, though various sections have been performed separately in their originating countries and elsewhere. The Olympics Arts Festival failed to donate the necessary money for the full performance, even though the other five countries had fully paid not only for the local stagings but for the shipping costs to Los Angeles.

The Rome section is in two acts and four scenes and runs about two hours. It was planned so that it could have a life of its own, independent of the larger work of which it was the concluding section. It is a very Wilsonlike meditation in image, dance and music on the end of war, and on rebirth and renewal. There are spoken sections in the language of the audience, and the vocal parts are sung in both Latin and Italian. Compared to *Akhnaten,* a somber and somewhat brooding work, *the CIVIL warS* is far lighter and more lyrical, altogether appropriate in character for my "Italian" opera. The text, by our librettist Maita di Niscemi, is a compilation based largely on poems of Seneca, letters written during the American Civil War, and some texts written by Wilson himself. The main characters include a Snow Owl, Robert E. Lee, Abraham Lincoln, Mary Todd Lincoln, Garibaldi, and Hercules.

I won't try to explain this, but if the reader knows Wilson's work, perhaps explanation will not be needed. This work was written for the Rome Opera, and the rehearsal period included a lengthy workshop with singers and actors in the summer of 1983.

During one of those workshops, there occurred one of those incidents that can sometimes exert a crucial influence on the outcome of a work. I should preface this by mentioning that Bob Wilson is a Southerner, from Texas, while I, being from Baltimore, am technically a Southerner as well. The fine soprano Jessye Norman, who at that point was involved in *the CIVIL warS* production, is yet another Southerner (from Georgia). Given the Civil War atmosphere of much of Bob's epic work, there thus was a high degree of national, political and cultural feelings involved.

During one rehearsal, I found myself whistling that old Southern revival hymn that begins "We are climbing Jacob's Ladder . . . soldiers of the Cross." Bob turned to me and said, "That's 'Jacob's Ladder.' "

I said, "Oh, you know it too."

And he said, "Yes. We used to sing it in Sunday School."

The tune began to haunt me, and when it came time to compose the third section of *the CIVIL warS*—a sorrowing, contemplative section based on a letter written by Robert E. Lee—I simply took "Jacob's Ladder" and built an entire movement upon a reharmonization of it. I wrote it for Jessye Norman but, as yet, she has not had occasion to sing it (she had been scheduled to do it in the canceled Los Angeles production). So far, Ruby Hinds has been the only one to sing it—and she does so beautifully.

A second work, written just after the Rome section of *the CIVIL warS,* was a score for the Cologne section of the same piece. This was really the accompanying music to a theater work with text by the contemporary German writer Heiner Müller. The music was recorded; Michael Riesman overdubbed numerous synthesizer parts with Kurt Munkacsi producing. So far, I have transcribed two of its seven sections for orchestra and intend to add three more to form an orchestral suite. One of the pieces, transcribed by Michael, has entered my Ensemble's repertory.

The next work I undertook, in the summer of 1984, was *The Juniper Tree,* an opera based on the story by the Grimm brothers. It was commissioned by Robert Brustein's American Repertory Theater in Cambridge, Massachusetts, and is particularly interesting for two reasons. First, it was written as a collaborative work with the composer Bob Moran, a long-time friend. Second, it was the first opera in which I used an English text. Moran and I enlisted the writer Arthur Yorinks as librettist, and the work became a three-way collaboration.

Written for a chamber orchestra (about twelve players) with a small group of soloists and chorus, *The Juniper Tree* is a two-act work lasting about ninety minutes. Most of the music was written in Nova Scotia with all three coauthors present. Moran and I worked in neighboring cabins and, after dividing the scenes between us, consulted each other freely on the progress of our individual work. At one point, for example, Moran took a theme I had used in one scene and based a set of variations on it for use in another. Though we are sympathetic to each other's work, our music isn't really that much alike so, rather than eliminate our stylistic differences, we elected to emphasize them, giving the work a broader musical range than if one of us had composed it alone. Another innovation for me was to have a real writer, Arthur Yorinks, acting as librettist, which relieved me and Moran of that part of the creative process. Maita di Niscemi had performed that role to an extent with *the CIVIL warS,* but in a more abstract, less conventional way. Yorinks produced a terse, economical text that captured the character and spirit of the Grimm brothers' original tale, making our work that much easier.

The production, presented at Brustein's American Repertory Theater in Cambridge, turned out to be a very handsome affair and has proven popular with audiences. André Serban was our director and, using the delightful and imaginative sets of Michael Yeargan as well as the lighting design of Jennifer Tipton, gave an interpretation of the work that nicely balanced the light and the gruesome sides of the story. The production traveled the next year to Houston and Philadelphia. New productions (i.e., with new designers and directors) are planned in Omaha, Nebraska, and the West German cities of Freiburg and Bielefeld. In short, it looks like *The Juniper Tree* is becoming something of a minor "hit" in the world of new opera.

As of this writing, the new opera written with the author Doris Lessing and based on her book *The Making of the Representative for Planet 8* has been completed. I am reluctant to report very much about it, since it has yet to receive its first production (to be undertaken by the Houston Grand Opera in 1988). Speaking generally, though, it is a three-act work, about three hours in length, for a full opera orchestra, small chorus and four soloists. Mrs. Lessing made a free adaptation from her book so that it could function as a stage work. Eiko Ishioko and Manuro Dumberger are the designers. I met Eiko during my work on *Mishima*, greatly admired her designs for that project and persuaded her to join us in this one. The design team, along with Mrs. Lessing and myself, began meeting in 1985 to develop our ideas, and in October 1986 I completed the score. Casting, building of sets and rehearsals are still before us. This will be my second full-length opera in English which, as can be seen, has become one of my present preoccupations.

As I look at my work in the theater and the various forms it has taken, I see that the roles I have played over the years have been specifically tailored to each project. Generally, though, I can describe them in one of the following ways.

First, as a composer of incidental music for theater works, I play a part as a contributor, much as the designer or lighting person might, but I do not enter into it as an author of the work in any way. This can still require detailed study of the work and long hours in the theater during rehearsal periods but, in a crucial way, my music does not form the work. Most of my work with the Mabou Mines is of this kind.

Second, I have worked as coauthor with directors and writers. Pieces such as *Einstein on the Beach, The Juniper Tree* or the new opera with Mrs. Lessing are conceived jointly by two, sometimes three, persons and we share, more or less equally, the artistic responsibility for the outcome.

Third, I have worked as the principal author with a group of collaborators, as in the operas *Satyagraha* and *Akhnaten*. Here the initial idea and impulse was mine, and I invited people of different capacities to aid me in the execution. This is closer to the traditional role of the opera composer. But when one considers to what extent collaboration can contribute to the final shaping of a work, it will be obvious that this process is far different from what has brought new works to opera houses in the past.

Finally, there are a few works such as *A Madrigal Opera* that are completely written in terms of the music but await the contribution of other as yet unknown authors in order to be completed for the theater. The results can, of course, be unpredictable. But for those who have the nerves for it, having an open-ended piece of this kind can be very exciting.

At this writing, it has been over twenty years since I began working in the theater with the original members of the Mabou Mines, allying myself firmly with the progressive world of experimental theater. The emphasis of this work has been on collaboration throughout, as my work extended into music theater, film and dance. This predilection of mine for working with other artists is certainly one of my distinguishing features, and accounts, I believe, in large measure, for the difference my work bears from that produced in more traditional ways.

The standard operas that are mainly performed by repertory opera houses were conceived differently. For the most part, these operas in the Italian and German traditions were the work of one man with one vision (the contributions of librettists notwithstanding). The opera houses of the past simply produced these works and did not function as workplaces where artists from different fields collaborated on joint projects. Most modern operas written for present-day opera houses are conceived in exactly the same way. Indeed, it is difficult not to see that they are usually built on Italian and German models in terms of construction, intent and execution. It is not so odd, then, that music theater works coming from a new and very different tradition, be they by Robert Wilson or David Byrne or JoAnne Akalaitis or myself, or by anybody else, should be greeted with surprise and even alarm—when they are acknowledged at all—by most producers of traditional work.

As matters now stand there is, on the one hand, a continually evolving world of music theater rooted in the progressive and experimental world of twentieth-century theater. On the other hand, we have the traditional world of repertory opera, which occupies most of the opera companies now operating in Europe and the Americas. One would think that designers, directors, authors and composers would move easily and eagerly from one world to the other, thus leading eventually to the integration of the two. In fact, this is beginning to happen as some directors such as Wilson, Serban and Freyer (all men with whom I have worked) are invited to lend their talents to new productions of opera classics, usually bringing with them their own designers and production teams. However, stiff resistance to genuinely new ideas is more widespread than is generally acknowledged, and I must conclude that the majority of opera producers, both in the U.S. and Europe, simply have no acquaintance with contemporary theater practice. It occurs to me that they have never seen the Living Theater or Meredith Monk, Bob Wilson or Peter Brook, or Mabou Mines, or Richard Foreman, etc., etc.

To me, this is an astonishing thought, but it may actually be so. Still, I feel very positive about our inherited and changing world of music theater. New works not modeled on the past are being created, producers are beginning to appear in cities and countries all over the world, and the public for these new works is very much *there*. When new works can outsell classics of the Italian and German repertory, as is actually happening all around us, it is hard not to sense a growing momentum toward a new and revitalized future for the music theater of our time, and I think this will have the proper effect on our opera houses. I don't doubt that the world of traditional repertory opera will eventually be dragged—probably screaming—into the twentieth century with the rest of us.

Of course, by then it will be the twenty-first century, and that will be a whole new story.

MUSIC CATALOG

LIST OF COMPOSITIONS SINCE 1965

(*Note:* PGE denotes works written for the Philip Glass Ensemble)

1965

Music for *Play* (Beckett). For two soprano saxophones.
Music for Ensemble and Two Actresses. For wind sextet and two speakers.
Piece for Chamber Orchestra

1966

String Quartet

1967

Strung Out. For solo amplified violin.
Music in the Shape of a Square. For two flutes.
In Again Out Again. For two pianos.
One Plus One. For amplified tabletop.

1968

Two Pages. For electric keyboards (later, PGE).

Music for the *Red Horse Animation* (Breuer). For the Mabou Mines Theater.

Gradus. For solo soprano saxophone.

How Now. For piano or ensemble.

1969

Music in Contrary Motion. PGE.

Music in Fifths. PGE

Music in Similar Motion. PGE.

Music in Eight Parts. PGE.

1970

Music for Voices. For the Mabou Mines Theater.

Music with Changing Parts. PGE.

1971–1974

Music in Twelve Parts. PGE.

1975

Another Look at Harmony, Parts One & Two. PGE.

Music for *The Lost Ones* (Beckett). For the Mabou Mines Theater.

Music for *The Saint and the Football Player* (Thibeau & Breuer). For the Mabou Mines Theater.

1975–1976

Einstein on the Beach, opera in four acts. For PGE, vocal soloists and chorus. Created with Robert Wilson.

1977

Dressed Like an Egg (Akalaitis; based on writings of Colette). For the Mabou Mines Theater.

Fourth Series Part One. For chorus and organ. Commissioned jointly by the Holland Festival and Festival Saint-Denis (Paris).

North Star. Music for the documentary film *Mark Di Suvero, Sculptor* by François de Menil and Barbara Rose.

1978

Fourth Series Part Two. For solo organ [same as Dance #2 from *Dance,* see listing for 1979].

Fourth Series Part Three. For violin and clarinet. Written for the radio adaptation of Constance DeJong's novel *Modern Love*.

Modern Love Waltz. Written for Constance DeJong's performance from her novel *Modern Love*. (A chamber ensemble arrangement of this was made by Robert Moran.)

1979

Fourth Series Part Four. For solo organ. Commissioned by Bremen Radio. (Later adapted by Lucinda Childs for her dance company and renamed *Mad Rush*.)

Dance. PGE. In five parts combining film, live and recorded music. A collaboration with choreographer Lucinda Childs and sculptor/painter Sol LeWitt.

1980

Satyagraha, opera in three acts. For orchestra, chorus and soloists. Commissioned by the City of Rotterdam for the Netherlands Opera.

A Madrigal Opera. For six voices, violin and viola. Commissioned and presented at the Holland Festival, 1980.

1981

Music in Similar Motion. New orchestration for chamber orchestra.

Glassworks. Recording for CBS Masterworks.

1982

Habeve Song. For soprano, clarinet and bassoon.

Koyaanisqatsi. For the Western Wind Ensemble, Albert de Ruiter (solo bass), chorus and orchestra. A film produced and directed by Godfrey Reggio for the Institute for Regional Education.

The Photographer. Originally for chamber orchestra, then PGE. A music theater piece written with director/author Rob Malasch and commissioned by the Holland Festival, 1982.

1983

Akhnaten, opera in three acts. For orchestra, chorus and soloists. Commissioned by the Stuttgart State Opera.

the CIVIL warS (Rome Section), opera with prologue and three Scenes. With Robert Wilson. Commissioned by the Rome Opera.

Music for *Cold Harbor* (Dale Worsley and Bill Raymond). Tape. For the Mabou Mines Theater.

Glass Pieces. For orchestra. Ballet choreographed by Jerome Robbins for the New York City Ballet from existing music.

1984

Music for *Company* (Beckett). String quartet commissioned by the Mabou Mines Theater.

the CIVIL warS (Cologne Section). With Robert Wilson. Commissioned by the Cologne State Theater.

Music for *Mishima*. Tape. A film written by Paul and Leonard Schrader; directed by Paul Schrader.

The Olympian. For chorus and orchestra. Commissioned by the 1984 Olympic committee for the opening and closing ceremonies of the Summer Olympics in Los Angeles.

The Juniper Tree, opera in two acts for chamber orchestra, small chorus and soloists. Based on the tale by the Brothers Grimm, written with composer Robert Moran and author Arthur Yorinks. Commissioned by the American Repertory Theater, Cambridge, Massachusetts.

1985

Songs from Liquid Days. Song cycle recorded for CBS Masterworks, written with lyricists Laurie Anderson, David Byrne, Paul Simon, and Suzanne Vega.

A Descent into the Maelstrom. PGE. Dance/theater work based on the story by Edgar Allan Poe, with writer/director Matthew Maguire and choreographer Molissa Fenley. Commissioned for the Australian Dance Theater by the Adelaide Festival.

Mishima Quartet. For string quartet. Extracted from the *Mishima* film score.

1985–1986

The Making of the Representative for Planet 8, opera in three acts, for orchestra, chorus and soloists. Written with author Doris Lessing and based on her novel of the same name. Commissioned by the Houston Grand Opera.

1986

In the Upper Room. Tape. A dance work written for and commissioned by Twyla Tharp.

Phaedra. Tape. A ballet score based on the *Mishima* film music. Conceived and choreographed by Flemming Flindt and commissioned by the Dallas Ballet.

1987

Pink Noise. A collaborative acoustic installation by Philip Glass and Richard Serra. For the Ohio State University Gallery of Fine Arts, Wexner Center, Columbus, Ohio.

Concerto for Violin and Orchestra. Written for Paul Zukovsky and Dennis Russell Davies. Commissioned by American Composers' Orchestra. Premiere: April 4, 1987, Carnegie Hall.

Cadenzas for Mozart's *Piano Concerto No. 21* (K. 467). Commissioned by Rudolf Firkusny.

The Light. Symphonic work. Commissioned by the Michelson-Morley Centennial Celebrations for The Cleveland Orchestra; Christoph von Dohnanyi, Music Director.

Powaqqatsi. For large orchestra, children's choir and mixed ensembles. A film by Godfrey Reggio for the Institute for Regional Education.

The Fall of the House of Usher. Chamber opera in two acts. Based on the story by Edgar Allan Poe, libretto by Arthur Yorinks. Commissioned by the American Repertory Theater, Cambridge, Massachusetts, and the Kentucky Opera Association.

1988

Music for *A Thin Blue Line*. Chamber orchestra. A film by Earl Morris.

Planet News. Solo piano music for the poet Allen Ginsberg.

A Thousand Airplanes, science-fiction music drama. For
the Philip Glass Ensemble and one actor. Written with author David Hwang
and artist Jerome Sirlin.

NOTE: The above list does not include a variety of smaller pieces written for friends and informal occasions—works not meant for public use, usually not available apart from an original score, and not performed beyond the occasion for which they were intended.

DISCOGRAPHY

Music with Changing Parts
Chatham Square   1001/2

Music in Similar Motion/Music in Fifths
Chatham Square   1003

Solo Music
Shandar   83515

Music in Twelve Parts—Parts 1 & 2
Caroline   CA 2010

Strung Out for Amplified Violin (Paul Zukofsky, violin)
Music Observations   CP 2

North Star
Virgin   V 2085

Mad Rush/Dressed Like an Egg
Soho News   9H001

Mike Oldfield—Platinum—North Star
Virgin   V2141

Einstein on the Beach
CBS Masterworks   M4 388 75

Einstein on the Beach (excerpts)
Tomato   Tom 101

Dance Nos. 1 & 3
Tomato   Tom 8029

Glassworks
CBS   FM 37265

The Photographer
CBS   FM 37849

Koyaanisqatsi
Antilles/Island   ASTA 1

Satyagraha
CBS Masterworks   I3M 39672

Mishima
Nonesuch   9-79113-1 F

Songs from Liquid Days
CBS   FM 39564

Company (Kronos Quartet)
Nonesuch   9-79111-1 F

The Official Music of the XXIIIrd Olympiad, Los Angeles 1984
The Olympian
CBS   JS 39322

Dancepieces
CBS   FM 39539

Akhnaten
CBS

Music in Twelve Parts (complete)
Virgin   Release due 1988

Powaqqatsi
Nonesuch   Release due 1988

INDEX